HELIGOLAND

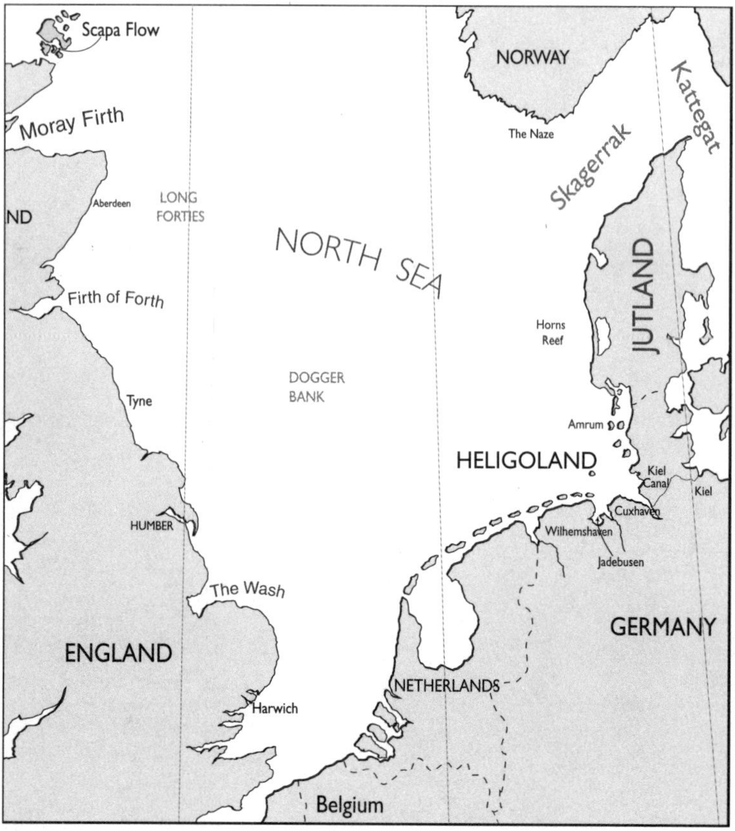

Heligoland is only 290 miles from the British coast.

HELIGOLAND

The True Story of German Bight and the Island that Britain Betrayed

GEORGE DROWER

SUTTON PUBLISHING

First published in the United Kingdom in 2002 by
Sutton Publishing Limited · Phoenix Mill
Thrupp · Stroud · Gloucestershire · GL5 2BU

British Library Cataloguing in Publication Data
A catalogue record for this book is available from the British Library

ISBN 0-7509-2600-7

To the people of Heligoland

Typeset in 11/14pt Melior.
Typesetting and origination by
Sutton Publishing Limited.
Printed and bound in England by
J.H. Haynes & Co. Ltd, Sparkford.

Contents

Acknowledgements

In Heligoland research for this book was done at the Lesehalle Bücherel, and the Nordsee Museum; in Hamburg, at the Museum für Hamburgische Geschichte; in Belfast, at the Public Record Office of Northern Ireland; in London, at the British Library, Imperial College, the Imperial War Museum, Institute of Historical Research, London School of Economics, the Public Record Office (Kew) and the RAF Museum. To the librarians of those establishments I am grateful. Additional data was provided by the Falkland Islands Archives, in the Falkland Islands; Hatfield House, Herts; the National Maritime Museum, Greenwich; and the Royal Commonwealth Society Collection at the University of Cambridge. I am grateful for the co-operation of: the late Sir Bernard Braine; former Bürgermeister Henry Rickmers, and Sue Wichers of the Helgoland Regierung; and my special thanks go to David and Mary Brooks for their welcoming dinners.

Introduction

'There are warnings of gales in Viking, North Utsire, South Utsire, Forties, Dogger, Fisher . . .'. Those sea area reports, which are read out on the UK's Radio 4's Shipping Forecast, all have their own recognisable personalities and quintessentially British-sounding names. A curious exception is the one called 'German Bight'. It is a wild 20,000-square-mile area of sea and coast which stretches between two headlands: near the Dutch island of Texel, to the Jutland port of Esbjerg. For many centuries seafarers knew this tempestuous corner of the North Sea as the 'Heligoland Bight'. That was until 1956 when, in the absence of any British government objections, the Meteorological Office arranged for it to be renamed. For secretive reasons it was not Germany which preferred to keep Heligoland Bight airbrushed out of its history, and with it the remarkable story of the forgotten island at its heart – from which the Bight's true name derives.

Then on 18 August 1965 a file marked 'Secret' landed on the desk of the Foreign Secretary, Michael Stewart. At that time Britain was having to protect the inhabitants of Gibraltar against an economic siege by Spain, which was demanding sovereignty of the Rock. Yet the Foreign Office was willing to become more radical in its steps to cope with such 'End of Empire' dilemmas. Soon it would contemplate handing over the

Falkland Islands to Argentina. Secretly, in order for Britain to conduct hydrogen bomb tests, it had arranged for the eviction of the coconut gatherers from Christmas Island, and was already preparing to deport the inhabitants of Diego Garcia from their homeland, to lend it to the United States to develop into a military base.

Stewart was intrigued to see that this report concerned none of those. It was from the British Ambassador to Germany, Sir Frank Roberts, who had just attended a 75th anniversary celebration in a North Sea island which even the Foreign Secretary had never heard of. The ambassador, who had been astounded by the good-natured welcome he had received in this former British colony, reported that: 'Everywhere I heard comments from the Islanders on the tradition of the benevolence of the British Governors.'

In August 1890, when it was still an enchantingly obscure British possession, Heligoland had become the focus of international attention as the hapless bait in an astonishingly epic imperial deal to persuade Kaiser Wilhelm II's Germany to hand over substantial elements of the continent of Africa. In Britain the audacious, and quite unprecedented, territorial swap provoked public protests that August. Even Queen Victoria furiously remonstrated that the two thousand inhabitants of this sophisticated island were being callously sacrificed like pawns in an arrogant diplomatic chess game.

Unexpectedly, the story of Britain's involvement with Heligoland continued after the transfer of sovereignty in 1890. There was cause bitterly to lament Lord Salisbury's decision to yield it in both world wars, when the strategically vital island was turned against Britain. It was becoming, as Admiral of the Fleet 'Jacky' Fisher, exclaimed, 'a dagger pointed at

England's heart'. In its waters was fought the Battle of Heligoland Bight, the first surface scrimmage of the First World War; and next, the Cuxhaven Raid, the first organised seaplane attack. Started on the island was 'Project Hummerschere', an ambitious scheme in the interwar years to construct a German form of Scapa Flow – so important that it was visited by Hitler in 1938. During the Second World War there came to be further significant historic records: for example, in 1940 the RAF's first mass night bombing raid of that conflict was made over the Bight.

And then, unbeknown to many, Britain next inflicted on Heligoland a misdeed far worse than a mere swap. Between 1945 and 1952 the Heligolanders were exiled to mainland Germany while the British – probably illegally – used the island as a bombing range for high-explosive and chemical weapons, and evidently as a test-site for various elements of Britain's prototype atomic bomb. Even now the quaint mile-long island still bears the scars, albeit now hidden by lush vegetation. Such was the severity of the bomb damage suffered in April 1945, when the 140-acre former British colony was attacked by the RAF with a thousand-bomber raid, that the windswept upper plateau remains buckled and twisted like the cratered flight deck of a crippled aircraft carrier. Despite such devastation, there remain a few indelible clues to its British colonial past: a street named after an English governor, and a church wall bearing a shrapnel-scarred bronze tablet honouring Queen Victoria.

For all its commercial sophistication, Heligoland is a beguiling place, guided predominantly by the rhythms of the seasons. Its people are a tough, independently minded, close-knit community of seafaring folk: strong, stoic, quiet and slow-moving. Their first loyalty is to their island and their outlook so innately maritime that they instinctively keep their sturdy houses and tiny gardens neat and shipshape. On the walls of their hotels, guest houses and even private houses hang maritime pictures – sometimes of old British merchant ships. Traditionally, despite Heligoland's constitutional links to the states of Denmark, Britain and then Germany, they have continuously sustained a deep perception of themselves and their island as a distinct and viable nation. Not untypically for inhabitants of small islands, their downfall has been their reluctance to sustain an effective representation of themselves in influential political arenas abroad until it is too late.

Known to the Germans as 'Helgoland', for simple linguistic reasons, the island lies tantalisingly close to Germany's North Sea coast. Even so, the severity of the weather in the Heligoland Bight means tourist ferries dare to make the 30-mile crossing only during the summer months. German trippers willing to brave the often stormy trip arrive from Hamburg and the coastal ports of the coasts of Lower Saxony and Schleswig-Holstein. By late morning the graceful white ferries have converged on the roadstead, where they ride at anchor until the late afternoon; then, fearful of being caught in the Bight after dark, they wisely scurry off home. To visitors, the island seems to represent an earlier, more innocent world, and one which has no need for cars or even bicycles. Goods are moved on four-wheeled hand-trolleys, rather like miniature corn wagons. Each year tens of thousands of tourists are drawn to the island, some of them attracted by its defiantly anachronistic allure as one of Western Europe's last outposts of duty-free shopping. Some trippers go for the chance of a few hours' bathing on the nearby dependency, Sandy Island, and a few for the exceptionally clear sea air, which is claimed to be the secret of the islanders' remarkably healthy old age.

Heligoland became a British colony in 1807, and from the very outset it was strategically important because of its location in the 'corner' of the North Sea near the estuary of the Elbe and three other great rivers. During the Napoleonic wars the island played a crucial role as a forward base for the officially endorsed smuggling of contraband to the continent, and also as a centre for intelligence gathering. After the wars it established itself as a tourist resort, on the initiative of an entrepreneurial islander, and settled down to life as a British colony. For Britain, a major world power with more island colonies scattered across the globe than it knew what to do with, Heligoland was not unique. But for neighbouring Germany, it was very much a novelty. Artists, poets and nationalists venerated Heligoland, all too often – to the bemusement of the islanders – devising ludicrous fantasies that it embodied the essence of the Germanic spirit. In 1841 Heinrich Hoffmann von Fallersleben wrote Germany's (old) national anthem there (while it was still under British rule!) Few were more enchanted with the romance of the place than Kaiser Wilhelm II; some years before he was crowned, he visited the island and vowed to make it German. Bismarck, his Chancellor, regarded Heligoland in terms of its strategic disadvantages as a British outpost, and coveted it for many years, not least to provide security for his pet project, the Kiel Canal. Indeed, he even suggested to Prime Minister William Gladstone that the island might be exchanged for an enclave in India called Pondicherry. This was refused.

But in August 1890 Lord Salisbury (who was both Prime Minister and Foreign Secretary) prepared to hand over this enchanting island to Germany in order to halt further German encroachments into East Africa, thereby preventing the ruthless German colonialist Dr Karl Peters – himself born near Heligoland – from gaining control of the headwaters of the Nile. This astonishingly arrogant deal – concerning which the islanders' opinions were never sought – included Zanzibar and various border areas in East Africa. Salisbury certainly did not get everything his own way. His fiercest critic was no less a personage than Queen Victoria, who in private furiously condemned Salisbury for even considering handing over the island. British newspapers and cartoonists were nearly as scathing in their criticism.

One cause of the interest in the island was its actual physical composition. The power of the waves in the Bight was such that Heligoland (and Sandy Island) was perpetually changing its shape. Coastal erosion was ongoing: sometimes barely perceptibly, but occasionally, especially in winter, dramatically, as prized sections of the cliffs disappeared overnight. And yet somehow Heligoland retained a magical quality of indestructibility. No matter what Nature (or Allied bombers) could hurl at it, the island would always survive. For decades none of this has ever needed to be known to British travellers because few, if any, caught even the most distant glimpse of the island. Passengers on civilian airliners never see Heligoland through the portholes because all the aircraft that shuttle between England and the main northern German cities – Bremen, Hanover, Hamburg and Berlin – cross the North Sea coast over the Netherlands. And even the car ferries operating between Harwich and nearby Cuxhaven often sail past the island at night.

In view of the number of significant events and personages with which it has been associated, it is astonishing that Heligoland has remained so undiscovered. It is only 290 miles from Great Yarmouth, yet very few people in Britain even know of its existence at the centre of the stormy Bight. Each year, on 9 August, the islanders gather at their town hall, the Nordseehalle, for a dignified public commemoration of the 1890 cession. But no British person ever attends it. By an extraordinary series of oversights, Heligoland has repeatedly missed out on opportunities to make the headlines in Britain. It broke a remarkable assortment of historical records: in addition to having the quaint distinction of being Britain's smallest colonial possession, Heligoland was also Britain's only colony in northern Europe. The first sea battle of the First World War was fought in its waters, while in the Second World War it was reputed to have been the first piece of German territory upon which RAF bombs fell. Then, in the postwar era, it secretly figured in Britain's atomic bomb programme.

So often it slipped through the net. In Victorian times its people were seldom invited to colonial gatherings, and later, when the British Commonwealth began to take shape in the 1920s, it did not participate in that either because it no longer had any constitutional links with Britain. Both the 25th and the 50th anniversaries of its transfer into German hands coincided with more dramatic events in the First and Second World Wars respectively, and so the occasions passed unnoticed in Britain. Several interesting consequences have flowed from this lack of wider British knowledge of Heligoland. Almost invariably it has allowed Whitehall a freer hand, almost always at the expense of the interests of the island. In the nineteenth century the preposterously untrue German claims – some of them made by Kaiser Wilhelm II himself – that Heligoland had originally been German, went ignored or unchallenged and, however baseless, gained common currency.

Government secrecy has certainly played a part in the island's history. At first it was as a matter of traditional diplomatic practice that details of the 1807 accession treaty were not publicly disclosed until 1890. More recently there are grounds for wondering whether official attempts have been made to brush aside embarrassing details of Britain's treatment of Heligoland. Dusty ledgers at the Public Record Office at Kew clearly show in fine copperplate handwriting that several 'sensitive' documents concerning the attitudes of the islanders to the swap deal have been destroyed. However, the Heligolanders have clear memories of the misdemeanours committed against their island. This is their story of the island that Britain knew as the 'Gibraltar of the North Sea'.

1

HMS *Explosion* Arrives

Some 30 miles from the coasts of Schleswig-Holstein and Lower Saxony, Heligoland rises like a fist from the swirling waters of the North Sea. Its cliffs tower some 200 feet above sea level, their red sandstone vivid against the cold flatness. Nearby are Germany's East Frisian Islands (Borkum, Memmert, Juist, Norderney, Baltrum, Langeoog, Spiekeroog and Wangerooge), separated from the mainland by mud and sand flats. Strung parallel to the Lower Saxony coast, this chain of low-lying islands once formed an offshore bar stretching from Calais to the Elbe. Between the coastal islets stretch the muddy estuaries of the rivers Elbe, Ems, Weser and Eider. In this area, known as the Heligoland Bight, strong currents, high winds blowing down from the Arctic and relatively shallow waters combine to produce not only severe weather but also steep waves. Historically, in some winters the rivers would freeze over, and with the thaw large sheets of ice would tear free and flow downstream to the open sea. Even in medieval times such dangerous waters required daring and specialist piloting skills that very few locals other than the Heligolanders were perceived to possess. Centuries later those exceptionally grim sea conditions were vividly brought to the attention of British mariners in the spy novel *The Riddle of the Sands* by the famous adventure writer and yachtsman Erskine Childers.

By the late summer of 1807, during the Napoleonic wars, England's situation had become more dangerously isolated than ever. On land, Bonaparte's armies were sweeping across Europe, relentlessly shattering the powerful coalition the British Prime Minister, William Pitt the Younger, had constructed just two years earlier with Austria, Russia and Sweden. Austria was defeated at Austerlitz in 1805, Prussia partly broken at Jena in 1806, and the Russians overcome in East Prussia in July 1807. Under the terms of the momentous Treaty of Tilsit in July 1807, Napoleon demanded that Russia become an ally of France; its territory was considerably reduced and occupied by French troops, as was what remained of the Lower Saxony part of Prussia. So swiftly did Napoleon's forces ride into Lower Saxony later that month that Sir Edward Thornton, Britain's plenipotentiary in Hamburg (effectively its ambassador) had to flee overland to Kiel, narrowly escaping capture. When, soon afterwards, French troops occupied Portugal and then Spain, Napoleon assumed that in some form or other he had secured control of the entire coastline of mainland Europe from the Adriatic to the Baltic.

So far, of all the forces ranged against Napoleon, only the Royal Navy had succeeded in making any significant strategic impact. The attacks on French shipping off Egypt at the Battle of the Nile in 1798 and on the Danish fleet at the Battle of Copenhagen in 1801 proved that Britain was able to make audaciously devastating strikes by sea. Forced by the destruction of the French and Spanish fleets at the Battle of Trafalgar in October 1805 to cancel his long-planned invasion of England, Napoleon decided to bide his time and rebuild his navy. In the meantime he devised an equally ambitious scheme that was intended to subjugate Britain by economic means. In November 1806 he decreed that the so-called 'continental system' was to be imposed along the entire coastline of Europe; this was intended to stop any of France's enemies, as well as neutral countries, from trading with Britain. By placing Britain under blockade, he hoped to ruin the international trade that formed the bedrock of her prosperity, and thus force her to accept his terms for peace. In January 1807 the British government retaliated by declaring a counter-blockade, by which Royal Navy warships would prevent vessels of any neutral country having commercial dealings with any French port, or with any port belonging to the allies of the French.

The stop and search duties this required British warships to undertake were, in certain significant respects, similar to other functions at which they were accomplished. Although such ships could often be subordinate in design to French ships, their signalling systems were more efficient and their discipline superior, making them formidable opponents in action.[1] The skills involved in maintaining a maritime embargo they had perfected during the long years of blockading France's invasion fleet, most notably in the unforgiving seas off Brest and Boulogne. Nevertheless the additional burden of having to impose a counter-blockade against the entire continent greatly stretched the navy's resources. But Admiral Thomas Russell was determined to keep the might of his squadron concentrated on its job of blockading what remained of the Dutch fleet, sheltering near the island of Texel, and since March 1807 the only vessel he could spare to take station off the mouth of the Elbe was a solitary frigate.

The work was dangerous, but it had to be done. Such were the risks of sailing in bad weather so close to shore (which was unlit at night), the spectre of shipwreck was ever-present. Indeed, of the navy's total loss of 317 ships in the years 1803–15, 223 were either wrecked or foundered, the great majority on account of hostile natural elements. Notwithstanding the sea-keeping qualities of the Royal Navy's ships, their capacity for endurance was far from endless. Such was the merciless pounding of the seas on hulls, rigging and spars, Admiral Russell knew that scarcely a month would go by when he did not have to send one or more of his vessels to the safety of the home dockyards for repairs.

The royal dockyards had just about been able to cope with these casualties because as well as building new ships they also had the capacity to repair damaged vessels. From the Baltic they received virtually all the high-quality basic products required, such as timber, flax, hemp, tallow, pitch, tar, linseed, iron ore and other necessities.[2] But all that was suddenly thrown into jeopardy in the summer of 1807 when Sir Edward Thornton sent reports to London indicating that France was planning to seize Denmark's fleet. As a neutral country, Denmark was in an invidious position between the warring factions. As a significant naval power, whose fleet had been rebuilt since 1801, she was regarded as a potential prize by both sides. On 21 July 1807, hearing – possibly via Talleyrand – that Napoleon and Alexander I of Russia were in the process of forming a maritime league against Britain in which Denmark would play a part, the War Minister Lord Castlereagh issued demands for the surrender of the Danish fleet.

Having battled around the Skagerrak in atrocious seas only to encounter frustrating calms in the

Kattegat, Admiral Gambier's task force of twenty-one ships-of-the-line, carrying nearly 20,000 troops, eventually arrived off Copenhagen on 2 September. When the Danish government rejected calls for surrender, a heavy naval bombardment of the city began. The most fearsome weapons used by the British, to devastating effect, were bomb-ketches equipped with huge mortars that lobbed 10-inch diameter fragmentation shells. These burst on contact and cut down personnel indiscriminately. By 5 September some two thousand of Copenhagen's inhabitants had been killed, many more were wounded and, to bitter parliamentary criticism, the remains of the Danish fleet was seized and brought into the Yarmouth Roads. This brutal pre-emptive strike had been a flagrant breach of Denmark's neutrality, and it threatened to be politically disastrous. Soon the key states under French influence – Russia, Prussia and Austria – declared war on Britain.[3] Significantly, on 17 August Denmark abandoned its neutrality and also declared war on Britain. The British had already been taking stock of Denmark's possessions, wondering which might be strategically useful, and Denmark's new stance soon focused British attention on Heligoland.

The fact that Britain had never before needed to fight a war in Europe on such a scale meant that a weakness now appeared in its campaigning. Numerous hitherto obscure parts of Europe were now suddenly of tremendous strategic value – but Britain had little or no intelligence about them. Rather astonishingly, although Heligoland was only some 300 miles from the Norfolk coast, scarcely anyone in Britain knew anything about the island, or even what it looked like. It seems quite probable that the only detailed chart of it the Admiralty had in its possession was a copy of one which had been made for the Hamburg Chamber of Commerce in 1787. This chart had recently been received from the second-in-command of Admiral Russell's flagship, HMS *Majestic*, Lieutenant Corbet D'Auvergne; he had acquired it from one Captain Dunbar, who happened to purchase it over the counter of a commercial ship's chandler during a visit to Copenhagen in 1806.[4] Fortunately for Admiral Russell, Lieutenant D'Auvergne was not just an exceptionally enterprising officer. He happened to be the younger brother of Rear-Admiral Philip D'Auvergne, otherwise known as the Duke of Bouillon, who was at that time controlling a network of spies gathering intelligence for Britain via the Channel Islands. The Jersey-based Bouillons were Belgian aristocrats who well knew the frailty of small national entities, having fled to England as long ago as 1672 when they were deposed from their homeland by the French.

The scarcity of detailed knowledge about the south-east part of the North Sea was slightly more surprising because Britain had had – albeit intermittently and fleetingly – various contacts with Heligoland over many centuries. There is a possibility that the island even received its name from a seventh-century English missionary called St Willibrod. The first written reference to the island appeared in AD 98, when it was recorded under the name 'Hyrtha' by the Roman historian Tacitus. At the very end of the seventh century, after Willibrod's accidental arrival there after a shipwreck in about AD 699, it acquired the name Heligoland (meaning 'Holy Land'), possibly because Willibrod himself came from Lindisfarne, on Northumberland's Holy Island, or perhaps because it had been a sacred place of the old Norse heathen gods.

Although for innumerable years thereafter various Viking chiefs vied for sovereignty of the island, such a hold as they were able to achieve was often precarious and disinterested. As a consequence there were often lengthy phases when the Heligolanders were left alone, and so virtually governed themselves. In a sense King Canute the Great of Denmark increased the island's constitutional promiscuity. By virtue of his becoming King of England in 1017, Heligoland came within the ambit of the English Crown for the period of his reign, which ended in 1036. In so far as there were subsequent links they were occasional, almost entirely of a commercial nature, and took the form of trips made by small merchant ships between the island and London's Billingsgate Market. In Britain it was only such traders who knew of the existence of Heligoland, together with a few mariners who had sought shelter there in bad weather or had perhaps transhipped some cargo in its waters. This remained the situation for centuries. In 1553 Richard Chancellor, the pilot-general of the exploration vessel *Bonaventure*, en route via Russia to search for a north-east passage to India, noted its existence in his journal – but he only happened to catch sight of it from a distance when his ship was blown off course by a storm. In Napoleonic times there was great need for a wider knowledge of Heligoland but no one had ever bothered to write down – in any language – any sort of history or pilotage notes.

Another beguiling feature of Heligoland's capriciousness was its ever-changing geographical appearance. By Napoleonic times it had changed dramatically from just a few centuries earlier. About the year 800 it had become home to a civilisation as advanced as any in northern Europe, with several villages scattered over the island. Covering some

24 square miles, it was wooded and fairly low-lying. In the south-west corner there was a huge mound, above which there towered two adjoining promontories, one of red stone and the other of white. Radiating outwards from the centre of the island were ten rivers. At the sources of the northernmost of those rivers were temples that had earlier been used for worshipping Tosla, Mars, Jupiter and Venus; in the south could be found a monastery and five churches. In inlets around the coastline were six anchorages, the three most important of which were on the leeward side of the island protected by three castles. But according to a map of Heligoland produced by the cartographer Johannes Mejerg in 1649, the gnawing away of the coastline by wave erosion and storms had been so voracious that by the year 1300 the sea had devoured all but 4 square miles of the hilly south-west corner of the island. All that remained at its fringes were the monastery, a church and the castle. By 1649 these too had vanished, leaving just an 'H'-shaped island, half red and half white, from which extended sandy reefs shaped like giant lobster claws.[5] And thus it stood until New Year's Eve 1720. That night there was an epic storm, and the sea surged through, permanently severing the narrow gypsum isthmus that had hitherto joined the western and eastern rocks. From then on Heligoland consisted of two distinct geographical sections, the main part of which was sometimes called Rock Island. Its low-lying dependency, just a few hundred yards to the east, was termed Sandy Island.

The final element in Heligoland's air of capriciousness was derived from the indefinability of its sovereignty. In 1714 Heligoland notionally became a possession of the Dukes of Schleswig-Holstein, who were Kings of Denmark. Danish rule was fairly remote

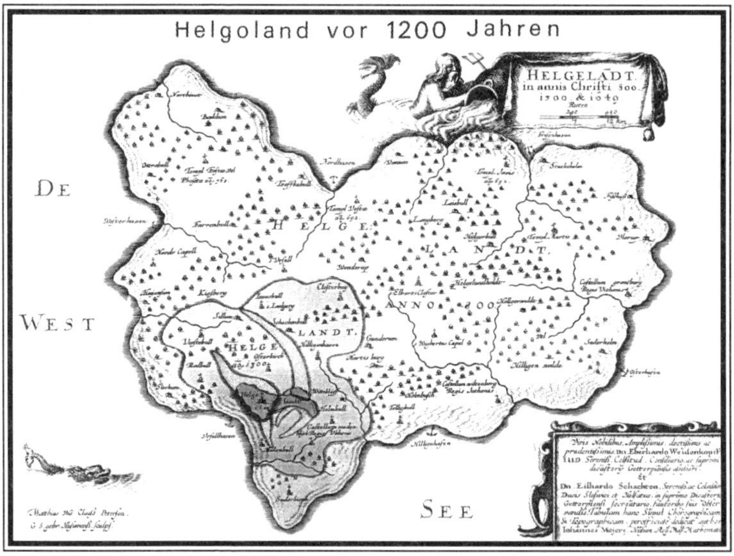

Map 1 Once a large North Sea island: sea erosion meant Heligoland's land area in 1649 was reduced to a fraction of what it had been. The small south-western corner was all that remained. (*Helgoland Regierung*)

and the Heligolanders were allowed the freedom to govern their own island as they thought best. Indeed in practical terms the ties that bound Heligoland, Denmark and Schleswig were slight. The island became a *de facto* No-Man's-Land, free to all, and afforded a welcome refuge for the people of other islands who were hounded by Danish tax-gatherers. The people made what they could by privateering, fishing and pilotage. Yet in Britain nothing was even known of the form of government which existed on the island. By Napoleonic times the Danish government had granted to Heligoland a few public works such as, in 1802, a fine cliff-side oak staircase joining the Lower and Upper Towns.[6]

Thus, in early September 1807, when Lord Castlereagh was poised to order the seizure of the island, all he had to go on was Lieutenant D'Auvergne's chart of the waters around it. The whole map measured just 15 inches by 9, less than 3 square inches of which covered the main island. It showed a blur of houses, but crucially gave no indication of where any fortifications might be. This all left disturbing questions about how much conditions there might have altered since 1787 when the chart had been drawn. For example, had the lobster-shaped reefs around Heligoland moved? There were military questions too. How many guns was it armed with? How many troops was it garrisoned by, and how spirited a fight might they make in defending it? So far the only written information available to Castlereagh was Chancellor's reported sighting of the island as long ago as 1553! But, by extreme good fortune, the person best able to provide the sort of answers Castlereagh needed had just arrived in London.

Even by the standards of the best and brightest of the Foreign Office in that era, Sir Edward Thornton was an exceptionally talented diplomat. The son of a Yorkshire innkeeper, and later a tutor to the household of the Foreign Secretary, Thornton had distinguished himself in the United States as the British *chargé d'affaires* in Washington. Since 1805 he had been Britain's plenipotentiary to Hamburg and the Hanse towns, but through his enthusiasm for his duties he had extended his understanding of potentially significant places beyond Lower Saxony. In the process he had made it his business to learn about nearby Heligoland, even though it was a Danish possession. It was in that regard that by 20 July 1807 he was corresponding with the picket ship HMS *Quebec*, stationed by Admiral Russell in the Bight. On 14 August 1807, having made a dangerous overland journey from Kiel to the mouth of the Elbe, Thornton and three of his diplomatic officials escaped in a small boat into the Bight where they encountered the *Quebec*. As they clambered aboard, Thornton and his party were greeted by the frigate's captain, Viscount Falkland. Allowed to remain as guests, they could see for themselves how the warship struggled in those waters to go about her business of intercepting suspicious-looking merchant ships. The potentially immense strategic importance of Heligoland suddenly became apparent on 19 August when news was received from a passing ship that Denmark had declared war on Britain two days before.

By lunchtime on 19 August the seas were sufficiently settled for Thornton's party to transfer to the brig HMS *Constant*, which two days later landed them in England.[7] Arriving in London, Thornton was invited to a hastily convened meeting with the new Foreign Secretary, George Canning, with whom he discussed what he knew about the situation on the island. Heligoland's future hung in the balance. Despite the fact that Britain was now at war with Denmark, Canning was reluctant to order an invasion of the tiny outpost, as he had been stunned by the fury elicited overseas by the attack on Copenhagen. Thornton sought to persuade him of the strategic advantages of capturing it, arguing that:

> its position and great elevation, compared with the low shoaly and dangerous coast of the North sea, meant it was absolutely necessary for every vessel bound to or from the Eider, Elbe, Weser and Jade rivers to make the Island of Heligoland; so that men-of-war stationed or cruising off it can as effectively secure the blockade of these rivers, at least, as if they were at anchor in the mouths of them.

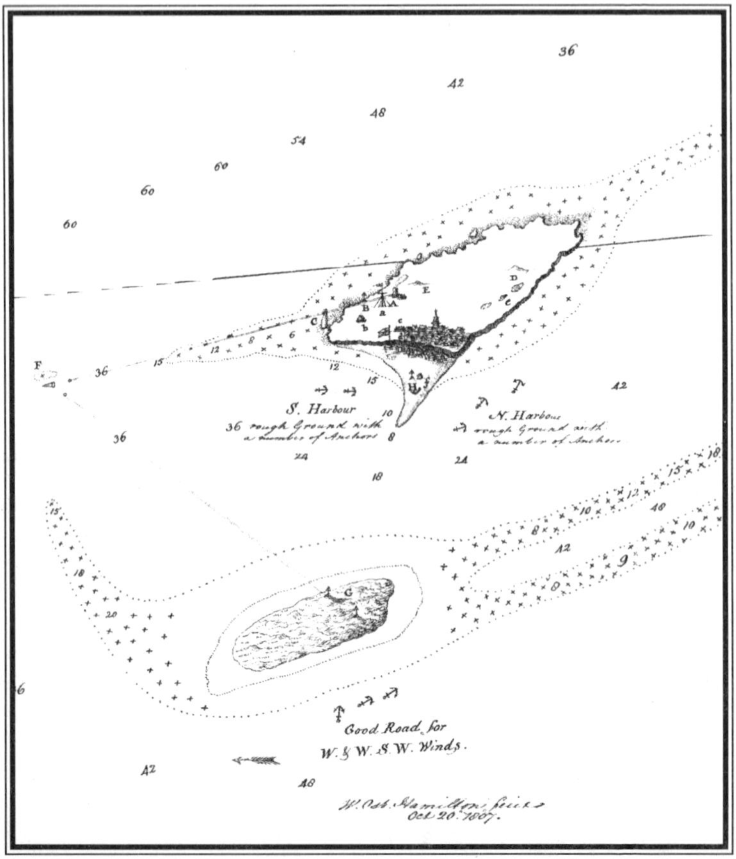

Map 2 So unknown had Heligoland been to the Royal Navy that this 1787 Hamburg chart was practically the only one it had when Admiral Russell captured the colony in 1807. That October, the governor designate personally added to the chart the improvised signal mast (marked 'a' on the clifftop) that the islanders had voluntarily salvaged from HMS *Explosion*. (*Public Record Office*)

Pondering on what had been said, Canning realised that it might become necessary to have a base from where his warships could conduct a rigorous blockade, especially against the Elbe. That river, being linked to the Baltic Sea by a small barge canal, offered the only overland route for naval stores for the Russian and Baltic ports, as long as the navigation of Denmark's Sound and Belts was obstructed by British cruisers. Furthermore, it might even be wise to deny Heligoland to the French. By the weekend Canning had decided the invasion of the island should proceed. On Sunday 30 August 1807 a messenger arrived at Thornton's lodgings with a letter from Canning urgently requesting him to 'commit to paper your ideas upon the subject of taking Heligoland, and send them to me at this office as soon as you can convey tomorrow morning'.[8] Thornton wrote hastily through that night. Working only by flickering candlelight, he distilled his observations and recommendations into a brief report. By noon the next day Canning had his report. Significantly, part of it read:

> The garrison consists of just one Danish officer and twenty-five soldiers. There are two or three cannon mounted at one end of the rock, which have been hitherto used for the purposes of signalling rather than with any view to defence. . . . There is little doubt that the appearance of an English gun-brig would immediately determine the inhabitants to surrender; and a vessel that could throw shells into the town would put the surrender beyond all question.[9]

Most crucially Thornton also urged that after taking over the territory Britain should abide by the administrative status quo: 'If any civil officer should be named for the purpose of internal regulations, he should be a person acquainted with the language and customs of the inhabitants.' And such an officer 'should not interfere with the government of the island'. His heartfelt conclusion read: 'I would take the liberty to recommend that its internal government should be continued as it exists at present without any alteration.'

Just a few hours after those recommendations were received at the Foreign Office and had been copied and despatched post-haste to Admiral Russell, a far harsher military assessment arrived at the Admiralty. On 1 September 1807 they received a report from a virtually unknown British military official, Colonel J.M. Sontag. His hastily written secret paper, *Attack upon the Danish Island of Heligoland*, agreed that: 'The taking possession of that island is of the greatest importance for Great Britain as it will enable the Navy to remain on that station the whole winter and afford an excellent shelter for their ships.'[10] In terms of storming the island, Sontag advocated a far harsher approach than Thornton's, suggesting that the inhabitants might be starved into surrender. The Heligolanders did not gather in their winter provisions until September, and the colonel noted that if a campaign began soon, 'the want of provisions – for they need to obtain every necessary of life from the mainland – would compel them to surrender in less than two months'. Sontag was clearly a ruthless man, for he also suggested bombarding the island with a pulverising Copenhagen-style mortar attack: 'To gain possession of it, it will be necessary to employ one or two frigates with some small ships of war to form the most strict blockade; one battalion of troops of the line, and also two bomb-ketches.'

Vice-Admiral Sir Thomas Russell's flagship, the 74-gun *Majestic* – a veteran of the 1801 Battle of Copenhagen – had been keeping a sea watch just off Texel, the easternmost of the Dutch Frisian Islands. At 10am on 3 September 1807 the fast despatch vessel *British Fair* hove into view and came alongside. From it Russell received two 'most secret' dispatches. One was his sealed orders from the Admiralty, the other a copy of Thornton's memo describing the island to Canning. Although Russell had been appointed commander-in-chief of the North Sea earlier that year, for an officer of his fighting qualities the Texel blockade had been especially frustrating because of the reticence of the Dutch squadron to allow him any opportunities for combat. The prospect of making some tangible strategic advance with regard to Heligoland was far more to his liking. Clearly eager to attack the island, he had been expecting that the orders to do so would arrive at any moment, as he had learnt from Viscount Falkland that Denmark had declared war. Consequently, on 30 August 1807, acting without authority from London, Russell ordered the *Quebec*, with the brigs *Lynx* and *Sparkler*, to establish an interim exclusion zone around the island to deprive it of all supplies and provisions.[11]

In fact it was only by chance that the admiral, who was to be fundamentally influential on the future of Heligoland, had ever gone to sea at all. By birth he had seemed destined to lead the life of a prosperous country squire. The son of an Englishman who had settled in Ireland, at the age of five Thomas Russell inherited a large fortune which by carelessness, or perhaps the dishonesty of his trustees, had disappeared before he was fourteen. This was probably what caused him to join the Royal Navy. Initially serving as an able seaman, he rose through the ranks to become a midshipman on a cutter in the North Sea. Although a blunt character, the misfortunes of his early life had beneficially imbued him with a powerful humanitarian spirit. By 1783 he was commanding a sloop off the North American coast, where he displayed both bravery and exceptional ship-handling skills in capturing in a storm the *Sybile*, a French warship considered to be the finest frigate in the world. For doing so Russell was offered a knighthood, which he modestly declined as he had not the fortune to support the rank with becoming splendour. In 1791, ten years before he was made a rear-admiral and did accept a knighthood, he commanded a frigate in the West Indies and won further distinction by securing the release of a British prisoner in Haiti's St Domingo by threatening to bombard the town to ruins.[12]

In the letter authorising the seizure of Heligoland the Admiralty also informed Russell that, to assist him with the capture, they had already ordered to set sail from Yarmouth the troopship *Wanderer*, carrying 100 marines, and the bomb-ketches *Explosion* and *Exertion*. On 3 September 1807, by which time Russell was under way on the 160-nautical mile voyage from Texel to Heligoland, he sent a despatch to the Admiralty, reporting that he had just 'given chase to five vessels to windward, to make out whether they may not be the bomb-ketches and their escorts, only to steer away for Heligoland, on the presumption they are destined for the capture of the island'.[13] So the *Majestic* confidently pressed on, Russell remaining as yet unperturbed by the non-appearance of the reinforcements. He had, after all, the copy of Thornton's letter in his pocket claiming that Heligoland's garrison consisted of only some twenty-five troops.

At 2.30pm on 4 September HMS *Majestic* arrived off Heligoland and anchored between Sandy Island and Rock Island, menacingly close to the Lower Town. The *Quebec* lurked nearby with the brigs, all ready for action. What Russell had no means of knowing at that moment was that the Heligolanders were mightily displeased with their current lot. Even before the exclusion zone policed by Viscount Falkland had been imposed their supplies had been running low. For some weeks Napoleon's 'continental system' and the resulting French pressure on Denmark had meant the islanders had been greatly impeded in their traditional occupations of fishing and piloting and so had been unable to make much of a living. Winter was approaching and they were, in effect, in the early stages of starvation. Initially, when the *Quebec* had arrived offshore a few days earlier, the island's Danish Commandant, Major Von Zeske, had been determined to hold Heligoland for his country as long as he was able. But his resolve was now waning fast, influenced by the Heligolanders' apparent reluctance to see their homes demolished before a surrender that appeared to be inevitable. Realising that his position was hopeless, at 6pm Major Zeske accepted a flag of truce and consented to a meeting with British officers the next morning.

The bomb-ketches and the troopship had still not arrived as Russell made ready to storm the island. He ordered a makeshift party of marines and seamen to be hastily assembled from the existing squadron. He was already anxious about the weather conditions and also became concerned that Major Zeske might be tempted to procrastinate, with the natural hope that so large a warship could not long continue to anchor so close to the town. His sense of urgency was clear in his letter demanding the island's surrender, which his representatives handed to Major Zeske at dawn on 5 September 1807. Hoping that the aristocratic status of his negotiators might itself have some effect on Zeske's position, Russell stated that the letter was 'being delivered to your Excellency by Captain the Right Honourable Lord Viscount Falkland, assisted by my First Lieutenant, Corbet D'Auvergne (brother to His Serene Highness Rear Admiral the Duke of Bouillon)'. Expressing an evidently sincere concern to spare the islanders from bloodshed, he implored Zeske to 'suffer me for the sake of Humanity to express a hope that your Excellency will not sacrifice the Blood and property of your inhabitants by a vain resistance, but that you will, by an immediate surrender, avert the horrors of being stormed'.[14]

Mindful of Thornton's memo to Canning urging that the island's 'Internal government should be continued without any alteration', Falkland and D'Auvergne agreed with Zeske that all such rights and customs would be safeguarded and respected. Unusually, there was an ongoing tradition that the islanders were not obliged to serve on board Danish naval ships, a privilege which should henceforth mean they would be exempt from service with the Royal Navy. The British representatives were in no mood to make any other allowances with regard to the military surrender: the garrison must lay down their arms, surrender themselves as prisoners-of-war and without their weapons leave forthwith on their *parole d'honneur* not to serve against Britain during the war. Zeske attempted to secure an undertaking that after the conflict the island would be returned to Denmark but this the naval officers refused to accept. At 2pm on the afternoon of 5 September the delegation returned to the *Majestic* with Zeske's signature on the Articles of Capitulation, which Admiral Russell briskly ratified.

British possession of the island began immediately with the arrival of a 50-strong landing party led by Corbet D'Auvergne. Even so, the commencement of British rule could scarcely have been more makeshift. To keep a record of events in the new colony he was furbished by the *Majestic*'s purser with an unused muster book – traditionally used to record the ship's company's wages and attendance data; D'Auvergne duly took a quill pen and neatly altered the words 'His Majesty's Ship' to 'His Majesty's Island of Heligoland'. He began by recording that, such was the high regard for Russell among the captains of the squadron, they had – without the Admiral's consent – named the highest part of the new possession 'Mount Russell'. The cliff-top that guarded it was now 'Artillery Park' and 'D'Auvergne Battery', below which was the inhabited part, now called 'Falkland Town'.

The capture of Heligoland had been a peripheral but psychologically significant naval triumph, and news of it came as a welcome change at a time when virtually all the gains elsewhere in Europe were being made by Napoleon. Seizing this opportunity to raise the British public's morale, the Admiralty circulated to the Press extracts of reports written by Sir Thomas Russell himself. Within a fortnight of the territorial acquisition these were prominently published in the *London Gazette* and even the *Gentleman's Magazine*. By such means the public learnt of the admiral's dash from Texel, the Danish representative's surrender of the island, and Russell's appointment of D'Auvergne as Acting Governor, because 'his perfect knowledge of both services, zeal and loyalty and a high sense of honour made him the most competent officer for the role'. The extracts concluded with the news that, on the morning of 6 September, at the very moment the British occupation was starting, the reinforcements arrived: 'the *Explosion*, *Wanderer* and *Exertion* hove in sight round the North End of the Island'.

But it might well have been a different story. By the time these extracts were on sale in the streets of London, Zeske and all the prisoners-of-war had been removed from the island, and shipped to mainland Europe for release. What was never revealed was the fact that the garrison's strength was not 'twenty-five Danish soldiers', as Thornton had predicted, but 206 – more than eight times that![15] In fact, Colonel Sontag's assessment of the need to bombard the island had fairly accurately predicted such a figure. Fortunately, Sontag's report only reached Russell when HMS *Explosion* and the other reinforcements arrived, by which time the garrison had surrendered. Significantly absent from any of the officially sanctioned extracts published was any mention of the islanders themselves.

The Admiralty most carefully hushed up the real details of the reinforcements' arrival. Russell had correctly reported in his letter of 6 September that 'the *Explosion*, *Wanderer* and *Exertion* hove in sight round the North End of the Island' – but his despatch did not conclude there. The sentence continued with the astonishing words: 'when the two former almost instantly struck and hung on the Long Reef'. What happened next was recorded in Lieutenant D'Auvergne's muster book. The good-natured islanders rushed to their boats to try to save the ships, even though they had been sent from Britain to threaten them with death. *Wanderer* was floated off, but the bomb-ketch *Explosion* had been too severely damaged below the waterline.[16] Two days later, in fresh breezes and squalls, she broke free from the reef and drifted across the narrow anchorage to Sandy Island where she finally ran aground, a listing wreck.

The spontaneity with which the islanders had rushed to help, and the immediate rapport between them and the British seafarers, fostered excellent relations between the two sides. Indeed, the islanders welcomed the British almost as if they were long-lost relatives. (In a sense, of course, they were, as both the British and the Heligolanders were, to a greater or lesser extent, distant descendants of the Frisians.) This goodwill greatly helped D'Auvergne in his hurried efforts to strengthen Heligoland's defences, lest the French should attack the island or Denmark attempt to recapture it. Under his directions the islanders themselves assisted in improving the ramparts of the cliff-top battery, which was to be the primary defensive position. The inventory of the captured Danish armaments provided grim reading. Of the dozens of abandoned cannon, virtually all were too rusty or poorly maintained to be functional.

Instead D'Auvergne turned his attention to the wreck of the bomb-ketch. With the islanders willingly providing most of the manpower, he set about salvaging all that might prove useful. First the *Explosion*'s fearsome 13-inch heavy mortars were brought ashore, as were her 68-pound cannon. Hauled aloft via the public oak staircase to Artillery Park they were duly installed at D'Auvergne Battery. Then, with great ingenuity, the islanders extracted the wreck's towering top foremast and floated it over to Falkland Town; here, they hauled it up to the windswept plateau atop the 200ft-high red cliffs and raised it as an improvised signal staff, complete with yardarm. Ironically, at noon on 22 September 1807, it was there that the British flag was raised in commemoration of the coronation of King George III, with the Heligolanders loyally in attendance as the guns fired a twenty-one gun royal salute.[17]

Evidently an inspired choice for the role of governor, D'Auvergne was quickly winning the approval of all the islanders. By his conspicuous zeal, excellent judgement and suavity of manner, he managed, to a considerable degree, to reconcile the inhabitants to the changes which they were experiencing.[18] One obscure incident helped to win him their affection. A few days after the surrender of Heligoland he was informed, on the authority of the magistrates, that there were forty families who had nothing to eat, not even bread, and no means of affording relief. D'Auvergne ordered the purser of the *Majestic* to deliver forty bags of bread to the island and directed him to see it impartially issued to the most needy families. On 16 September he wrote to Russell that virtually all the islanders were 'destitute of almost every species of provisions except fish', and to get them through the approaching winter he requested a shipment of 110 tons of rye, potatoes, flour and beef from England.[19] Aware that all supplies from Denmark had been cut off, Russell readily agreed to the request (and remarked that in view of the *Explosion*'s demise he would take a pilot from the island with him to ensure the supplies arrived safely).

D'Auvergne's kindness towards the islanders was in many other respects supported, indeed encouraged, by Russell. On appointing him Acting Governor on 5 September the admiral's written instructions had emphasised the need to treat the islanders with respect: 'You are to see that the inhabitants are treated with the greatest kindness; to conciliate their affections; and secure their attachment to our Government; as I hope it will never be given up.'[20] Two days later Russell wrote to the Governor, movingly expressing his heartfelt good wishes to the Heligolanders:

> Sir,
> Being on a point of sailing for England I am to request that you will acquaint the civil magistrates of your Government that I am so sorry that untoward circumstances have prevented my having the pleasure of being personally known to them.
>
> Assure them that I shall do the utmost of my ability to represent them as a people worthy of the attention of our Government; and worthy of the privilege of a British Colony.
>
> We have all noticed with joy the prompt, cheerful and effectual assistance given by your Inhabitants yesterday to HM ships the *Explosion* and *Wanderer* when aground, for which I pray Sir, that you will publicly advertise my thanks to them.
>
> I commit you and them to God's Holy care, and am with great respect.
>
> *Signed*
> Admiral, Sir Thomas Russell

The content of that moving letter was never made public by the Foreign Office, nor was the grateful letter of thanks sent a few weeks later to Governor D'Auvergne, and signed by every member of the Heligoland government:[21]

> By these victuallings is the danger of famine decreased, which lay very heavy upon the breast of every inhabitant. Your Excellency has, while you procured us these benefits, given us a practicable proof of the gentle affectionate intention you maintain for us.

> We acknowledge it with the warmest thanks that the Britannic Government gave us such a convincing proof of their humanity and generosity, and we hope that governance according to their general kindness all further months will see to commence.

Perhaps, then, it was not surprising that the British public also never got to hear the story of the forty bags of bread, or its postscript: that Russell had to personally intervene with the Admiralty to stop the mean-spirited Victualling Board from debiting the *Majestic* for those bags of bread for the starving.[22] Even the two-page Articles of Capitulation were kept secret, as was the admiral's declared hope that the island 'will never be given up'. There were other official clampdowns on the release of news. The loss of the *Explosion* and the consequent court-martial that September of its commander, Captain Elliot, were never brought to light. Nor was the trial of Viscount Falkland for an unrelated matter, although the disgrace resulted in altered place-names on Heligoland. Within a fortnight of the island's capture Russell personally made sure that all the names of British officers, including his own, were deleted from the map.[23]

But the British public was informed that Heligoland had a certain potential to be developed into an invaluable naval base. This was the opinion of Sir Thomas Russell himself, who had famously declared in his published despatch to the Admiralty on 5 September 1807, the day the island was captured, that Heligoland might prove to be the 'Gibraltar of the North Sea'. Two days later he advised the Admiralty of its benefits: 'It is possessed of a secure haven, formed between it and Sandy Island, for vessels of twelve feet draft; and a safe roadstead for 20 sail of the line the year round, with the exception of three or four points and with even these you may put to sea. It blows tremendously hard at this moment at N.S.W. which is nearly the least shelter, yet we ride easy with a scope of two cables.' It should not be forgotten that Russell was a superb ship-handler. Others were not so fortunate – as was seen with the wreck of the *Explosion*. Certainly in poor weather the island's 'harbour' – the quarter-mile channel between Rock Island and Sandy Island – was not safely tenable for large ships. Even when escaping out to sea to ride out the storm in open water they were at risk of being caught on the reefs. On 13 September D'Auvergne noted in his muster book that strong gales and heavy seas forced *Majestic* and her escorts to weigh anchor and make for the open seas; as they did so, the *Quebec* had to fire signal guns to warn the squadron that it was heading into danger.[24]

Of greater concern to the islanders was the arrival of the supply ship *Traveller*, bringing the 110 tons of food requested from England. It appeared on 7 October, and as it lay in the harbour D'Auvergne set about clearing out an old Danish storehouse to receive the provisions. That night a hard gale blew, with heavy running seas. Several fishing vessels and a galliot from London were forced ashore on Sandy Island. Then, at lunchtime, the *Traveller* parted a cable and showed a distress signal. The islanders immediately took to their boats and hurried to *Traveller*'s assistance with two anchors and cable, and it was only through their efforts that the ship and its precious cargo were saved.[25]

Heligoland might simply have remained a bustling naval station with warships coming and going at all hours, and escorting into the harbour any merchant vessels they managed to apprehend. But back in London the War Minister, Viscount Castlereagh, had other ideas. Keen to improve the artillery defences of the captured island, he hoped that in the process Heligoland could be brought under Army control, perhaps with a view to its eventually becoming a peacetime British colony. The artillery officer selected by the Adjutant-General to represent him in this respect was Colonel William Hamilton, the commander of the 8th Royal Veteran Battalion. Hamilton landed on the island on 16 October 1807 and his reception from the Heligolanders was markedly more reserved and less trusting than that shown to the original founding officers of British rule there: Thornton, Russell and D'Auvergne. That evening Hamilton wrote to Castlereagh, describing his 'considerable uneasiness' at the situation of the town so close to the barracks. 'In my opinion, it would be advisable to make a separation by a strong stockade with a blockhouse for a guard: which might be so placed as to command the town, and prevent any danger of surprises, should the inhabitants have any hostile intentions.'[26] For the construction of this fortification he advised: 'Timber for the stockade and blockhouses might be purchased from the Baltic, and the wreck of the *Explosion* also usefully might be used for military purposes.'

However, Colonel Hamilton was very impressed that the islanders, with their boats, had helped to disembark the 150 artillerymen he brought with him to replace the naval garrison.[27] Crucially, he also noted that the inhabitants appeared to be satisfied with the status quo, largely because they had faith in D'Auvergne's humane and good-natured governorship. This observation did most to overcome his scepticism about the islanders. The realisation that D'Auvergne's departure in February 1808 was sincerely regretted by every individual on Heligoland further made Hamilton determined, when he took over as the new governor, to continue with that apparently workable approach.

By then the defensive firepower provided by HMS *Explosion*'s salvaged mortars was heavily augmented with the arrival and installation on the cliff-tops of twelve large mortars and thirty-six cannon. However, for the moment the greatest danger came not from the Napoleonic forces but from Danish privateers preying on British-endorsed merchant vessels in the surrounding waters, beyond the range of the island's artillery. This problem persisted until June 1809, when four enemy ships were successfully deflected from approaching the island by HMS *L'Aimable*, a frigate commanded by Lord George Stuart, who in late September 1807 had replaced Viscount Falkland as commodore of the Elbe blockade squadron.

The potential for bad weather was itself likely to deter any but the most determined invasion force – especially in winter when the seas made Heligoland perilous to approach. During a violent storm on 7 December 1809 seven vessels were swept ashore at Sandy Island, including a Swedish galliot from Gothenburg and a vessel laden with sugar from England. In addition, a large sloop carrying goods from the West Indies sank in the harbour. The winds were so fierce the following night that several vessels were driven off the dangerously confined waters of the roadstead and perished in the Bight. Just how quickly a ferocious storm could engulf the waters around the island was described to readers of *The Times* on 15 June 1811. After a morning of remarkably fine weather, some dark and gloomy clouds were perceived about 4pm to arise on the horizon from the south, and by about 4.30pm the gloom was so great as 'almost to equal nocturnal darkness', claimed the writer.

> All of a sudden a white foam was perceived on the surface of the sea, drifting along with astonishing rapidity, and on its approach it blew such a hurricane of wind as has scarcely been witnessed by the oldest inhabitant on this island. In a moment every light article on the ground was carried into the air; for about half an hour the sea appeared one mass of foam, when a tremendous storm of thunder and lightning ensued, followed by a heavy pouring of rain. This calmed the wind, but we much fear that any vessel that came within the sweep of this violent whirlwind must have suffered greatly.[28]

During the autumn of 1810 alarming intelligence reached Hamilton. On Napoleon's orders a formidable Franco-Dutch expeditionary invasion force of twelve gun-brigs and twenty-four gunboats was being prepared in the rivers Ems and Jade, where special navigation marks had been placed in the shallow waters to enable ships to be moved at night. The invasion squadron put to sea on 20 November 1810.[29] As soon as he received intelligence that they were on the move, Lord Stuart went in search of them, his ship *L'Aimable* being accompanied by a schooner, six gun-brigs, and two gun-boats. The next day he got sight of the enemy, but as he closed in on them they fled. Three of the invading gun-brigs were driven ashore at the Jade estuary, while the rest scurried upriver to Varel (near the port later known as Wilhelmshaven). Stuart was left to prowl around at the mouth of the Jade, watching for the enemy. It was a celebrated defence and it won Stuart much applause in newspapers in England.

The 1810 invasion attempt had been ordered by Napoleon, who was becoming increasingly exasperated by Heligoland's effectiveness in breaching the 'continental system'. With a view to clamping down on the flourishing trade in contraband, in December 1810 Napoleon formally annexed from Prussia the north-west of Germany, including the mouths of the rivers Jade, Weser and Elbe. Insofar as the island came to be known of in Britain, it was as an entrepot for smuggling goods, in defiance of the French blockade, to and from Europe. In fact this trade did not commence until many weeks after Britain had seized the islands, and began by means of a certificate granted on 7 November 1807 by Governor D'Auvergne to a few London merchants to export British manufactured goods via Heligoland to Rostock.

Originally it was the far-sighted Edward Thornton, in his memo of 30 August 1807, who first advised that the island could be used for commercial as well as military purposes. By early 1808 the trickle had swelled into a powerful flood. Attracted by the island's proximity to the coastline of mainland Europe, nearly two hundred British agents and merchants had converged on it. With them they brought such immense quantities of goods that Heligoland seemed to be filled to overflowing. Scarcely a place could be obtained for storage, so great was the demand, and virtually any price the Heligolanders chose to ask was readily paid by the merchants. One entrepreneurial islander bought the hulk of the *Explosion* in a public auction on Sandy Island, and wondered if that too could not be utilised for storage.[30]

Never in all its history had Heligoland known so much prosperity; to its inhabitants, it seemed as if all their Christmases had come at once. The whole island hummed with activity. The first inkling D'Auvergne had that a 'gold rush' was looming came in December when he was approached by merchants seeking permission to build a brewery on the island.[31] Mariners' requirements for sustenance were such that by this time the island had only one church but thirteen inns! Sometimes there seemed to be dozens of merchant vessels of all shapes and sizes jostling for decent anchorages in the harbour. Not only were the Heligolanders now enjoying high rents for warehousing and for providing personnel with accommodation, but the island was receiving a few useful infrastructural facilities.

In 1808 the British government spent £500,000 on improving the anchorage and erecting warehouses. By means of small coastal craft enormous quantities of British goods were systematically smuggled into the ports of Holstein. Great ingenuity was used in getting colonial produce into the Elbe. The Hamburgers arranged for bogus funerals in a riverside suburb – until inquisitive officials discovered that on the return journey the hearses were packed with coffee and sugar. Much trade also flowed eastwards through the island, and in 1810 vast amounts of German corn reached England through Heligoland. Such was Britain's pre-eminence at sea that, despite all Napoleon's scheming, the 'continental system' eventually broke down. It had been a foolish economic weapon. By attempting to reinforce the French economy at the expense of other European states it prompted enormous antagonism. Indeed, the disastrous Russian war of 1812 was a direct outcome of the Russians' refusal to endure Napoleon's decrees any longer.[32]

With the Napoleonic wars drawing to a close, the British government turned its attention to the question of what to do with the colonies it had acquired during the years of conflict. Now Foreign Secretary, Lord Castlereagh showed great moderation in the peace negotiations with France, appreciating the folly of compelling the vanquished to accept crushing terms. Criticised in the House of Commons for this apparent leniency, he replied that the object of a peace treaty was peace and that if France were deprived of all her colonies and her natural resources she would certainly seek revenge. He secured all that he thought Britain needed: Gibraltar, Malta and the Ionian Islands. These, he hoped, would be enough to safeguard British naval power in the North Sea and in the Mediterranean, and to control the sea route to India.[33]

Once again, Heligoland's fate in British hands was to be greatly influenced by Sir Edward Thornton. During the latter years of the war he had carefully begun to form a union of the northern powers against Napoleon. In the process, in October 1811 he journeyed to Sweden on a special mission in HMS *Victory*, to attempt to negotiate treaties of alliance with both Sweden and Russia. Thornton, like Castlereagh, believed that for strategic reasons Heligoland should be retained, and in 1813 it was he who was entrusted by Castlereagh to negotiate the terms with Sweden and Denmark by which Norway was ceded to Sweden and Heligoland ceded to Great Britain. He made sure that Anholt was returned to Denmark, as was St Thomas, a Danish possession in the Caribbean which Britain had seized in 1807. In his crucial memo to the Foreign Office that year Thornton had urged that the gains of the inhabitants, either from their fisheries or their pilotage, should be given up to them without tax. He made certain that this and several similarly benevolent measures were incorporated into the Treaty of Kiel, signed by Britain, Sweden and Denmark in January 1814, by which Heligoland was ceded to the British Crown. The island looked set to begin a new life as a peacetime British colony.

2

Gibraltar of the North Sea

The crew of HMS *Explosion* must have wondered if they had been shipwrecked on the shores of a mysterious lost world, inhabited by distant relatives. The islanders who suddenly converged on the stricken bomb-ketch in a shoal of wooden boats seemed harmless enough. As they threw rescue lines aboard and helped to evacuate the ship, the crew of *Explosion* saw them clearly for the first time. In appearance the Heligolanders were almost Rubensesque: hearty and good-natured, beaked-nosed, with healthy tanned faces, burnished by an outdoor life. They looked rather Frisian, although also slightly Danish.

In 1666 Samuel Pepys, then Secretary to the British Admiralty, referred to that northern wind-blown maritime province of the Netherlands as 'Freezeland'. And thus it remained – a place about which the British knew, or cared, very little. Culturally the outer reaches of Friesland's influence were the Frisian Islands, which extended along the coast of the Netherlands from Texel, and off the Lower Saxony coast around the Elbe. The Frisian peoples were predominantly seafarers, and their native language was reputed to be dialectically the closest European language to English. Indeed, the similarities between English and Frisian were so extensive that Willibrod had found no difficulty in conversing with the islanders centuries before; nor, superficially at least, did the crew of the *Explosion*.

And yet, despite their close links with the Frisians, the islanders always perceived themselves as Heligolanders, not Frisians. There was some justification for this, because Heligoland had never been constitutionally associated with any of the Frisian Islands. They even had their own dialect, Heligolandish, which they instinctively used when chatting among themselves. To those not of their island, even to Frisian people who spoke a similar language, Heligolandish was virtually incomprehensible. In the absence of a dictionary of Heligolandish (indeed, one was only compiled in 1954), early on in his governorship Colonel William Hamilton had to persuade the Colonial Office to supply him with a translator.[1]

By 1811 the British had completed a census of Heligoland. This revealed that the civic population consisted of 2,061 persons living in 461 dwellings, and that 390 of them were pilots and fishermen, operating 100 boats and 9 schooners.[2] Flesh was put on to the bare bones of those statistics by the distribution within official circles of a description of Heligoland. Even that found the islanders something of a puzzle. They were good people: quiet, strong, honest, courteous, friendly and law-abiding. And yet, though welcoming, they were also beguilingly inscrutable and obscurely impassive. They kept their thoughts to themselves. A stoical bunch, their national character had been carved by the sea, like the geography of their homeland. Their island's defiant ability to withstand the worst that the elements could throw at it made them perceive it as having magical qualities. Their pride in the island extended to their homes, which were all kept scrupulously clean. They regarded their island as the centre of the only world that mattered, and even the most skilled Heligolandish sailors seldom ventured into seas beyond the Bight. So content were they with their tiny island homeland that they regarded it – perhaps rather absurdly – as being a nation itself. Such pride derived substantially from the island's exceptional geographical qualities. This they celebrated in their own popular rhyme, which translates as: 'Green is the land, red is the rock, white is the sand; these are the colours of Heligoland.'

In the archive of dusty official papers surrendered by the island's former Danish administration, Governor D'Auvergne was delighted to discover seventy protocols and documents. In the absence of any sort of written constitutional history of Heligoland, these were the clues he needed to learn the arrangement of the previous structure of government. The island's affairs were run by six Magistrates, who in turn nominated seven Quartermasters. As well as commanding pilot boats and other craft engaged in public service, their duties included keeping clean the streets in their 'Quarters'. The Magistrates also nominated sixteen Aldermen, who acted for the Quartermasters in their absence. Together the Magistrates, Quartermasters and Aldermen formed the membership of the island's parliament, the Vorsteherschaft, which assembled so rarely that it did not even have a meeting-house.[3]

The Heligolanders evidently did not realise, or did not mind, that such a system discouraged individualism, and thereby inhibited the growth of indigenous leaders who could effectively speak on their island's behalf. In any event, at the time of the Treaty of Kiel, Sir Edward Thornton made sure the island's Danish style of constitutional system would continue virtually unchanged under British rule. Initially that suited Britain too, as her new colony had a well-established constitutional system. Although quite sophisticated, it was not greatly dissimilar to those in most of Britain's other colonial possessions, most of which had a governor, a council and an assembly; so, from 1814, Heligoland joined the ranks of Britain's smallest colonies – remote places such as St Helena and the Falkland Islands. Like them, it received a minuscule annual grant to cover the cost of employing a handful of British people to assist with the territory's administration. The Colonial Office was so rigorously parsimonious that for many years the civil staff expenditure remained fixed, with scarcely any permitted alteration. In 1848 the total cost of the civil establishment's salaries on Heligoland, as paid for by the Colonial Office, was just £1,023 – an amount scarcely changed from 1836 when it was just £963.

Governor	£500
Clerk to Governor	£136
Two Clergymen @ £50	£100
Two Magistrates @ £30	£60
Town Clerk	£60
Signalman	£60 10*s*
Navigation bosun	£33 6*s* 8*d*
Mail Carrier	£69 6*s* 8*d*
Keeper of the Blockhouse	£3
Total	£1,022 3*s* 4*d*

Unwittingly, Governor D'Auvergne's generosity in facilitating the distribution of the forty bags of bread in 1807 had defined the dynamics of the crucial conflicting attitudes regarding Heligoland. On the one hand there were the islanders who, though independently minded, were instinctively well disposed, and indeed even affectionate, towards Britain; and on the other there was mean-spirited officialdom in London which was inclined to be predominantly concerned with the cold realities of Britain's wider interests. Caught between the two were the governors, and it was they who played a vital role in reconciling those sometimes conflicting forces. Moreover it was the humane means by which they did so that cumulatively improved the situation. The islanders quickly realised that in January 1814 when, the war having ended, all the contraband merchants departed, bringing to an abrupt end a buccaneering business activity which had seen some £8 million-worth of goods transferred through Heligoland in each year of the 'continental system'. Almost immediately, the islanders were left with virtually no employment. Even for the better-off that winter, Christmas dinner consisted of a plate of seagull and cabbage. They were further reduced to a deplorable state by the weather, as the island was encircled by great shoals of ice. In the absence of much Colonial Office support, on his own initiative Governor Hamilton launched an appeal for financial subscriptions to assist the islanders.[4]

Subsequent governors did what they could to present the Heligolanders in a favourable light. Hamilton's successor, Lieutenant-Colonel Sir Henry King (governor 1815–40), did so for twenty-five years. The sympathies of the next governor, Admiral Sir John Hindmarsh (1840–57), were with the poorest of the working class. He was followed in office by Major Richard Pattinson (1857–63), who invariably took the side of Heligoland's pilots in maritime disputes, especially when they were unfairly accused by ship-owners of hazarding vessels in the Elbe.

For decades the colony had been unusual in the British Empire insofar as it made remarkably few complaints against the Colonial Office.[5] But all that began to change in 1864 when Whitehall began planning to reduce the island's heavy £7,000 national debt burden – which had been growing alarmingly since the Napoleonic wars – by means of a tax on gambling. Local politicians, perceiving the imposition of such a betting levy to be an infringement of their 'Ancient Rights' of no taxation, refused to co-operate. In March 1865 a deputation proceeded to London to voice their opposition. Their protests were endorsed by the island's newest governor, Major-General Sir Henry Maxse (1863–81), an energetic and fearless former soldier who had witnessed the Charge of the Light Brigade and distinguished himself in the Crimean War. In the dispute he took the side of the islanders. At his request, in June 1867 the Colonial Secretary, the Duke of Buckingham and Chandos, arrived on the island on the Admiralty yacht *Enchantress*, becoming the first British minister ever to set foot there. What he heard and saw caused him to decide that a simpler form of government should be established on Heligoland, and accordingly that was done by an Order in Council in February 1868. For taking a humane stand on their behalf Maxse became something of a hero to the islanders – so much so that they named a street after him. It is still there.

Regardless of the differences some of the island's elders had with London, the inhabitants were mostly well satisfied with the post-1868 state of things, although naturally there was always likely to be a slight general hankering for the good old times of wrecking, gambling and no taxation. Britain continued to make no attempt to stifle local identity. Indeed, it affably accepted, and indeed encouraged, such distinctiveness. Its benignly disinterested stance towards the territory meant the islanders felt they were enjoying the best of both worlds. On the one hand their relatively strong sense of independence was respected, while on the other, their status as a British colony – unlike all the other Frisian Islands and neighbouring North Sea coastal ports – meant they were uniquely associated with the world's greatest maritime power. Queen Victoria's head appeared in the corner of all their distinctive green, red and white stamps. London had no objection to the Heligolanders evolving a flag of their own, depicting the island's native colours of green, red and white, and formally approved of that tricolour having the British Union Jack motif in one corner. That flag became one of the Heligolanders' most prized possessions. It tangibly linked their little island with Britain's immense naval power, and they scarcely missed an opportunity to fly it proudly – if rather provocatively – from the ensign staffs of their fishing-boats when visiting neighbouring ports.

In 1868 the island saw the establishment of half a dozen English coastguards under a Royal Navy officer. The officer was also appointed Wreck Receiver – and thereby, on the subject of wreck and salvage, enabled ship-owners to obtain justice. Instead of being an alleged nest of wreckers, Heligoland became renowned for the order and regularity preserved when wrecks occurred. There was a sense that the presence of uniformed British coastguard officials on the island somehow brought Britain and Heligoland closer together. During gales the islanders used to drag their small lobster boats up to safety among the houses of the Lower Town, while their sloops had to ride out the worst of the storms at moorings that might frequently be carried away. Hitherto the island's fishermen had lived heroically, often using their boats as lifeboats, manoeuvring them skilfully through the shoals that beset the island to save some schooner or brig driven aground. The arrival of the coastguards to do this work further strengthened the link of common seafaring experience between Britain and Heligoland.

And yet still there were few in Britain who really knew much about the island. Artistic works were made of it, but for one reason or another the British public seldom got a chance to view them. In 1837 a grotesque etching entitled 'The Death-boat of Heligoland', of drowning mariners in a tempestuous sea, was created in the style of the seascape artist J.M.W. Turner, although it only appeared as an illustration in a collection of poems by Thomas Campbell. The exhibits displayed at the 1851 Great Exhibition at Crystal Palace and the 1886 Colonial Exhibition in London gave the general public the opportunity to get some idea of the nature of Britain's colonies. Heligoland, unfortunately, was too diminutive to be considered worthy of representation at such gatherings. In 1856 a sculpture of Alfred the Great clutching a Heligoland-style Frisian boat was unveiled at the Royal Academy. It was then permanently sited within the confines of the Houses of Parliament, but in a spot so obscure that no one had a chance to associate it with Heligoland. In the 1880s Hamilton Macallum, a distinguished Royal Academician, visited the island and was well received at Government House. The many images of it he painted during his visit were exhibited in London –

but in the Grosvenor Gallery where only a privileged few had a chance to view them. During the nineteenth century the few charts the Admiralty produced of Heligoland were seen by only a few seafarers. The nearest the island ever came to 'official' pictures were the water-colours and sketches done by Lieutenant-Colonel Edward Frome of the Royal Engineers, who in the 1850s was apparently stationed on the island with the temporary garrison during the Crimean War scare. These were never shown in public, and could only be privately viewed at the Royal Commonwealth Society's collection in Cambridge (from where they were eventually stolen in 1989).

By Victorian times many more British people knew of the existence of Heligoland and were generally well disposed towards the island. But it really captured the British public's imagination when Miss L'Estrange wrote a detailed and enchanting exposition of life on Heligoland. She was the daughter of an invalided British officer who had been stationed there until 1821. Her slim book, *Heligoland, or Reminiscences of Childhood*, somewhat surprisingly, became a best-seller and was reprinted four times in the 1850s. Nevertheless, in contrast to the Napoleonic period, when (weather permitting) dispatches from the island would appear in *The Times* twice a week, often whole years would pass without the island being mentioned by any British newspaper.

Somehow there were very few Britons interested in actually making a visit, although the facilities for doing so were well-enough organised. According to a newspaper advertisement of 1836, passengers with the General Steam Navigation Company could travel from the City of London to Heligoland within 30 hours. The company ran a fleet of five ships, one of which would call twice a week to collect passengers from the foot of Lombard Street, at Custom House stairs. Departing down the Thames on a Wednesday morning aboard one of their ships bound for Hamburg, for example, passengers for the island could disembark en route at Cuxhaven and after a short trip on a mail boat, weather permitting, arrive in Heligoland at lunchtime on the Thursday.

In contrast, German curiosity about the island had begun to grow. Ironically, the roots of their curiosity can be traced back to an incidence of British parliamentary meanness. In 1825 Joseph Hume's persuasive denunciation in the House of Commons of what he insisted was the excessive cost of the island's garrison had resulted in the removal of the two hundred soldiers later that year.[6] It was a move which further required the islanders' to revive their fishing skills, as well as the trades of their forefathers as pilots, capitalising on their specialist knowledge of the shifting sands and perilous mudbanks of the estuaries of the Bight's great rivers. Even so, something more was needed to develop the island's natural resources. Quite unexpectedly it was a Heligolandish carpenter who in 1826 came forward to create the foundations of a scheme that would eventually transform the island's economic fortunes. Jakob Andersen Siemens had done quite well for himself on the mainland and now began to wonder how he might help his homeland. Could, he mused, a sea-bathing establishment be set up on Heligoland's dependency, Sandy Island?

The winters were usually stormy. May and even June were often wet and foggy. Even so, a few visitors came in the first summer season between early July and late September. In 1828 they numbered just a hundred. In a decade that figure had become a thousand, and the number kept rising until by the third quarter of the nineteenth century it was nearing fourteen thousand. The salubrity of the summer climate and the excellence of Sandy Island's sea bathing assisted Heligoland's evolution into one of the most fashionable and fun-loving bathing resorts of northern Europe. The visitors were from every rank in society, from princes to tradesmen, and most came from Hamburg and the other towns on the neighbouring coast. The paddle-steamer trip from Hamburg, down the winding Elbe, across the estuary and thence into the Bight, was in distance remarkably similar to the trip Londoners might regularly make to Margate on the Kent coast. Significantly, few of the summertime visitors to Heligoland were British; they were virtually all German.

Because the British Empire embraced dozens of small island colonies – many of them tropical – across the world, Heligoland was naturally perceived by most British people in benignly matter-of-fact terms as being relatively unexceptional, but to the Germans it was a vivid novelty. Not only was it a unique offshore (rather than inshore) North Sea island, it was physically totally unlike anywhere else in Lower Saxony. In contrast to the mile upon mile of deserted fields that made up the drably featureless Frisian coastline, 'perhaps covered in snow, bathed in a murky light',[7] the Germans regarded Heligoland as geographically unique, with its towering red cliffs, rocky shore and capricious sands. These beguiling attractions were enhanced by the oscillating tides and the presence of countless gulls and migratory seabirds which seasonally flocked to the island from distant lands. The mesmerising, magical sense of a charmed island which had somehow survived the rigours of fierce storms yet remained beautiful all added to the sense of the place as a whimsical paradise.

In contrast to their British counterparts, German writers, artists and musicians were heavily influenced by the North Sea island. Composers who went there for spiritual fieldwork included Anton Bruckner (who in 1893 even wrote a work aptly entitled *Helgoland*), Franz Liszt, Hans von Bülow, and even the Austrian Gustav Mahler. Among the Germanic artists drawn to the island were the painter Gustav Schönleber. *Sturmläuken auf Helgoland*, a dramatic oil painting depicting Rubensesque Heligolanders hurrying along a street in a violent storm, was created by Rudolf Jordan. Famous writers also came: men of such stature as Franz Kafka, August Strindberg and Hebbel bis zu Kleist. A particularly enthusiastic visitor was the influential German travel writer Reinhardt – the originator of the hymn 'Watch of the German Fatherland' – who published a glowing account of his trip.

To the bemusement of the independently minded islanders, creative Prussian intellectuals presumptuously depicted Heligoland as the exemplification of German virtues and the 'Germanic spirit'. None did it more preposterously than the German lyricist August Heinrich Hoffmann. But few Heligolanders could have predicted his achievement back in 1841 when he first arrived on the island, virtually unnoticed. Born at Fallersleben in Lüneberg in 1798, he had been employed as a professor of the history of language at the University of Breslau. In 1840 he published a political critique expressing National-Liberal views, as a consequence of which he was forced to leave Prussia, and he decided to travel abroad for three years. On 28 August 1841, while sheltering as a political exile in Heligoland, he wrote the song 'Deutschland, Deutschland über Alles' ('Germany, Germany over all'), under the pen-name Hoffmann von Fallersleben. It was an emotive work that pleaded for a single unified Germany to take precedence over all the numerous states into which the country was fragmented at the time. In due course, a number of years later, the song became Germany's national anthem. This had the effect of bolstering the growing but absurd myth that Heligoland was, by association, something to do with Germany.

Ironically, one unexpected consequence of adhering to Sir Edward Thornton's well-meant entreaty that the colony be administered more or less as it had been in Danish times was that in two symbolic respects its sovereignty could be misconstrued as having German elements. Shortly after the island's surrender in 1807, the British discovered a lighthouse on the highest point of the plateau. It took the form of a red-brick tower upon which was kept alight a coal fire. Surprisingly, captured papers revealed that its maintenance (and that of a similar lighthouse on Neuwerk Isle at the mouth of the Elbe) was financed by the Admiralty of Hamburg, which for countless years had been paying for 700 tons of high-quality coal to be procured for it each year from Scotland.[8] At Colonel Hamilton's recommendation the tower was replaced by a more effective, state-of-the-art rounded lighthouse, similar in type to those then being built around the coast of Ireland. However, because of Joseph Hume's repeated criticisms in Parliament about the amount of money spent on the island, since 1825 the authorities in Hamburg had again been permitted to pay for the light's running costs, although it remained the property of Trinity House.

There was further blurring of the island's national identity. Again to save money, the Colonial Office had allowed Heligoland's postal affairs to be run by the City of Hamburg. With the British government paying the maintenance expenses, the postal authorities of Prussia undertook to design, engrave and print all the necessary labels and stationery at their own Royal Printing Office (ironically, it was they who printed Queen Victoria's head on the stamps). That rather Byzantine *modus operandi* led to some astonishing scams. By 1870 a series of special stamps, which had first been issued in 1867, were being widely forged, notably by a gang of criminals known as the Spiro Brothers. Their plates somehow fell into the hands of a printer in Hamburg. Then a Herr Goldner, a dealer in that city, was allowed to purchase the plates of ten stamps of different value from the Royal Printing Office in Berlin. All the stamps were defunct, but immediately he obtained possession of them he set about producing reprints, charging double the ordinary price for supplying them postmarked. This arrangement caused ill-feeling between Government House on the island and the Hamburg Post Office, while much-needed revenue was being forfeited by the farming-out of the production of those symbols of nationhood.

In 1848 the Germans were rethinking their naval strategy; although it was not evident at the time, this would have a profound influence on the future of Heligoland. In that year a former German diplomat, who had recently embarked on a career in politics but was still virtually unknown, wondered if the effectiveness of the German Navy could be increased by widening the barge canal that wound across the Jutland peninsula separating the North Sea and the Baltic Sea. His name was Otto von Bismarck. Farsightedly he set about quietly acquiring the land rights which could eventually serve as the territorial basis for the construction of the Kiel Canal. 'I travelled back to Berlin with the cession of an old strip of land on the Jade in my pocket, thinking not a little of my achievement', he later admitted.[9] But for many years subsequently, Bismarck was entirely distracted from his canal scheme by more pressing affairs of state.

In the meantime, however, the planners of Germany's fledgling coastal navy were increasingly having strategic nightmares about the Royal Navy's devastating raid against the Danish fleet at Copenhagen in 1801. The central question buzzing in their minds was how they could best forestall the British from making such a ruinously effective pre-emptive attack against their own warships. Ironically, their sense of strategic vulnerability was increased by the inauguration in 1869 of a new naval base called Wilhelmshaven. It was Germany's equivalent to Chatham, but its location a few miles inland in the muddy Jade estuary made it potentially vulnerable to a blockade by the British, who could use Heligoland as a forward base, just 48 miles north across the Bight. With that strategic disadvantage in mind Admiral Ludwig von Henk, one of the developers of the new German Navy, in 1882 wrote a pamphlet entitled *Heligoland's Strategic Significance to Germany*, in which he argued that it was vital for Germany to acquire the island.

Rather surprisingly, even senior German naval officers were so awed by the power Britain could presumably wield via Heligoland that they overlooked the likelihood of the island being implicated in regional wars *even when Britain remained neutral.* This was brought home to Governor Ernest Maxse on 9 May 1864 during the Franco-Prussian war when a ferocious sea-battle occurred between Austro-Prussian and Danish warships just off the coast of Sandy Island. Earlier that week the British government had hosted a reconciliation conference in London, at which the combatant nations had agreed to a limited armistice. So there was consternation in the Colonial Office at 2 o'clock that afternoon when a telegram suddenly arrived, via a newly installed North Sea telegraph cable, direct from Maxse. Excitedly he reported: 'The Danes have won the action. One Austrian frigate is in flames, and she, together with the other Austrian frigate, and gunboats, is making for Heligoland. They are almost in English waters.' Soon the battered vessels were lying at anchor in the roadstead just off the island. Momentarily there must have been some alarm that the fight might continue within the British jurisdiction, or even that the Danes might take advantage of the confusion to recapture Heligoland. But eventually the bedraggled Danish fleet sailed off, perhaps deterred by the sight of the frigate HMS *Aurora*, pugnaciously riding at anchor as guardship just south of the island with all her guns run out and ready for action.

Mischievously trying to provoke a conflict with Britain, soon afterwards German nationalists wrote reports in continental newspapers falsely claiming that this British warship had manoeuvred to deceive and impede the Austrian squadron. Then, in the 1870 Franco-Prussian war, in which Britain was also neutral, Heligoland's non-involvement was again compromised. Unsuccessful though the French were on the battlefields, they had a substantial navy and put it to practical use blockading Germany's navigable estuaries in the Bight. Not since the 'continental system' of the Napoleonic wars had there been so many ships anchored in the Heligoland roadstead. The opportunistic islanders sought every chance to sell provisions to the crews of the French blockading vessels. These breaches of neutrality became so blatant that in 1871 the German Ambassador in London demanded an enquiry into reports that the Heligolanders had been supplying coal to the French warships. Governor Maxse had previously turned a blind eye to the islanders' activities, and the island's parliament was furious when Whitehall ordered him to put a stop to such violations of British neutrality. Even so, just as he had done in 1864, Maxse used the island as an ideal observation post to keep London informed by telegraph of the locations and movements of the rival warships.

Despite unnervingly close encounters in those two wars, Britain still failed to fortify the island. As long ago as April 1860 official meanness frustrated Governor Pattinson's initiative to muster a local voluntary militia. He successfully raised a corps of twenty-five recruits but by January 1861 the scheme had collapsed because, despite numerous written pleas from Pattinson, the Colonial Office refused to pay for the much-needed ammunition to be sent from the Army depot at Purfleet. In October 1871 – according to the German newspaper *Kreuz Zeitung* – a battery of 12-pounder Armstrong guns was sent to the island from England, but they were only to be used for firing fog signals and salutes, and were not perceived as having any defensive function. There were anxieties that the accompanying stocks of gunpowder would run out anyway, Britain being too tight-fisted to ensure that supplies were regularly delivered.[10]

For a while it looked as if the Colonial Office might yield to requests from Maxse's successor, Colonel

Terence O'Brien (Governor 1881–8), for the construction of a harbour for local needs. In 1883 the eminent civil engineer John Coode was sent to Heligoland to complete a feasibility study. Knighted for his construction of the breakwater in the treacherous tidal waters off Portland Island, he was an ideal choice of harbour designer. He made a huge, beautifully coloured plan of the Lower Town, on which he showed how east and south piers might be constructed for a cost of some £60,000.[11] Nothing came of it, and ships were still obliged to anchor in the roadstead and land their cargo and passengers in open boats, even in stormy and dangerous weather. At Westminster there were a few calls for the island to be fortified. But more hope came in March 1885 from a report by the Parliamentary Select Committee on Harbours of Refuge. Acknowledging Heligoland's great value to British fishermen working the Dogger Bank and Heligoland Bight, the Committee observed that the island had the potential to be of even greater importance if a proper graving dock were constructed there for the repair and maintenance of British fishing vessels.

Partly relenting, the Colonial Office grudgingly permitted the construction of one of the piers Coode had recommended. In terms of defending against coastal erosion, as the relentlessly gnawing waves caused the collapse of cliff-tops on the island's west side, it would do nothing. When Governor O'Neil personally drew charts proving that Sandy Island was vanishing by half an acre every decade, Whitehall's response was that Sandy Island was a commercial beach resort and thus not its responsibility.

Britain's reluctance to spend even minimal sums on such improvements was keenly noted by nationalists in the German parliament. Doubtless they were reminded that in the past Britain had been known to abandon unwanted colonies. In the Anglo-Dutch treaty of 1824, for example, all the British settlements in Sumatra had been handed over to the Netherlands, and Dutch predominance recognised in other occupied islands in the East Indies in exchange for Malacca being handed over to Britain. And had not the Ionian Islands, which had been captured by the British in 1809 and made a British Protectorate in 1815, been annexed to Greece in 1864?

Nationalists within the German government saw their chance in February 1871, when a peace treaty was being negotiated between Germany and France. Their thoughts turned to an extraordinary place called Pondicherry. Known as the 'Paris of the East', Pondicherry was the capital of 'French India' and consisted of a beautiful enclave of some 115 square miles not far from Madras on the south-east coast of India.[12] Their idea was that Germany should deprive France of Pondicherry in the peace talks, and then offer it to Britain in exchange for Heligoland. It was a bizarre scheme, and it did not get far. On 6 June 1871, when rumours of the Pondicherry scheme were brought to the attention of Parliament, Lord Enfield, a Foreign Office spokesman, declared: 'No proposal has been received for the cession of Heligoland to Germany, and there is no correspondence on the subject.' Hansard records the chamber's approving response to that dismissal with hearty growls of 'Hear, hear'.

At that time Count Bismarck was vigorously opposed to the acquisition of Heligoland, or indeed of any colony. When the prospect of overseas territories for Germany was urged upon him, he famously replied: 'I want no colonies. For us colonial enterprises would be just like the silks and sables in Polish noble families, who for the rest have no shirts.' Colonies were, he was convinced, a meaningless distraction from his ambition of unifying and expanding Germany. Various difficulties in the 1870s had left him no time even to overcome the resistance to his pet project, the Kiel Canal, in the imperial councils.[13] But by the 1880s Bismarck was well established as the 'Iron Chancellor' and he had Kaiser Wilhelm I's support.

In February 1886 the Reichstag was considering a bill on the subject of the Kiel Canal, which it was widely expected to approve. The 61-mile shipping waterway was to be constructed between the Elbe above Brunsbüttel and the Baltic Sea at Holtenau above Kiel, thus linking the North Sea and the Baltic. As well as gratifying the political wishes of the 'extenders of the realm', who envisaged it as a tangible demonstration of Prussian imperial power, it would also reduce dramatically the sailing distance between Kiel and Wilhelmshaven from 480 miles to just 80. An entire fleet of ironclads could be quickly and safely moved across German territory from one sea to the other, and would no longer have to sail through the Skagerrak and Kattegat on the 'Great Belt' route along the Danish coast, where they were at risk of attack from other vessels and mines. Actual construction of the canal would begin in 1887, but in the meantime, to remove the potential risk of a British blockade of the Elbe estuary (and thereby the western end of the canal), Bismarck became convinced that Germany must somehow get control of Heligoland.

On 5 May 1884 he had written to Count Münster, the German ambassador in London, instructing him to invite Gladstone's government to consider abandoning the island. Münster, who had long advocated Anglo-German cooperation, was delighted with this instruction and replied on 8 May: 'During my appointment here I have always, although the possession of Heligoland lay near my heart, carefully avoided discussing the question with the statesmen here.' The only time the ambassador had had any discussion on the subject with any English statesman was in a conversation with the present Colonial Secretary, Lord Derby, who himself brought up the question. Münster was shooting with Derby at Knowsley when the minister happened to receive some official letters, including one from Colonel O'Brien, the Governor of Heligoland. Lord Derby remarked: 'This perfectly useless piece of rock in the North Sea, the smallest of our colonies, gives me the most trouble of any.' To which Münster replied: 'If the rock seems so useless to you, you should make it useful by building a harbour or else hand it over to the Germans.' Derby quipped: 'If Germany would undertake to build a harbour of refuge, which would cost at least £250,000, there might be some use in talking about it.' Münster pretended to attach little importance to the matter, but now assumed his new instruction from Bismarck gave him an easy opening for a more serious discussion at a convenient opportunity.[14] He decided the most effective tactic would be to play upon Britain's evident disinclination to spend money on fortifications.

On 17 May 1884 the veteran Foreign Secretary Lord Granville met Münster at the Foreign Office for a routine if formal discussion on various matters of mutual concern. Towards the close of the conversation, the German ambassador said he wished to have a further talk with Granville, on a subject that he said might startle the Foreign Secretary. From a memorandum left much later by Lord Granville, we learn that Münster said:

> Heligoland was a place of no importance to Britain in its present state, whereas it would be of immense importance to Germany, to Britain, and to the whole of the world, if it were made into a good harbour of refuge. This would be an expensive work for Britain to undertake. Britain could not be expected to go to such an expense, whereas Germany would be quite ready to undertake it. Count Bismarck wished to cut a canal into the Baltic, which would also be a great advantage to Britain, as the most powerful maritime nation in the world, and Heligoland, which of course would always be open to British ships, would be a necessary key to such a plan.

Inauspiciously, he had made no mention of the wishes of the islanders.

'I suppose that the cession of Gibraltar would strengthen our good relations with Spain!' retorted Granville gruffly, quite astonished by this audacious request. Nervously, Münster took his words to mean that Granville was ill-disposed towards the scheme. Granville declined to commit himself to any expression of opinion upon a question so controversial, and it was agreed that the matter should, for the present, go no further. Münster begged Granville not to discuss his request with any other British ministers, and believed that his request had been adhered to. In fact, Granville reported it to Gladstone. On 24 May, just a fortnight after the meeting, Bismarck told Münster to drop the request because the timing did not seem right. At the time he remarked confidentially to an assistant, Count Hatzfeldt, that Germany had no legitimate claim to the island. Bismarck wrote: 'I pressed Count Münster strongly today to say no more about Heligoland, for a desire of this kind can only be presented to a nation when it is in friendly mood towards us. Our wishes regarding Heligoland rest on *no legal basis* and would drag down our justified demands regarding overseas affairs to the same level, if they were lumped together for public discussion.'[15] Bismarck too failed to mention the well-being or the wishes of the islanders. Lord Derby had an inkling that Bismarck might offer Britain a certain part of Africa in exchange for Heligoland.

The sudden and unexpected death that week of Lord Ampthill, the popular British ambassador in Berlin for the past thirteen years, caused a serious break in the functions of the Embassy because the good understanding between Britain and Germany had tended to hinge on his personality. In January 1885 the question of Heligoland was again opened by Münster, acting on instructions from Berlin, but with the same result. What Bismarck did not know was that had he persisted he might have achieved what he wanted. Granville wrote to Gladstone, regarding this repeat request: 'Count Münster said that he would put the question to us in a few days. I was prepared with an answer had he done so. I should have told him that I had mentioned the subject to Mr Gladstone alone, and that when current political questions were settled we should be prepared to give a friendly consideration to the question.'[16] Evidently then, in 1885, the Liberal government was contemplating a graceful surrender. But the time did not seem quite right and so nothing happened.

The island thus remained caught between the two powerful nations with their widely contrasting perceptions: Britain saw no necessity at all to spend money on fortifications and a proper harbour, while Germany saw every need, to ensure its security. And yet Heligoland itself was progressing from strength to strength. By 1890 the island was free of debt. Sir Terence O'Brien, an energetic and popular governor, presided over a period of economic success, albeit as a consequence of the sound fiscal foundations established in Governor Maxse's time. The key to Heligoland's new prosperity was the now established ability to collect revenue through local taxation, which meant the colony's debt could be eliminated. As its financial position improved, O'Brien even succeeded in extracting a £2,000 grant from the UK Treasury for much-needed capital projects and public works.

The large bathing establishment had fallen into decay and had been purchased by the community from its previous owners; it was rebuilt in a modern form with swimming baths added. A vertical lift was built to carry passengers and goods between the lower and upper towns. All the principal streets were re-paved and public lighting was improved; a new pier was erected for £700, which provided visitors with something of a promenade. Also built were the Conversation House, where balls and concerts were frequently held, and an excellent reading room, amply stocked with newspapers and books for the islanders that used it – especially in winter. Taking shape were a new hotel and casino. The submarine telegraph cable that had been laid in 1859 to link Heligoland with Cromer in Norfolk and Busem in Schleswig-Holstein now had added to it – at the colony's expense – a telegram office, while a conical-shaped Lloyds shipping signal station was built around HMS *Explosion*'s old mast high on the red cliffs near the lighthouse. Alone of all Britain's smaller colonies, Heligoland was free of debt by the late 1880s; indeed, it even boasted a secure reserve fund (of £2,500). So why was the constitutional future of this sophisticated possession about to become a subject of feverish speculation?

3

Rivalries in Africa

Knowing the strategic importance of their island, the Heligolanders could not have been totally surprised by the speculations about its prospects as a naval base, but they could never have anticipated that its future would be linked to rivalries in Africa. Ironically, for a people whose homeland rarely produced any people of noticeable leadership qualities, the character who was to play a vital part in that international power struggle in Africa had been born near the Elbe in 1856.

Since leaving the river as a youngster, Karl Peters had developed a passion for adventure; he had successfully studied for a science doctorate, and became a campaigning journalist. Not content merely to advocate German colonisation overseas, Dr Peters was determined to be at the forefront of the process. Eventually he became Germany's foremost explorer. In 1882 he was an inaugural member of the German Colonial Association but he soon perceived it to be insufficiently adventurous and in 1884, with a few friends, he founded the Society for German Colonisation, the function of which was to acquire, as urgently as possible, new lands for Germany's overseas empire. Their initial scheme for colonising the interior of Angola was dismissed by the German Foreign Office because it would impinge upon territory claimed by Portugal, so Peters and his associates fell back on their alternative: a momentous expedition to East Africa.[1] This was notionally organised on behalf of Peters's German East Africa Company, for which he sought a charter from Bismarck; it would prove a bitter rival to Sir William Mackinnon's Imperial British East Africa Company.

Germany was astonishingly late in getting into the colonial business. When Wilhelm I was declared an emperor in 1871, Germany was in the curious position of claiming to have created an empire within Europe, without yet having started to establish one overseas. It might easily have acquired an extensive, 'ready-made' empire that year had it not been for the opposition of Chancellor Bismarck. For during the peace negotiations at Versailles he turned down the chance to seize not only Pondicherry but also many other French colonies, including Cochin-China, Tahiti, the Marquesas Islands, Reunion, Madagascar and Algiers.[2] Over the next few years Bismarck consistently resisted all the proposals for overseas annexation that colonial enthusiasts continued to press upon his attention. When the rulers of Fiji and Zanzibar, in 1872 and 1874 respectively, asked for the protection of the German Empire, he promptly declined to give it. Much occupied with domestic and military questions, and above all with the problem of Germany's consolidation, he was unwilling to give any thought to projects of colonial expansion. To him it was folly to talk of an overseas German Empire before the German Empire in Europe had been properly established. In 1873 he remarked to Lord Odo Russell, the British ambassador in Berlin, that colonies would be a source of weakness, because they could only be defended by powerful fleets and Germany's geographical position would not assist her development into a first-class maritime power.

There is no doubt that Bismarck was wise to adhere to that policy for many years, but by the mid-1880s the political and commercial pressures to endorse the acquisition of colonies had become too great. In 1885 Germany established island colonies in the Marshall, Caroline, Marianne and Solomon Islands in the West Pacific, and in April that year acquired a large slice of New Guinea and some adjacent islands which it renamed the 'Bismarck Archipelago'. Nevertheless these new colonies were economically unviable, as were the territories it had acquired the previous year in Africa, namely Togoland and the Cameroons and, most notably, German South-West Africa.

Bismarck was persuaded that German South-West Africa was immensely mineral-rich, even though at the time scarcely anything but sand had been found there. The strategic key to the colony was Angra Pequena, a tiny coastal settlement at the mouth of the Orange River. German contact with Angra Pequena had commenced in 1883 when a Bremen entrepreneur established a factory there. The Foreign Office in London was soon asked if Britain had any intention of claiming the settlement. For several months the Gladstone government refused to bother to reply. In April 1884 Bismarck arranged to endorse Angra Pequena as a German possession and finally, in late May, the Colonial Secretary Lord Derby declared that even if Britain did not wish to take formal possession of the place herself she considered that she had the right to prevent other nations from doing so.

In Britain the Angra Pequena affair caused some resentment towards Germany on the part of MPs and the general public alike. Nobody really thought that South-West Africa had any great intrinsic value, but Bismarck's attempt to breach Britain's monopoly of the

South African coast was regarded as an affront to national prestige. It had been precisely because this crisis was brewing that on 24 May 1884 Bismarck wrote to Ambassador Münster, strictly ordering him not to antagonise Gladstone's administration by linking the cession of Heligoland with a relinquishment of Angra Pequena, because he feared that such a move 'would provide an excuse for making the justice of our African claims subservient to our claims regarding Heligoland'.[3] Bismarck was furious with Münster, believing that he had committed a grave blunder by disobeying orders to propose a wider scheme for overseas affairs, with or without Heligoland. Bismarck's true intentions at the time remain a matter of historical dispute: he believed the ambassador was over-preoccupied with securing Heligoland, while the historian A.J.P. Taylor sees it as an acute example of the irascible Chancellor giving muddled instructions to his subordinates.[4] Bismarck's anger was quite futile because Salisbury, who returned to power as prime minister in 1886, was determined to elude his upstart attempts to lure him into an equitable settlement of African disputes.

Thus, for a while at least, Bismarck had to set aside his schemes to acquire Heligoland, even though there were a few glimmers of hope when Britain wavered on the matter of colonial ownership, keeping alive the embers of his ambitions. Since 1868 there had been occasional press speculation in Britain about exchanging Gibraltar for Spain's North African colony of Ceuta, and in January 1887, after only two years of suzerainty, Britain restored to Korea Port Hamilton, a superfluous enclave it had somehow acquired on the Korean coast. But in the North Sea Britain appeared to be in no mood to relinquish anything. Bismarck pressed on with the construction of the Kiel Canal. The foundation stone was laid by Kaiser Wilhelm I in 1887, and by 1889 digging was well under way.

Entirely unexpectedly, Germany's opportunity came in March 1889. A dinner party in London was attended by the Chancellor's son, Count Herbert von Bismarck, a former diplomat who had been Germany's Minister of State since 1888. Also present was Joseph Chamberlain, a former senior Liberal minister who had recently returned from the United States where he had been a British plenipotentiary. Chamberlain had been greatly vexed that his former colleagues had missed an opportunity to take over South-West Africa. 'Why don't you', Chamberlain wondered to Bismarck junior at the dinner, 'exchange Angra Pequena for Heligoland?' As a Liberal politician Chamberlain had no authority to speak for the Conservative government, and it seems very unlikely that he was acting as a secretly approved *agent provocateur*. Nevertheless, he was sometimes perceived to be Salisbury's 'freelance' political ally.[5] Confusingly for the Germans, Prime Minister Lord Salisbury, also present at the dinner, said nothing to Bismarck on this subject other than – or so Count Herbert believed – 'If you wish, we can talk of it another time.' Count Herbert exultantly reported all this to Berlin, reminding his father that there were many people in Germany who were already anxious to get rid of the disappointing experiment in South-West Africa at any price.

The proposal excited the new Emperor Wilhelm II to a state of considerable enthusiasm, and for months Count Herbert and the new German ambassador in London, Count Hatzfeldt, waited in hope for the 'other time' which might bring a formal overture from the British government – but it never came. Joseph

Chamberlain had, it seemed, grossly overreached himself. There was nothing Salisbury wanted from Germany at that moment which could match the importance of Heligoland. From his point of view, the idea of giving up the island in return for the bankrupt wastelands of South-West Africa seemed preposterous. He remained firmly opposed to the cession under any circumstances.

In the spring of 1889 Salisbury was concerned at the appearance of rumours about a cession in the newspapers in both Britain and Germany, although there was no foreseeable prospect of discussing the constitutional future of Heligoland with Germany. Britain, he believed, needed to uphold the dignity of its sovereignty of the island and he alighted on a fairly trivial incident to make that point. During the summer a German warship omitted to salute the Union Jack as it steamed past Heligoland. Salisbury telegraphed Sir Edward Malet (who had been Ampthill's successor as ambassador in Berlin since 1884), repudiating the rumours about ceding Heligoland: 'We are absolutely opposed to such a move, but the ways of the German Navy rather give maintenance to such a rumour.' Without going so far as to demand a formal remonstrance, he advised Sir Edward to meet with the German Admiralty 'to suggest to them the expediency of more respectful behaviour in future'.[6]

So far there had been little reason for Salisbury to concern himself with East Africa. The most influential key to that quarter of the continent was the historic trading island of Zanzibar, whose sultan had sovereignty over a 10-mile wide strip of coast (and thereby some influence, albeit dwindling, with the mainland beyond it), down to the frontier of Portuguese East Africa. As long ago as 1878 the

Foreign Office had been presented with an extraordinarily favourable opportunity which, had it been accepted, would have spared Britain the diplomatic agonising that eventually affected Heligoland. In that year the founder of the Imperial British East Africa Company, the Scottish ship-owner Sir William Mackinnon, had attempted to establish a trading empire between Mombasa and Lake Victoria, taking in a large part of Zanzibar's inland possessions. Sultan Seyyid Barghash was willing to grant Mackinnon a seventy years' concession, transferring to Britain the administration of the entire hinterland of thousands of square miles of East Africa as far as the Great Lakes. Astonishingly Lord Beaconsfield, then Prime Minister, declined to accept on behalf of the British Empire an obligation so large. Instead, he opted to continue to have an informal influence in the coastal area, exercised through Sir John Kirk, who since 1868 had been Britain's trusted consul-general to the Sultan of Zanzibar. A former professional associate of Dr David Livingstone on the Zambezi, Kirk had the Sultan's complete trust and maintained British confidence upon a dependable foundation.[7]

This situation stood until November 1884, when a merchant ship arrived off Zanzibar and disembarked three passengers it had brought from Germany under assumed names. They were Dr Karl Peters, the intrepid aristocratic explorer Count Pfeil and Dr Jühlke. Peters and his cronies slipped across to the mainland unnoticed at Dar es Salaam, and in the space of a fortnight audaciously concluded treaties with various tribal chiefs by which they claimed German sovereignty over some 60,000 square miles of territory in the interior. Chancellor Bismarck, who had originally frowned on the German Colonisation Society, accepted the *fait accompli*, and in 1885 granted a charter to Peters's German East Africa Company and placed the Society's territories under imperial protection.[8] By October 1886 Britain and Germany had reached an agreement. The Sultan gave up his claim to illimitable empire on the mainland in return for the recognition of his authority over 6,000 miles of the coast to a depth of 10 miles, while Germany and Britain divided the rest of the hinterland between themselves. For a while rivalry with the British East Africa Company abated. Britain's principal sphere of influence was in the north (Kenya), and Germany's in the south (Tanganyika), although Germany also retained a hold in the Witu area in the north.[9]

So uninterested in clashing were the British and German governments that in July 1887 they drew up a practical Hinterland Agreement, which they hoped would discourage unsanctioned annexations of each other's areas.[10] Even so, they were powerless to limit the activities of their nationals such as Dr Peters and Mackinnon (whose ambition was to construct a Cape-to-Cairo railway), who as commercial pioneers were intent on extending their presence westwards towards Uganda. Lord Salisbury, who had hitherto taken a sanguine now-and-then interest in East Africa, now began to consider it more closely. Lady Gwendolen Cecil, his daughter, who many years later wrote a biography of her father, detected the change of emphasis in the physical appearance of his rooms at Hatfield and at the Foreign Office. By 1889 the walls were covered with huge maps of Africa.[11]

The key to Lord Salisbury's entire African strategy was Egypt. In 1882 William Gladstone, then Prime Minister, and Sir Edward Malet, the British Representative in Egypt, had assumed that their invasion of Egypt in that year 'to restore order' would provide an opportunity for securing the Suez Canal and the Indian Dominions, and would allow them to maintain Britain's superiority in the East. However, Britain's presence in Egypt became an irritant to European relations in Africa. During 1888 renewed attacks on Egypt's southern frontier by the Dervishes made it necessary for Salisbury to come to terms with the fact that Britain could not extricate herself from Egypt in terms that would satisfy both national and international interests.[12] His decision in favour of a prolonged occupation of Egypt was a momentous one, and recognised the probable necessity to achieve some sort of control of the Nile provinces. Salisbury became increasingly concerned about the headwaters of the Nile, particularly an unclaimed area called Tana-Juba which lay between the great expanses of Lake Nyasa, Lake Tanganyika and Lake Victoria. His worry was that should another power take control of Uganda and the Upper Nile, it could threaten Egypt's water supply and thereby Britain's Suez Canal route to India. This fear was expressed to him by Evelyn Baring, the Consul-General of Egypt, and most notably by Sir Percy Anderson, head of the Foreign Office's Africa department. Anderson had taken on this role in 1883 and had proved to be a most able and influential bureaucrat in shaping the overall view of that continent.

Salisbury's fears reached a higher state of alert in June 1889 when he learned that Karl Peters had crossed from Zanzibar to Witu and was heading inland, apparently in search of the German explorer Emin Pasha (Eduard Schnitzer), who was claimed to be lost somewhere in equatorial Sudan. In fact Peters was too late. It fell to the Briton Morton Stanley to find the famous explorer –

if indeed he was ever lost. In truth, Dr Peters's solicitude was just a pretext for another buccaneering *coup*. From the first his primary object had been to secure more treaties and more territories. He was hoping to establish a line of German settlements from the coast at Witu, along the Tana River to Victoria Nyanza and Uganda, thus securing for Germany – as Salisbury suspected – a powerful influence in the basin of the Upper Nile.[13] In March 1890 it was rumoured that the Imperial Commissioner, Hermann von Wissmann, was about to leave for Uganda, and on the last day of the month Germany announced that Emin Pasha was to lead a large caravan to Buganda. Then, in the first week of May, news was received that Dr Peters had agreed some sort of treaty with the Kabaka. By the following week it was evident that the East African hinterland disputes could no longer remain unsettled without the serious risk of friction with Germany, and of political embarrassment at home.[14]

Another relevant factor at this time was the fall of Chancellor Bismarck. The death of the aged Kaiser Wilhelm I in 1888 brought to the throne his son Wilhelm II, then just twenty-nine years old. The new Kaiser wished to pursue a policy of social reform and conciliation, and was determined that the Chancellor would obey it, but Bismarck, then aged over seventy and accustomed to both initiating and controlling policy, was uncomfortable in his new role. Bismarck urged upon the new Kaiser a policy of conservative resistance.[15] Serious quarrels developed concerning the rights of Cabinet ministers to an audience with the Emperor without the presence of Bismarck, who was not in favour of the social reforms put forward by the new Kaiser. The Chancellor, Wilhelm II later claimed, wished to call out the troops and shoot down the socialists in the streets, but 'I told Bismarck that I would never incur before the Almighty the responsibility of shooting down my people'.[16] Eventually, at the Kaiser's insistence, on 18 March 1890 Bismarck resigned. Effectively it was the end of a dynasty. His son Herbert von Bismarck followed suit, and was replaced as Foreign Minister by Baron Marschall. Bismarck's successor was Count Georg von Caprivi, who was even less of a colonial enthusiast than his predecessor had been. One of Caprivi's earliest utterances – to the annoyance of Germany's colonial enthusiasts – was to the effect that 'no greater misfortune could happen to Germany than that the whole of Africa should fall into her hands'.[17] For Salisbury these developments in the spring of 1890 created uncertainties but also significant opportunities.

Precisely when Lord Salisbury took the fateful decision to sacrifice Heligoland to secure the headwaters of the Nile is a mystery. From his daughter's description of his state of mind on 10 April it is clear that he was still hoping for a rapprochement with Germany, and to that effect was sending Sir Percy Anderson himself to Berlin to settle disagreements deriving from the July 1887 Hinterland Agreement on East African spheres of influence.[18] 'But rarely', wrote Lady Gwendolen, 'can a political enterprise of equal importance have left behind so few traces of the process of incubation.' On 18 April Salisbury returned to London from convalescence at Beaulieu. Did he then, as she suggests, 'with a brain cleared from the last lingering mists of influenza', make some reassessment of the East African situation, in particular the problem posed by the Tana-Juba hinterland?[19] There might have been domestic political considerations, too. Certainly at this time the celebrated explorer Morton Stanley was busily making rabble-rousing speeches at huge open meetings (such as one held at the Albert Hall on 5 May 1890) at which he condemned what he called British subservience to Germany in East Africa. The fact that Salisbury was simultaneously serving as both Prime Minister and Foreign Secretary meant that there was no need for documents to be exchanged between those offices, and so the decisions he made were shaped within the privacy of his own mind.

Salisbury prepared to play his diplomatic bargaining cards to best effect. On 13 May he engaged the German ambassador in a seemingly futile discussion in the Secretary of State's room at the Foreign Office. Count Hatzfeldt expressed concerns about the dangers of a 'steeplechase' in East Africa. For a while the irreconcilable claims of 'hinterland' and 'previous settlement' were spoken of. Then Salisbury broke off the conversation and, after some hesitation, offered to reveal for Hatzfeldt's personal benefit the 'sum of his wishes' with respect to East Africa. The Count, with ready curiosity, welcomed the offer and then listened with dismay to Salisbury's formidable list of demands. It began with a full statement of the boundary concessions demanded by Mackinnon's company at the edge of the Germany colony. Germany must recognise Uganda as within the British sphere; she must abandon Witu; and she must accept a British Protectorate over Zanzibar and Pemba Islands. In return Britain would drop her claim to a strip of territory by Lake Tanganyika, and would use her influence to persuade the Sultan to sell outright the coastal leases to Germany.[20]

Then, without further ado, and with no hint of an invitation from the wholly unprepared ambassador,

Salisbury threw down Heligoland on the table. The British government would, he said, be willing to 'hand the island of Heligoland to Germany'. Cleverly, Salisbury seemed to take Hatzfeldt into his confidence, by appearing to suggest that the cession of the island would be subject to some elements that were not necessarily within his control. He begged the ambassador to report to Berlin nothing of what had been said because he must 'first see the Directors of the British Companies'. At the time, of course, Stanley's rousing speeches were fanning colonial sentiments into a passion and misleading public opinion about the justice of German claims. Furthermore the handing over of Heligoland would need the approval of Parliament.

Berlin's initial response to these proposals was indignation. On 17 May 1890 Baron von Marschall telegraphed Hatzfeldt instructing him not to accept Salisbury's exorbitant African demands, but 'do not *a priori* adopt an attitude of refusal' towards it. The Heligoland element of the outlined package was never even mentioned. Within a week, in a move of supremely cool brinkmanship, Salisbury hinted that the entire British offer might be withdrawn. On 22 May 1890 Hatzfeldt replied to Berlin with startling news of a confidential discussion he had just had with Salisbury. Now, he wrote: 'the situation is much complicated by Stanley's hostile and inflammatory attacks, and Lord Salisbury is inclined to consider that it will be advisable to *postpone our negotiations* until the excitement is allayed'. Salisbury had so far consented to yield just a few trivial concessions near the Great Lakes, but Hatzfeldt reckoned that if Germany held her nerve 'even more might be obtained' after further negotiations.

But in Berlin there was curiously undiplomatic consternation. Overnight, the very prospect of Salisbury postponing negotiations caused Germany to capitulate almost totally. The following morning, 23 May 1890, a secret telegram from Foreign Minister Marschall arrived on the ambassador's desk. Its opening line stated 'Postponement of negotiations most undesirable.' It went on: 'I inform you that we are ready in return for the concession and probable further ones mentioned in your telegram, to hand over to England, Witu and Somali Coast with their respective hinterlands, and to concede a British Protectorate over Zanzibar, if England will hand over Heligoland and support us in demanding from the Sultan of Zanzibar the cession of the coast of the mainland.' On 25 May Hatzfeldt received another telegram from Marschall which provided an inkling of just how fundamental the North Sea island was perceived to be in all of this. 'The possession of Heligoland is highly important to us for military reasons because of the Kiel Canal, and the possession of the coastal strip leased to us by the Sultan is indispensable for the definite regulation of our position in East Africa.' If Germany's concessions were agreed to, including an acknowledgement of Britain's Protectorate over Zanzibar, Germany was 'ready for an immediate agreement on this basis'.

The unseemly haste to secure a deal was caused by the meddling intervention of Wilhelm II. As long ago as 1873, when still the Crown Prince, he visited Heligoland and was so captivated by the mystique of the place that he vowed to make it part of Germany. Even then his personal characteristics were becoming apparent: he was vain, self-willed, rash in utterance, and alternated between excessive self-confidence and nervous depression. From the moment he came to the throne in 1888 he luxuriated in the public image of himself as *der reise Kaiser* ('the travelling emperor'), and was delighted to be perceived by *Punch* as dashing when that satirical magazine ran its infamous 'Dropping the pilot' cartoon of the confident new Kaiser dismissing the elderly Bismarck. His pride knew no bounds in June 1889 when, as the eldest grandson of Queen Victoria, he was given the honorary rank of Admiral of the Fleet in the Royal Navy. In the spring of 1889 he had been crestfallen when the Bismarck/Chamberlain talks on the possible cession of Heligoland in exchange for Angra Pequena came to naught. He had hoped that the transfer of those territories would be completed in time to coincide with his triumphant acceptance of the prestigious – although meaningless – naval rank in June at Osborne. He wanted to wear the famous uniform of St Vincent and Nelson at the reception party at Cowes as the acknowledged new ruler of Heligoland.[21]

Hatzfeldt could no longer doubt whose interference was shaping Germany's negotiating strategy. On 29 May the ambassador received a secret telegram from Marschall, mentioning the Kaiser by name and promoting Heligoland – within a week – from being of 'high' to 'supreme' importance to Germany: 'The possession of Heligoland is of supreme importance to us and is by far the most serious matter in the whole negotiation. His Majesty shares the Chancellor's opinion that without Heligoland the Kiel Canal is useless to our Navy.' The extent to which Salisbury was aware of the Kaiser's meddling is unknown, but certainly his tactic of insisting that any agreement would necessarily be subject to the approval of certain forces within the Cabinet and Parliament, which were not necessarily within his control, caused invaluable uncertainty and anxiety in Berlin. Tension was heightened on 30 May when the German Foreign Office informed Hatzfeldt that Salisbury had written to the ambassador from Hatfield, blithely commenting that the British companies concerned were still not in agreement and, even more alarmingly, on 5 June that 'he wished to discuss it with his colleagues, some of whom were nervous with regards Heligoland on account of Parliament and public opinion'.

Wilhelm was becoming frantic, as can be seen from a cipher telegram he received from Marschall on 4 June, upon which he scribbled various irate annotations.

> At yesterday's conference between Count Hatzfeldt and Lord Salisbury the latter declared that he had found much anxiety amongst his colleagues concerning these concessions [Kaiser: '!'] and suggested that it would be better to postpone further this and the connected question of the Protectorate over Zanzibar [Kaiser: 'No! All or nothing!'] and leave it for a later agreement. [Kaiser: 'No!'][22]

Having convinced himself that no more concessions were to be garnered from Germany, on 5 June Salisbury closed the negotiations with Hatzfeldt, subject to the approval of his colleagues. It was a comprehensive draft agreement which covered not just Zanzibar but other parts of East Africa, and even reached as far as West and South-West Africa. In West Africa the boundary between Togo and the British Gold Coast colony was adjusted, and in the Cameroons there was a realignment of the western boundary between the German and British possessions. In South-West Africa the boundary between that German colony and British Bechuanaland was delimited, and Germany was given access from her Protectorate to the Zambezi by the cession to her of a strip of territory known as the 'Caprivi Strip'. In East Africa new boundaries were defined. In the north Germany was to cede in favour of Britain all claims in respect of Witu and the Somaliland coast; and the immense region from the coast to the Congo was to be divided in such a manner

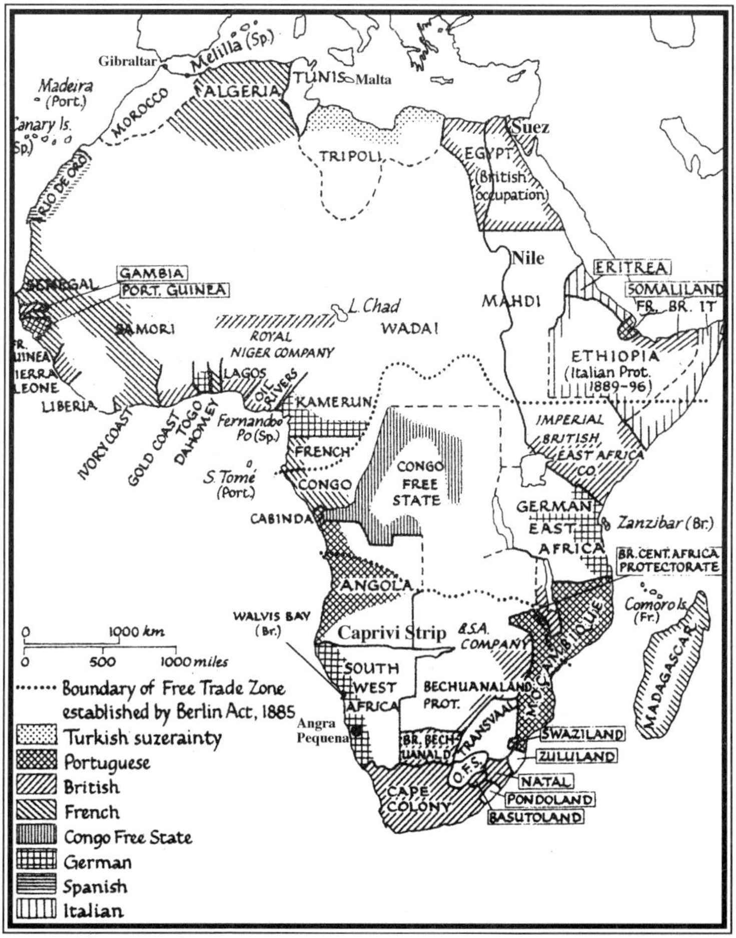

Map 3 Africa in late 1890. *(A Short History of Africa, Penguin, 1988)*

that Britain took the territory lying north and Germany that lying south of a line from the River Umba across Lake Victoria to the frontier of the Congo Free State. Further, Germany agreed to acknowledge a British Protectorate of Zanzibar and the neighbouring island of Pemba.[23] In return Britain undertook to persuade the Sultan to grant to Germany his coastal territory in East Africa. Eventually the Sultan agreed to cede his rights in the area for a payment of £200,000.

The Kaiser had more reason to be pleased than both Karl Peters's German East Africa Company, which was effectively barred from Uganda, and Sir William Mackinnon's equivalent organisation, which found its ambitions for a Cape-to-Cairo route sacrificed for the sake of the Anglo-German agreement.

During all these discussions the questions of the rights, interests and especially the wishes of the Heligolanders had been virtually ignored. Their opinions had been given almost no consideration. In fact the islanders were regarded as something of a nuisance, who ought not to be allowed any opportunity to make trouble.[24] Declassified Foreign Office papers show that on 18 June 1890 there was an exchange of letters about the islanders between Sir Percy Anderson in London and Sir Edward Malet, the British ambassador in Berlin, in which they spoke of the need to be watchful of possible 'agitation by the natives'. It was curiously redolent of Governor Hamilton's initial apprehension of the islanders all those years ago – except that this time there was genuine reason for them to be hostile.

4

Queen Victoria Opposes

Queen Victoria's public image as a distant and rather frosty monarch obscured the reality that she had a keen and indefatigable sense of responsibility towards all the peoples of the British Empire, even though, throughout her long reign, she visited virtually none of her extensive collection of overseas colonies. Ironically, although Heligoland was the most diminutive of all her imperial possessions, it might quite possibly have been the one she had seen more of than any other. She never actually stepped ashore there but on her rare trips on the royal yacht to visit relatives in Germany, via the port of Bremerhaven, she might have been unable to resist glancing at the enchanting little island on the horizon.

Today, high on the island's plateau, there is evidence of a once-distinctive landmark that the queen might have noticed. In the centre of the Upper Town stands the rebuilt war-torn church of St Nicolai. Cemented into a brick wall by the main door is a shrapnel-scarred bronze tablet. Donated by the Heligoland-born shipping magnate Rickmer Rickmers, it commemorates the construction of a distinctively pointed steeple on the church's tower with the inscription: 'For the honour and glory of God, and in great admiration of our gracious Queen Victoria.' There were other reasons for Victoria to have enjoyed a quiet affection for the island. In 1863 the islanders had sent the Prince of Wales their best wishes on his engagement, and received him kindly when he visited them in 1886. Three years later, when she learned that the Governor had asked the Treasury to supply a portrait of the Queen for Government House, Victoria quietly ordered one to be sent at her own expense.

From the correspondence between the Queen and Salisbury, which was only made public many years later, it is evident that Salisbury was remarkably slow to inform Victoria of the relevance of the island to the Anglo-German Agreement negotiations. Perhaps it was because he wished to wrong-foot her or because he had a premonition that the swap scheme would provoke royal displeasure, but he saw to it that she was only belatedly informed of the details. As long ago as 13 May he had presented to Ambassador Hatzfeldt his proposals for a grand Anglo-German Agreement, of which Heligoland was the crucial centrepiece. Sir Percy Anderson had already commenced detailed negotiations in Berlin. On 23 May Salisbury sent a cipher telegram to Victoria in which he informed her of another meeting he had just had with Hatzfeldt: 'The emperor wants to cut us off from the great central lakes, which I could not allow.'[1] In fact the first proper inkling the queen had of the extent of Heligoland's role in all this came as late as 4 June 1890 when she happened to be speaking with Lord Cross, the Secretary for India, who had just arrived at Balmoral Castle from a Cabinet meeting in London. According to her *Journal* they 'talked of Africa and what we required, which he showed me on the map. Germany wants more; he said there was an idea of giving up Heligoland as an equivalent, its being of no use to us; but this has not been brought forward yet.'[2]

The next communication she had on the subject came on 8 June. A telegram from Salisbury informed her that the previous day the Cabinet had held a meeting at which the Anglo-German draft agreement had been the principal subject of discussion. The full Cabinet had decided that – other than a few minor border modifications – so far as East Africa was concerned they were broadly satisfied with what had been negotiated. She was told by her Prime Minister that the next steps to be taken were conditional on the Cabinet being quite satisfied that it was wise to part with Heligoland. At this point Salisbury and his closest colleagues became aware of the queen's rage. On 9 June she sent Salisbury a blisteringly annotated telegram from Balmoral:

> Have received your account of the Cabinet. Understood from Lord Cross that nothing was to be done in a hurry about Heligoland, and now hear it is to be decided tomorrow. It is a *very serious* question which I do not like.
>
> 1st. The people have been always very loyal, having received my heir with enthusiasm; and it is a shame to hand them over to an *unscrupulous despotic Government* like the German without first consulting them.
>
> 2nd. It is a very bad precedent. The next thing will be to propose to give up Gibraltar; and soon nothing will be secure, and all our Colonies will wish to be free.
>
> I very much deprecate it and am anxious *not to give my consent* unless I hear that the people's feelings are consulted and their rights are respected. I think it is a very dangerous proceeding.[3]

Victoria certainly had plenty of reason to doubt whether Germany's 'unscrupulous despotic Government' could be trusted to safeguard the human rights of the Heligolanders. Mary Kingsley, the niece of the royal chaplain Charles Kingsley (better known as the author of *The Water Babies*) was an intrepid travel writer. From her perceptive accounts of her journeys through territories in West Africa, Victoria would have been aware of Germany's cruel methods of inflicting bloody punishments on dissenters. The German authorities could not even be relied upon to behave humanely towards their fellow-citizens in Europe. Indeed, on 13 May, the very day that Salisbury was meeting with Hatzfeldt at the Foreign Office to offer to hand over Heligoland, British newspapers carried stories about a gas workers' strike in Hamburg that was crushed with much bloodshed.

Salisbury was apparently so determined to hand over Heligoland as the price for securing stability in East Africa that he was willing to sacrifice his conscience to his ambition. Remarkably this was the same man who in April 1864, as a fortuneless young MP called Robert Cecil, had written a brilliant article in the *Quarterly Review* condemning the German expansion into, and brutal military occupation of, Schleswig-Holstein.[4] In the years since he wrote that piece, it would doubtless have been brought to Salisbury's attention that the plebiscite provided for in the 1864 Treaty of Prague, by which the Danes of North Schleswig were to be given an opportunity to decide their own fate, had never been held. The Danish 'optants', who had the right to choose Danish citizenship, were forced to do military service in the Prussian Army or to leave the country, and the Danish language was steadily being displaced by German in the schools. Elsewhere on its frontiers, such as Poland and Alsace-Lorraine, wherever the German Empire included non-Germans, there had often been harshness and repression on the one side, provoking discontent and hostility on the other.

In respect of Germany's empire overseas, matters were even worse. The Chancellor of the Exchequer George Goschen wrote to Salisbury on 10 October 1888: 'German insolence with native races constitutes a very serious difficulty. Look at Samoa! I felt as if they behaved disgracefully there. And would not the proposed partnership, unless most carefully guarded, expose us to some of the evil results of the German method of action?'[5] Lord Salisbury was fully aware that Germany was not to be trusted in that regard, as is evident from a letter he wrote to the British Consul at Zanzibar, Gerald Portal, on 25 November 1888: 'The whole question of Zanzibar is both difficult and dangerous, for we are perforce partners with the Germans whose political morality diverges from ours on many points.'

Bowing to pressure from the full Cabinet, which, on 7 June, after heated and lengthy discussion, insisted the question of Heligoland required more 'careful sifting', Salisbury appointed a special ad hoc Cabinet Committee. This pivotal ministerial group consisted of Salisbury himself; the Chancellor, George Goschen; the Leader of the Commons, W.H. Smith; the Chief Secretary for Ireland, Arthur Balfour; the Secretary of War, Edward Stanhope; and the First Lord of the Admiralty, Lord George Hamilton.[6] They assembled at a specially convened meeting in Downing Street to confer with naval experts on the question and reported to a Cabinet meeting on Tuesday 10 June. Her Majesty's furious telegram was duly read out to the assembled ministers. Doubtless her inference that she was ready to refuse to sanction Salisbury's swap scheme offered heart to those members of the Cabinet uneasy about relinquishing Britain's North Sea possession. Salisbury must have been alarmed by this because he probably thought Victoria would be more likely to reject the proposals if they were not unanimously endorsed by the Cabinet.

Some details of that momentous meeting on 10 June did come to light many years later. Salisbury's biographer Aubrey Kennedy wrote in 1953 that the Admiralty had admitted this 'untenable advanced base' was valueless to Britain, but the curious point was made that the island was a splendid recruiting ground for the Royal Navy. Its inhabitants were described as 'born seamen favourable to the British connection, and splendid material for bluejackets'. The meeting completed, Salisbury hurried to his desk and skilfully composed a letter to the queen in which he summarised the decisions taken about the Heligolanders, and the wider implications of the swap scheme with regard to Britain's position in Africa. In accordance with his instructions the letter was ciphered and telegraphed to her at Balmoral that evening.

He began by reporting that his colleagues were of the opinion that in any agreement arrived at with Germany the 'rights of the people of Heligoland should be carefully preserved'. That, he assured her, had been done. Next he detailed the specific safeguards for them he had demanded on 5 June, and which Kaiser Wilhelm had provisionally decided to accept. Salisbury informed Victoria that 'no actual subject of your Majesty living now will be subject to naval or military conscription. The existing customs tariff will be maintained for a period of years and every person wishing to retain his British nationality will have the right to do so.'

Purposely blurring Victoria's concerns, expressed in her 9 June telegram, about the risks of setting a precedent of being guided by the electoral decisions of colonial peoples, Salisbury assured her that anything like a plebiscite would be very dangerous as it would admit the right of the inhabitants of an imperial post to decide for themselves as to the allegiances of that possession. To that effect it might be used by discontented people in Gibraltar, Malta, Cyprus and even India. Certainly in the context of the times it would have been rather unusual for the wishes of the colonial peoples to be consulted. The crucial issue of the wishes of the Heligolanders Salisbury now side-stepped. The Cabinet, he claimed, thought it was 'impracticable' to obtain the formal consent of the two thousand inhabitants. He then embarked on a series of untruths by telling her that the information available to the Cabinet suggested that 'the population, which is *not British, but Frisian*, would readily come under the German Empire if protected from conscription'.

This was quite untrue. The inhabitants were as distinct from the Frisians as the island itself was totally detached from the Frisian Islands. Furthermore, as citizens of the British Empire the Heligolanders were already substantially British. Salisbury then rounded off this section of the telegram with the dubious remark: 'On these grounds the Cabinet *unanimously* recommend the arrangement for Your Majesty's sanction.'

In this way Salisbury convinced Queen Victoria that there was now no effective constitutional means by which she could impede the process of the Heligoland swap, and on 11 June 1890 she reluctantly sent the following telegram to her Prime Minister in London: 'Your cipher about Heligoland received. The conditions you enumerate are sound and the alliance of Germany valuable; but that any of my possessions should be thus bartered away causes me great uneasiness, and I can only consent on receiving a positive assurance from you that the present arrangement constitutes no precedent.' The following day Salisbury replied, claiming that he and his colleagues well understood that Heligoland could not be a precedent: 'It is absolutely peculiar. The island is a very recent conquest.' On 12 June Victoria despatched her final telegram on the subject of the negotiations: 'Your answer respecting Heligoland forming no possible precedent I consider satisfactory. I sanction the proposed cession or almost exchange. But I must repeat that I think you may find great difficulties in the future. Giving up what one has is always a bad thing.'

Victoria was right to feel uneasy. She probably never knew how fully Salisbury had deceived her. The reality was that there was no unanimity – nor even a majority – in Cabinet in favour of the cession. From German foreign policy documents, released many years later, it has become possible to understand what happened. On the evening of 11 June, the day after the special Downing Street meeting, Count Hatzfeldt, the German ambassador, sent a secret telegram to Chancellor Caprivi. Salisbury had just informed him that 'the Cabinet has declared, with *certain reservations*, its adherence to the agreement arrived at privately between the Prime Minister and myself. This fact is of importance, for Lord Salisbury repeatedly and confidentially informed me yesterday that certain

Ministers *had opposed him* to the end.' Nevertheless, on 17 June a preliminary agreement on Africa and Heligoland was initialled in Berlin by Sir Percy Anderson and Count Hatzfeldt.[7]

Had Salisbury done a secret deal with his dissenting Cabinet colleagues? His next move was extraordinary and indicates that he was prepared to go to astonishing lengths to buy their public silence. To mollify those ministers who were ill at ease with the Heligoland cession and the outline Anglo-German Agreement, Salisbury now took the radical step of deciding that these two aspects should be split so Parliament could consider them separately. Cunningly, in accordance with his negotiating position with Germany, he arranged to make acceptance of the overall Anglo-German Agreement package subject to a vote on the Heligoland issue, which would be called soon after extensive parliamentary debate in both Houses of Parliament. Throughout the negotiations with Germany, Heligoland had been the tantalising bait he had used to lure the Germans away from East Africa. However, in Westminster during the summer he would offer the prospect of settling boundaries in Africa as the prize for ditching Heligoland.

It seems quite likely that Salisbury was encouraged to opt for a strategy of separating the two debates by George Goschen, Chancellor of the Exchequer. Certainly in order to soothe parliamentary and public opinion he was urged by Goschen to provide an explanation of the deal 'so as to explain it more fully to the common herd'.[8] Unusually, Salisbury authorised the publication of carefully selected official correspondence concerning the swap. More exceptional was the inclusion of recent communications between himself and Queen Victoria, including a cipher telegram that he had sent her on 12 June.[9] In his dealings with Parliament on the question of Heligoland, Salisbury was clearly prepared to be quite unprincipled. From the outset he ruthlessly sought to besmirch the hapless island by grossly exaggerating its frailties and minimising its virtues. These deliberately harmful misrepresentations began in the first parliamentary phase of the transfer of Heligoland.

Since the spring of 1890 there had been repeated stories at Westminster and in the British press about Sir Percy Anderson's mission in Berlin to harmonise the colonial boundaries in East Africa, but at no time had Heligoland *ever* been mentioned in such a context. Thus the news that the two were to be linked in a swap was greeted with total shock and amazement. On the British side the divulgence was personally orchestrated by Salisbury himself. It was done at midnight on 17 June by means of depositing in the Vote Office of the Houses of Parliament a copy of a despatch dated 14 June which Salisbury, in his capacity as Foreign Secretary, had sent to Ambassador Malet in Berlin, instructing him that Anderson was returning to that city immediately to finalise the deal.

In that despatch Salisbury summarised the outline agreement which had been reached on the disputed spheres of interest in East Africa: the Witu coast, Zanzibar and the area at Lake Victoria north of the 1st degree of S. latitude. On Heligoland, Salisbury wrote with needless damnation:

> On the other hand, her Majesty's Government are prepared to propose a Bill to Parliament which shall transfer the Island of Heligoland to Germany. It has never been treated by the British Government as

> having any defensive or military value, nor has any attempt or proposal been made to arm it as a fortress. Her Majesty's Government are of the opinion that it would constitute a heavy addition to the responsibilities of the Empire in time of war, without contributing to its security. There is no reason, therefore, for refusing to make it part of a territorial arrangement, if the motives for doing so are adequate.

The few copies of the despatch had been deposited so very late at the Westminster Vote Office on the night of 17 June that not one MP had a chance to read it. However, it was soon noticed by hawk-eyed parliamentary correspondents from *The Times*. With almost unbelievable speed they rushed the long despatch to their newspaper offices and within hours it appeared in print in full.

Auspiciously, an eclipse of the sun that morning cast an eerie, though scarcely perceptible, shadow over much of southern Britain. It was patchy, visible in some counties, obscured by cloud in others. *The Times* newspapers, which appeared at the breakfast tables of the good, the great and the influential that morning, contained a relevant leading article which by some extraordinary feat its staff also had been able to put together in a few hours. Just as Lord Salisbury had expected, however, it was an historically distorted and scathing interpretation of his despatch to Malet. It stated as accepted fact: 'Indeed, the connection between the little Frisian island and Great Britain is extremely slight, and is not even sacred by long prescription. *It came to us as a part of the possessions of the Hanoverian Kings*, and remained British in 1814, because of its proximity to Hanover.' What the staff at *The Times* did not know was the sentence referring to the Hanoverian kings was precisely the one which the Prime Minister had used in his telegram to Queen Victoria on 12 June.

One consequence of the story of Edward Thornton's negotiation of the Treaty of Kiel never having been told was that Salisbury was able to distort history enough to deceive his queen. In fact, the Congress of Vienna (which dealt with Hanover) was signed on 9 June *1815*, while it was the Treaty of Kiel that was signed in 1814, by which *Denmark* agreed to make peace with England, Sweden and Russia. Heligoland had *never* been a jewel in any German crown. So was this faulty editorial in *The Times* an early example of deliberate governmental spin-doctoring? Perhaps it was just a careless late-night misinterpretation of what Salisbury's despatch had seemed to state. Its significance was far-reaching, as it reinforced Germany's historically groundless fantasies about their links with Heligoland. Salisbury had won the first round.

Queen Victoria's constitutional stance posed a far-reaching and fundamental question. How was Salisbury to reconcile his need for freedom to cede Heligoland with the newly perceived sense that the interests of the inhabitants should, in some form, be taken into account? Hitherto such transactions were exceedingly rare and the peoples of such colonies had not been an impediment to British government action. But now Salisbury calculated that in order to reconcile these elements he would subject the swap to parliamentary approval. Although it was scarcely recognised outside the esoteric world of Westminster at the time, this initiative was a profound break with the constitutional tradition whereby the British government made treaties and relinquished sovereignty over particular colonies in the name of the Crown *without requiring parliamentary ratification*. Ominously for the Heligolanders, it was the establishment of this precedent, rather than their enforced change of sovereignty, that most perturbed the minds of influential politicians.

In all this activity the Heligolanders had been kept entirely in the dark about the momentous decisions regarding their future. They were not even granted the courtesy of a ceremonial or private briefing. One day in June 1890 the astounding news burst upon the islanders – via newspapers brought from Hamburg via the mail paddle-boat – that Britain was arranging to hand over their homeland in return for the withdrawal of Germany's rather indefinite claims of recently acquired suzerainty over Zanzibar. The Heligolanders, who knew of William George Black's 1888 travel book *Heligoland and the Islands of the North Sea*, and his deep interest in all that concerned their island, urgently sent him a telegram asking him to do everything possible to put their case against cession. Quite by chance Black had just returned from his second visit to the island, and therefore knew better than anyone in Britain what the latest conditions were on the ground there. But not being a well-known public figure, he was not necessarily the best choice of champion for the islanders.

Publicly Black's protest began in the form of a letter published in *The Times* on 20 June. Twenty-one years later, in an article for the *National Review* in 1911, Black disclosed that in waging this campaign he had vainly sought interviews with leaders of the governing Conservative Party, but had been somewhat more successful in securing audiences with eminent opposition Liberals, notably former Prime Minister, William Gladstone, former Foreign Office minister, James Bryce, and – potentially most importantly of all – the current Liberal Party Leader, Lord Rosebery.

Rosebery was virtually the only senior politician still active who had ever visited Heligoland. He had gone to the island during the six months when he had been Foreign Secretary in the brief Liberal administration of 1886. Rosebery soon found a fine opportunity to reproach Salisbury in the Lords. On 19 June 1890 he asked him 'If any steps have been taken, or are in contemplation, to ascertain the wishes of the Heligolanders themselves with regard to the transfer?'[10] For a while the Prime Minister was able to side-step the issue by claiming 'the plebiscite is not among the traditions of the country'.

Never before had the British press taken so much interest in Heligoland. The news that Salisbury was intending to surrender the island prompted a stampede of journalists. As so few people knew anything about the island, despite eighty-three years of continuous British rule, the early correspondents concentrated on describing Heligoland to their readers. One illustrated paper, the *Leisure Hour*, ran a despatch reporting it to be a land 'where there are no bankers, no lawyers, and no crime; where all gratuities are strictly forbidden, the landladies are all honest and the boatmen take no tips'. An article in *Murray's Magazine* trivialised the place, recounting a story of a Lutheran pastor martyred by the Catholic islanders.

The *English Illustrated Magazine* provided a depiction in the most glowing terms: 'No one should go there who cannot be content with the charms of brilliant light, of ever-changing atmospheric effects, of a land free from the countless discomforts of a large and busy population, and of an air which tastes like draughts of life itself.' It just could not resist the temptation to shock its Victorian readers with titillating stories of nude bathing. 'One curious feature of bathing at Heligoland', it revealed, 'has now become much less common than it was. The ladies from the more remote parts of Germany used at one time to have a curious prejudice against bathing otherwise than in the costume of their mother Eve! And, in spite of government edicts, even now the practice has not been finally stamped out.'

Initially much comment was also made on the likely consequences of the exchange. Salisbury was reassured that a few newspapers praised him for his desire to end the dangerous Anglo-German rivalry in East Africa. The *Manchester Guardian* hoped that the Anglo-German Agreement would 'be accepted in both countries as a final settlement', while the *Daily News* considered that, if faithfully observed, it 'must make for the peace and prosperity of Africa'. The *Morning Post* on 18 June thought that greater than any territorial advantages must be reckoned: 'the good understanding' established between England and 'her natural ally'. It considered that the price Germany had agreed for Heligoland justified the deal.

In addition to accepting Goschen's advice to release certain official papers for public scrutiny, Salisbury himself fleetingly made a foray into public speech-making on the question of the Anglo-German Agreement in a foreign policy speech he gave in London that summer to the Merchant Tailors. A real bonus for the Prime Minister was the surprise endorsement his grand swap received from the celebrated explorer Sir Henry Morton Stanley, who was then in the early stages of a tour of Britain.

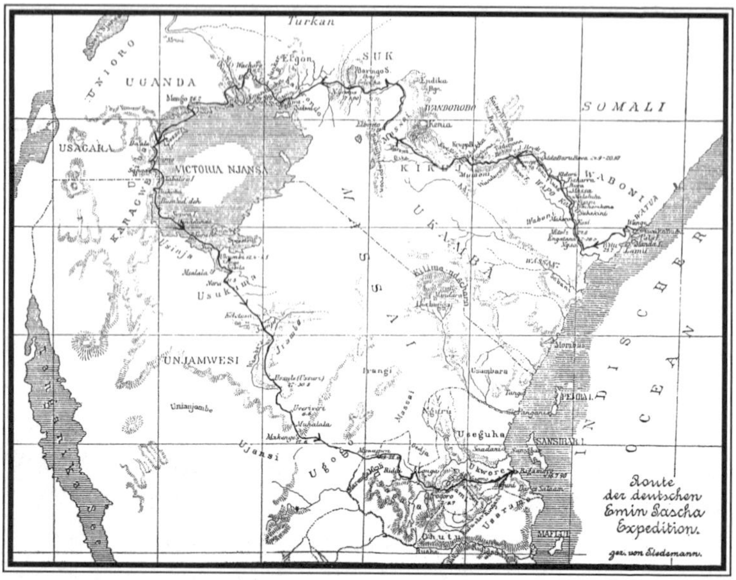

Map 4 German East Africa. Heligoland was pivotal in achieving the 1890 Anglo-German Agreement, which resolved several territorial disputes between the colonial powers.

Just as Salisbury had foreseen, the interest aroused by the cession of a British possession in time of peace meant that the debates in the English-language newspapers and in the Westminster Parliament were much more vigorous than foreign policy discussions normally were. The question of the wishes of the colonial inhabitants aroused the greatest passions. As well as the moral issue of taking the wishes of the Heligolanders into account, people began to contemplate the possible significance of the swap for the rest of the Empire, and to realise the potential dangers of setting a precedent by so doing. At first the reaction of Parliament was rather muted. On 18 June, the day after Salisbury's announcement, questions were asked as to whether a Bill would be introduced, and when; and whether the views of the inhabitants had been obtained. Evidently suspicions were growing that all was not right. Why, the Leader of the House, W.H. Smith, was asked, was the government refusing to disclose the opinions offered by the naval authorities?[11] And was it because of the Foreign Office's contempt for Parliament that the inaccurate map provided of Africa in the Tea Room had boundary changes marked that differed from those advocated by Lord Salisbury?[12] By 23 June, just six days after Salisbury's announcement, the First Reading of the Cession of Heligoland Bill was held, by which time a number of its key opponents were finding the range of their target. The merciless forensic questioning of three tenacious parliamentary figures, Mr Channing, Mr Howard Vincent and Mr Summers, now threatened to jeopardise the parliamentary progress of Salisbury's entire scheme. Unfortunately for the Heligolanders, the three were not especially well known or influential.

Even though Heligoland was less than 300 miles from the Norfolk coast, few if any Members of Parliament had ever visited the place. This lack of familiarity had been a crucial element in Salisbury's intention to bluster the legislation through. His bluff was suddenly called in that furious debate when Howard Vincent called for the Treasury to provide one of HM's ships in which members of the House, paying their own expenses, could visit Heligoland. Just as alarmingly for Salisbury, a request was made that a Commissioner be sent to ascertain the views of the islanders.[13]

Doubts about the views of the islanders were soon articulated in condemnatory letters in national newspapers. On 24 June Howard Vincent indignantly thundered in *The Times*'s letters page: 'For one I have no intention of voting for the hauling down of the British flag upon any portion of the globe unless personally convinced that the Empire gains more than it loses.' Newspaper editorials were also scathingly critical of Salisbury's refusal to take account of the colonial inhabitants' wishes.

On 19 June 1890 the *Daily News* incisively pointed out that from the 'first line to the last' there was not a word in the agreement about 'the rights of the Africans'. *Punch* was also scathing, producing a critical cartoon of the Salisbury scheme on 28 June. The *Review of Reviews* sourly noted that ministers were refusing to listen to the protests of the Heligolanders: 'It reminds one of the transactions between Russian grandees of olden times, when, to pay a gambling debt, an estate with all its serfs would be made over from one noble proprietor to another.' The envisaged transfer of sovereignty was most aptly summarised and condemned by the pioneering lady journalist Miss Friederichs, who had gone to Heligoland as a correspondent for the *Pall Mall Gazette*. She brought back, condensed into a single sentence, the sentiments of the islanders on the subject of their abandonment: 'You may give away a cat or a dog', said an indignant Heligoland dame, 'but not a whole people.'

For parliamentary purposes Salisbury had disentangled the question of the Heligoland cession from the rest of the Anglo-German Agreement on Africa, and on 1 July 1890, when the provisionally accepted Agreement was signed in a simple ceremony in Berlin, two documents were initialled: one covering Africa, the other Heligoland. The latter, written in large copper-plate handwriting, barely covered three folio-sized pages. So hastily had this vitally important document been cobbled together there had been no time to bind it in leather, so its covers were of simple bureaucratic red cardboard. Britain's signatories were the ambassador in Berlin, Sir Edward Malet; and the chief of the Foreign Office's African Department, Sir Percy Anderson. The Kaiser considered the acquisition of Heligoland so important that he insisted on his new Chancellor being the leading German signatory.

Outside very select official circles no one ever discovered that at the last minute a secret annexe was attached to the draft Heligoland Agreement – namely that in the event of any difficulties arising between Britain and Germany with respect to ownership of property on the island, such questions should be submitted to the arbitration of a Dutch lawyer, who would be nominated by the highest Dutch Court of Justice. The part of the proposed legislation that covered Heligoland, Article XII, was printed as follows in Foreign Office Paper C.6046 in July 1890. Covering just one page, it read:

1. Subject to the assent of the British Parliament, the sovereignty over the Island of Heligoland, together with its dependencies, is ceded by Her Britannic Majesty to His Majesty the Emperor of Germany.
2. The German Government will allow to all persons natives of the territory thus ceded the right of opting for British nationality by means of a declaration to be made by themselves, and [or] in the case of children under the age of consent by their parents or guardians, which must be sent in before 1st January 1892.
3. All persons natives of the territory thus ceded and their children born before the date of the signature of the present Agreement are free from the obligation of service in the military and naval forces of Germany.

4. Native laws and customs now existing will, as far as possible, remain undisturbed.
5. The German Government binds itself not to increase the customs tariff at present in force in the territory thus ceded until 1st January 1910.
6. All property rights which private persons or existing corporations have acquired in Heligoland in connections with the British Government are maintained; obligations resulting from them are transferred to His Majesty the Emperor of Germany. It is understood that the above term 'property rights' includes the right of signalling now enjoyed by Lloyd's.
7. The rights of British fishermen with regard to anchorage in all weathers, to taking in provisions and water, to making repairs, to transhipment of goods, to the sale of fish, and to the landing and drying of nets, remain undisturbed.

Another aspect of Heligoland which passionately excited its supporters in Britain that summer was its strategic significance. William Black was by no means the only public-spirited eminent person to send letters to newspapers arguing in support of the status quo. Quickest off the mark in springing to the islanders' defence in print was an earlier Governor, Sir Ernest Maxse. Writing to *The Times* on 26 May 1890 he claimed that: 'Had Germany possessed Heligoland, the blockade of the Elbe and Weser by the French fleet in the earlier part of the war would have been impossible. I was at Heligoland at the time and observed the French fleet, obliged as it was to lie outside English waters at a safe anchorage from whatever direction the wind blew.' He went on to advocate that Britain should spend a million pounds on the island to develop it into the 'Gibraltar of the North Sea'.

Maxse's intervention stimulated some fascinating exchanges of views in the letters pages of *The Times*. On 23 June the newspaper ran a letter from Sir John Coode, the engineer who had surveyed the coast of Heligoland and prepared a plan for a harbour for the Colonial Office in 1883. Coode now insisted that, were the British to make a base of the island, nothing less than £1 million on a harbour alone would be necessary, and at least £2 million would be required to fortify it. But Maxse was supported in his view that Heligoland was already of strategic importance in a letter to *The Times* from Admiral Philip Colomb (the elder brother of John Colomb, author of *The Defence of Britain*, who in 1880 had prophetically warned of the rise of German naval power).[14]

A particularly prominent opponent was Robert Heron-Fermor, an Inner Temple barrister who had written a specialised book on the foreign policies of Prussia and England, and who made a series of speeches condemning the planned cession on the grounds that it was strategically disadvantageous for Britain to do so. He commenced his agitation roadshow on 28 June 1890 and continued it unremittingly throughout the next month, speaking at specially convened public protest meetings in Brighton on 1 July and at least one other occasion, in London on 17 July, and at the National Liberal Club on 25 July. To further broaden the reach of his campaign he arranged to have extracts of his barnstorming utterances published in a pamphlet entitled *A Speech in condemnation of the Cession of Heligoland*.[15] To illustrate his talk he took on stage with him a map of Heligoland. Speaking at the Athenaeum Hall, Brighton, on 9 July, he said:

> What would be the consequence to England of the incorporation of Holland with the German Empire? Why, in the event of war, our whole East coast would be open to invasion. Because from the Thames to the Humber we have no harbours nor roadsteads where vessels could lie under the protection of guns. On the other hand the creeks and inlets of Holland swarm with places of refuge where fortifications could be thrown up, and an invading flotilla could lie concealed under their shelter in perfect safety.

To further stimulate public discussion that summer, other high-minded citizens produced pamphlets, with titles like *Heligoland for Zanzibar*, but Heron-Fermor's was the most energetic campaign. At the close of his meeting on 9 July a vote was taken – and only one hand was held up for the surrender of Heligoland. The overwhelming majority of those present were in favour of its retention. What perhaps even Heron-Fermor did not realise was that no one but he was making any attempt to measure British public opinion on the question of the cession of the island.

Such was the unease in public life, and at Westminster in particular, about the Heligoland element of the Anglo-German Agreement, Salisbury knew it was absolutely vital for him to present an overwhelmingly convincing case when he led the first full parliamentary debate on the subject. The Heligoland clause had its Second Reading in the House of Lords late at night on 10 July 1890. Salisbury had done his homework thoroughly, and seldom can a Prime Minister have made so much effort to concoct so many distorted facts, half-truths and lies. The crucial make-or-break speech with which he opened the debate covered the main strands of his argument.

He began with a historical review, claiming that in 1807 'Denmark was the owner of Schleswig, to which Heligoland naturally and by population belonged' (thus abandoning his earlier claim that it had once belonged to the Hanoverian kings).[16] He sought to denigrate the islanders by claiming 'their pecuniary interest comes down to motives which are less noble to dwell upon', thus implying, without evidence, that they had once made a living from deliberately wrecking ships.[17] In terms of the strategic position of the island, he drew comfort from the fact that there was still no harbour there, and thus only 'an open roadstead which is untenable in a north-west wind, which is the prevailing wind'. Yet the absence of a large constructed harbour had not prevented the island from being of value to Britain in the past. With no historical foundation Salisbury was now insisting that 'in respect of a war with Germany . . . it would expose us to a blow which would be a considerable humiliation; and it would not confer upon us any great advantage in the conduct of the war'.[18] Such was the lack of knowledge about Heligoland in Parliament that Salisbury was able to avoid mentioning Heligoland's primary value to Britain: simply by holding it, she prevented others from doing so. Nor was it mentioned that the continuance of that dog-in-the-manger strategic function was costing the Exchequer virtually nothing.

Where Salisbury was most vulnerable in his arguments was on the question of the wishes of the islanders; and the Leader of the Opposition, Lord Rosebery, duly concentrated on that issue in the debate. He claimed that if an island population of 2,000 was an acceptable level for a transfer of sovereignty, why not hand over a few of the smaller

Channel Islands? 'Whether you have 2,000 souls or one soul, you have some right to be considered in the transfer of your person and the territory in which you live from the flag under which you were born.' Referring to the proposed cession as a 'Capitulation'[19] Rosebery reminded the House that in a recent debate Lord Knutsford (now the Colonial Secretary) had insisted there was no desire for annexation on the part of the people of Heligoland. And yet now Salisbury was evading the question of the views of the islanders. 'We have', Rosebery observed, 'as yet failed to find out exactly how the noble Marquess arrived at the conclusion which he has confided to us.' Salisbury hedged unconvincingly: 'The manner in which I have arrived at the impressions I have stated, I am compelled to treat as *confidential*.'[20] Nevertheless, later that night the House of Lords approved the Bill.

Although the government was desperate to get the process completed in order to have the necessary legislation on the Statute Book before the summer recess, opposition to the Bill was even more intense in the Commons. Delays caused by the slow progress of parliamentary business on Ireland meant that the Second Reading of the Bill in the Commons did not commence until the evening of 24 July. Views varied. One MP, Mr Philips of Lanark, noted the implication of the government's stance that keeping Heligoland might mean needing to fortify it. 'But do we', he observed, 'garrison outlying islands around our coasts? No garrisons are needed; they are defended by the power of the British Navy.'[21] Another MP, Mr Storey, who was one of the few to mention the rights of the many thousands of Africans involved in the exchanges, scornfully condemned the transaction: 'Since the day Dick Turpin and Tom King met to divide the plunder of Hagley Hall I do not know of any more atrocious thing that has been done by those two great civilising powers in Africa.'[22] And yet, regardless of these and other protests against the proposed cession, notably by Messrs Channing, Vincent and Summers, the entire proceedings were dominated by what William Gladstone identified as a fundamental constitutional question of precedence.[23]

The elder statesman paid tribute to the Heligolanders as 'an interesting people of substantial existence with a good deal of character'. He noted that hitherto, on the very rare occasions when British possessions had been ceded, this had been done by the Crown, without the need to obtain parliamentary approval. He gave as examples Dunkirk, which Charles II had sold to France in 1662, and the Ionian Islands, transferred (as a Septinsula Republic Protectorate) to Greece in 1864. But now, said Gladstone, even though 'the nationality of the Heligolanders is more microscopic than any other subject to which the idea of nationality has yet been applied', by seeking parliamentary endorsement for their actions, Salisbury and his government were embarking on 'an absolute and entire novelty'. That the Commons were having such a debate at all was a perilous and unnecessary step, and he effectively washed his hands of it. The Secretary for Ireland, Arthur Balfour, disagreed. He claimed to approve of the setting of a precedent that created the safeguard of a full debate and a vote in both Houses. 'That precedent, I hope, will always be adhered to.'[24]

The controversy was so intense that the debate had to be continued in another session the next evening. Regardless of attempts by the hapless Leader of the House, W.H. Smith, to bring the debate to an end sooner, the arguments continued until just before midnight.[25] As the MPs cast their votes in the lobbies that night Heligoland's future hung in the balance. If Salisbury's grand territorial swap scheme could not be derailed in the Commons, the only person still able to impede the transfer of Heligoland would be the island's governor.

5

Swapped

Unfortunately for Heligoland, the prospects for the island looked bleak. The governor suffered a bout of illness which distracted him from his efforts to fight off the proposed swap. Arthur Stuart Barkly, who had arrived on the island in late 1888 to replace Sir Terence O'Brien (1881–8) as governor, had been much debilitated by diabetes while serving in Basutoland in the early 1880s.[1] He was a talented and humane colonial administrator, who had enjoyed a varied career. In 1885 he was made governor of the Seychelles, but soon had to leave because of ill health and was advised to take a year's sick leave. But money was tight, and he still needed to cover the cost of travelling with his wife Frances and their five young children. His financial worries seriously affected his health. In January 1886 he was appointed relief governor of the Falkland Islands, where he served for eleven months. After more than a year's absence, awaiting a new assignment, he was sent back to the Seychelles for another stint as governor.[2] Now he had the chance to improve his family's fortunes by having his salary paid in advance. But his prospects of financial recovery were dashed when he was taken ill again and was obliged to return to England. After a few months he was informed by the Colonial Office that he was being appointed governor of Heligoland, at the lower salary of just £1,275 a year.

So it was that in December 1888 Heligoland received its latest and – as it happened – last British governor. Arthur's problems were exacerbated by his beautiful wife Frances, who expected to live in a grand style irrespective of what her husband could afford. Thus, in addition to their children, the Barklys took to the island with them a nanny, a private secretary, a butler and two English maids. They did not arrive in style. The furious sea conditions around the island at the time of their arrival were an ominous foretaste of the upheaval caused by the cession. Frances Barkly later recalled:

> Never shall I forget that crossing; although I have had many long voyages in my eventful life, and I am quite used to rough seas. I really never expected to reach the island alive. The seas ran mountains high, and we seemed to go *through* instead of *over* them, as was actually the case. Crossing from Bremen to Heligoland in rough weather at that time of year was by no means devoid of danger, and wrecks on the coasts are very frequent. At last, the lights of Heligoland were to be dimly seen through the foam and dashing spray. The moon rose slowly through the dark clouds, and the effect of the silvery light was very fine, as we slowly approached the island. The waves and spray broke fiercely on its rocky shores, and dashed even over the Oberland. For some time the little steamer could not approach the anchorage, but battled with the waves; at last, the sea went down a little, and the captain managed to steam into harbour safely; the sturdy crew of English coastguardmen, somehow or other, lowered us into the lifeboat and rowed us ashore, where the Chief Magistrate, Colonel Whitehead, formerly of the 'Black

> Watch', was waiting to receive us. All the officials were with him, and most of the inhabitants of the island, bearing lighted torches, which had a weird and picturesque effect. It was Christmas Day.[3]

Since their memorable arrival in 1888, Arthur had become increasingly enchanted with Britain's North Sea possession and was always delighted to converse with the inhabitants in their broken English. Browned from their exposure to the sun, the people had a pleasing countenance that reminded Barkly of portraits by Flemish artists that he had seen in the National Gallery. Roaming about on foot, for there were no horses or mules on Heligoland, he would sometimes brave the incessant din of squawking seabirds and wander around the hummocky green plateau. There the islanders grew oats and potatoes in cultivated strips of ground, sheltered from sea breezes by hawthorns; guillemots, kittiwakes, auks and gannets would endeavour to plunder these vegetables. From the path along the rim of the red cliffs high above the pounding waves he could look over to Sandy Island. To the west he could see the lobster boats checking their pots in the oarweed for catches of Heligoland's legendary huge crustaceans. He could peer down at the harbour complex, home to the island's 107-strong fleet of fishing boats, including small sloops for catching cod and haddock. Jaunty Heligoland tricolours, proudly bearing the Union Jack in one corner, fluttered briskly at the vessels' ensign staffs.

Sometimes, on his walks around Government House, he would find himself at the wooden church of St Nicolai, with its ancient tenth-century font. From the high ceiling hung a celebrated collection of model Frisian ships; an especially venerated one had been presented by Governor Maxse in 1869. On the side of the church tower was the bronze plaque telling the world it had been built: 'For the honour of glory of God, and in great admiration of our gracious Queen Victoria.' From the vantage point of the tower, across the sapphire blue water, he could see vessels from the Elbe estuary plying the sea-route past the low-lying East Frisian Islands. The sight reaffirmed his belief that Germany was only interested in Heligoland in order to secure the mouths of the Rivers Ems, Jade, Weser and Elbe and the Kiel Canal, and to acquire the strategic waters for a radius of 30 miles around the island.

Down the wooden Pottchen stairs nestled the Unterland, which Barkly considered to be the livelier of the twin towns. Its quaint narrow streets had distinctive British names: Thames, Church, Prince of Wales and Maxse. The buildings huddled close together as if for protection from the wild winds of the North Sea. Characteristically the Unterland houses were clean and neat-looking, with clapboard walls, slate roofs and brightly painted verandas. Fish were hung on drying racks outside the boatmen's cottages, in preparation for being placed into barrels for consumption in the winter. Strolling along the main street Barkly would find colourful gift shops stocked with shells of every description, all manner of boxes and fancy articles made from the skins of gulls, and Schensky's photographs of the island. Many of the restaurants had tables set out in the open under small trees. When dining out, the Heligolanders liked to sip a small quantity of schnapps and follow it down by a draught of ale. After their meal they would move off to the Strand, where the excellent town band might start to play in front of the pavilion-style Reimer's Restaurant. In the evening some people would go to the Casino, or perhaps to a show at Her Majesty's Theatre, but more would proceed to the Conversation House, where from 9 o'clock till midnight or later there would be a public ball. Their relatively carefree alfresco lifestyle prevailed even when the tourist season was over. Although drink could be purchased anywhere the locals were almost invariably sober and well behaved.

Early in his governorship, Arthur Barkly set about improving the social conditions of the Heligolanders. He submitted legal orders for the protection of women and children, and on 1 February 1889 asked the Colonial Office to send him copies of the Falkland Island Ordinances, which he thought would provide for the islanders a less arbitrary legal system. Subsequently on 28 April 1890 he sent the Colonial Office a report on the administration of justice, suggesting amendments to the law.[4] He had learnt from his father how governors should care for the protection and well-being of colonial peoples. In Basutoland Arthur had won the nickname 'Lion' as the commander of Barkly's Horse, the regiment raised by his father, Sir Henry Barkly.[5] Fearlessly public-spirited, Sir Henry had been a governor in several Caribbean and Indian Ocean colonies. He showed his true mettle in 1873 when, as Governor of the Cape Colony, he resisted an attempt by the Colonial Secretary, Lord Carnarvon, to force that territory into a South African Confederation. Quite by coincidence, as a member of Carnarvon's 1879 Colonial Defence Commission, Sir Henry had recommended that Heligoland be fortified. Like Sir Henry, Arthur was a free-thinker, and by no means a malleable bureaucratic stooge. But did he have enough vivacity to challenge the Colonial Office and win?

Idyllic though his assignment in Heligoland seemed, money worries continued to haunt Arthur. By August 1889 he had accepted the fact that he needed to refund the balance of £470 advanced to him from the Seychelles. So desperate was his financial situation that each month he would write to the Colonial Office urging them to send his monthly salary sooner than the due date.[6] For decades the confidential communications between Whitehall and Arthur Barkly have lain unopened in a hefty leather-bound book of official correspondence at the Public Record Office. It provides several clues as to what his political masters thought of him professionally. Seemingly they found him irritating; not, surprisingly, because of his constant urgings for prompt payment, but rather because of his frequent absences from his post. Perhaps his beautiful and clever wife Frances demanded trips to more glamorous places, and certainly he went several times to Hamburg, possibly for his health. The consequence was that by early 1890 the Colonial Office was ready for the slightest error on his part.

Diabetes weakened Barkly's health that winter and he planned to take his annual holiday in the early spring. On 21 February he wrote to the Colonial Office requesting one month's leave, commencing from 1 March. The previous autumn he had requested – and been granted – a maintenance grant to have the exterior of Government House repainted. But, quite by chance, in early 1890 a dignitary passing through Heligoland happened to remark to the Colonial Office that the paintwork on the windows of that residence looked rather blistered. Barkly's superiors in Whitehall sought an explanation, and the Governor cited the inclement weather as the reason the work had not been done. Sensing official displeasure, on 10 March he wrote to the Colonial Secretary, Lord Knutsford, requesting permission for his leave to be postponed for a month, as weather conditions were still preventing the commencement of repairs to Government House.[7] Thus senior ministers had reason to know that Heligoland's Governor would be away from the island while the crucial negotiations about its future were in progress. Salisbury well knew that he would need to move very quickly if he were to get the swap agreement enacted before the Heligolanders could attempt to organise any effective veto.

Arthur and his family spent their leave in Britain. While at 1 Nina Gardens, his father's house in South Kensington, Arthur was appalled by the newspaper stories about the impending swap. Indignant that the islanders were not being consulted, he was also fearful for them; his knowledge of German cruelties in Africa gave him good reason to fear that the Germans could not necessarily be trusted to treat their colonial peoples well. Returning to Heligoland on 21 June he immediately met with the island's parliamentary Executive Council to check through the outline agreement. On 26 June he was off again, this time to Berlin – ostensibly to discuss details of the hand-over ceremony, but also to meet Sir Percy Anderson, the chief negotiator, to ascertain if there was any scope for amendments to be made. Despite all Arthur's efforts, there is no evidence that Anderson ever attempted to discuss the issue with the Germans, nor of any willingness to allow the islanders to indicate their choice by means of a plebiscite. The draft Anglo-German Agreement was signed, unamended, by Anderson in Berlin on 1 July. Arthur made one last desperate attempt to protect the islanders. On 10 July he wrote to the Colonial Office requesting that the existing ordinances provided for the administration of justice in Heligoland should be replaced, at the transfer of sovereignty, by ordinances similar to those obtaining in the Falkland Islands. Irritated by Barkly's attempt to interfere with the treaty-making process, Knutsford refused.

The Heligolanders regularly read the Hamburg newspapers, which circulated freely on the island, and were well acquainted with events in Europe. Thus, on 17 June there had been an excited response to a false report that Heligoland was to be ceded to Denmark. When the next day's papers disclosed that Germany was to be their new colonial master there was much apprehension. Newspaper stories soon appeared about German entrepreneurs with ambitions to turn Heligoland into a sort of Monte Carlo; they were said to be attempting to lodge licences in Berlin for hotels, restaurants, concert halls and casinos on the island. Of the 2,000 Heligolanders there were a few who reckoned the cession could be for the better, but many were concerned that the transfer would mean Heligoland losing its duty-free advantage. The fear that their island paradise would be spoilt under German rule was widespread. Professor Heinrich Gätke, who was also director of the island's ornithological institute (and also, since 1865, the official government interpreter), expressed concern that German militarisation might overwhelm the Oberland plateau with heavy guns, destroying its peace and quiet and making impossible the work of the island's world-famous migratory-bird sanctuary.

All that summer demands at Westminster for the views of the Heligolanders to be ascertained were being side-stepped with excuses about precedence and logistical difficulties. Whitehall could – if it had wished – have been guided by assessments of the islanders' wishes, provided by Barkly. But these were never requested. Rather, on 1 July 1890 Sir Edward Malet sent a secret telegram to the Governor enquiring what 'steps were being taken to prevent agitation'.[8] Salisbury well knew the islanders were far from indifferent about their impending change of nationality. When he spoke in the Lords debate on 10 July about the 'confidential' information he had received on the subject, his source was actually Arthur Barkly, from whom he had received a telegram, via Lord Knutsford, that very afternoon. Barkly had wired:

> They are very concerned as to whether it will be annexed to Schleswig-Holstein or treated as a separate territory (which is what they would much prefer), and whether or not the island is to be made a fortress, which they consider would greatly impede it as a bathing and health resort. They are perfectly contented and happy under British rule and desirous of no change.

Typically the Heligolanders were rather slow in making their deeper feelings known. It was not until 21 July – just three days before the crucial Second Reading debate in the Commons – that Barkly received, and immediately forwarded to England, a petition from the islanders addressed to Queen Victoria.[9] It declared: 'In parting from your Majesty, as subjects of the great British Empire, we shall never forget the manifold reasons we have experienced to feel contented and happy under your Majesty's government.' Correspondence now available for scrutiny makes it clear that Victoria was very touched by these sentiments, for she ordered Lord Knutsford to forward her reply to the islanders. It stated: '[Queen Victoria] gladly recognises the loyalty of the inhabitants which they showed under her Government, and she sincerely desires their sustained prosperity and contentment, to secure which she is satisfied that no effort will be wanting on the part of the German Emperor.' Barkly arranged to have that message publicly displayed on placards throughout the island, mindful that the last line carried a hint that she would be keeping a watchful eye on Wilhelm's future conduct.

But it was all far from over for Arthur Barkly, whose anxieties were deepening further. Accepting that there was no realistic hope of derailing the transfer of sovereignty, he energetically sought other employment for his staff. Evidently the Colonial Office negotiators had not given the slightest thought to their future. On 2 July they informed him that, with regard to compensation for the British officials losing their appointments, it was now too late to make further demands on the German government.[10] Would, he asked Malet to discover, the German government be willing to continue to employ Professor Gätke and the native officials? Other than Barkly himself, the one most in need of security was the Chief Magistrate, Colonel Edward Whitehead, who had with him on the island a wife and eight children. In vain Arthur attempted to get him a posting with the government of Gibraltar.

Paradoxically, in that summer of 1890, when Heligoland was on the verge of becoming the focus of international attention, its governor was obliged to spend an inordinate amount of time struggling with the staff at the Colonial Office, as he needed them to persuade the Treasury to reimburse him the £11 in expenses incurred during his recent four-day visit to Berlin.[11] Already close to penniless, Barkly was distraught to realise that no one in the Colonial Office had thought to make even a minuscule financial provision for him to get home. As late as 5 August 1890, by telegraph, he had to inform London that if he was to depart from the island by mail-boat on 9 August he could only do so if the ceremony of transfer was done early in the day. Even so his family, and that of Colonel Whitehead, were in the potentially humiliating circumstance of not being able to get home unless a passage allowance was paid for them out of funds from the Heligoland government.[12]

One consequence of the uncertainty as to whether the House of Commons would approve the Anglo-German Agreement bill (which it did by 209 votes to 61 on 25 July), was that the timetable for the hand-over was not determined until near the time appointed. On 23 July Arthur received a telegram from the British chargé d'affaires in Berlin informing him that the German emperor would visit the island some time after his return from Osborne. On 31 July he received a cable announcing that the Kaiser would be visiting on 10 August *when the island would be taken over*. It was presumed that his own administration would leave on 9 August, and advised him that 'The Admiralty have been informed'.[13] On 3 August the steam corvette HMS *Calypso*, fresh from naval duties off Plymouth, reached Sheerness, where her captain, Count Frederick Metaxa, was informed that she had been appointed the headquarters ship for coordinating the British withdrawal.

On the evening of 6 August *Calypso* anchored in calm water off Heligoland, as did the Admiralty yacht

HMS *Wildfire*, which had accompanied her from Sheerness. At 5.30 the next morning a 61-strong working party of seamen was landed ashore by the ship's steam pinnace, barge and cutter to bring off stores.[14] The events of that day and the next echoed the scene of eighty-three years earlier, when HMS *Explosion*'s mortars were heaved aloft to the plateau, but now the process was in reverse. One by one the Armstrong saluting guns were slung over the side of the Falm Esplanade near Government House, and lowered on ropes and pulleys down the steep red cliff there, before being taken out to the *Calypso*. In the course of the heavy and dangerous work the corvette's cutter was damaged, and a hundredweight boat anchor became irretrievably jammed in an underwater crevasse near the harbour.

Heligoland was virtually the first ever *colony* to be peacefully transferred in peacetime by Britain. (The Ionian Islands, which were handed over by Britain to Greece in 1864, had been a *Protectorate*.) This meant there were effectively no procedural or ceremonial precedents on which Arthur could draw when organising the British retreat. 'Should', he telegraphed London, 'the official portrait of Queen Victoria be removed?'[15]

Required by circumstance to turn himself into an imperial impresario, he often had only his initiative to guide him. He saw to it that the emblems of the British Empire were removed: the busts of Victoria and Albert were taken from the alcoves in the little post office, and royal coats of arms, where possible, were taken down from public buildings and brought aboard the cruiser.

In Germany there was great excitement about the Empire's forthcoming acquisition, which was already being dubbed 'Germany's pearl of the North Sea'.

Astonishingly most Germans at the time considered the island to be a far better prize than Zanzibar, or even Uganda. *The Times* correspondent in Hamburg reported on 8 August: 'The interest taken in the cession of Heligoland is increasing to an enormous extent, the island forms the chief topic of conversation, and the communications sent by reporters of newspapers of standing are read almost with the excitement of despatches from a battlefield.' When the *Hamburger Correspondent* disclosed that Wilhelm II himself would be landing on the island on 10 August, cession enthusiasm went into overdrive. As the Kaiser was visiting his grandmother Queen Victoria earlier in the week, a rumour (unfounded) also began to circulate that the hand-over ceremony might even be attended by a member of the British royal family. Evidently it was going to be an historic weekend, with the cession of the island to Germany on the first day, and the arrival of the emperor on the second to take possession of this 'Last jewel in the Crown', as it was widely referred to. The *Freia*, a magnificent steam-powered ferry built several years earlier, was already fully booked expressly for the 6-hour crossing from Hamburg. Numerous extra steamers, from Cuxhaven and Bremen, were chartered to carry spectators to the island to witness the transfer and imperial visit. On the island there were fears that there would be standing room only, and that there would not be enough food for the converging hordes of excursionists.

There was no let-up in the activity and animation on the morning of Saturday 9 August. The weather was beautiful and the island thronged to excess with sightseers. The Lower Town was decorated from end to end, with the Heligoland and German flags being most prominently displayed. The first move towards the official evacuation of the island by the British took place that morning when the Trinity House lighthouse-keepers and the families of the six British coastguardmen embarked on board the tender *Seamew*. At 1pm Arthur Barkly, in full dress uniform, was joined at Government House by Colonel Whitehead and the chief officials of the island, and soon they all proceeded to the landing stage to receive Herr von Bötticher, the German Secretary of State assigned to represent the Kaiser in accepting the transfer of authority. A guard of honour, consisting of a detachment of marines from the *Calypso*, was drawn up at Government House, while another guard of honour awaited Barkly at the landing stage, where he and his officials were met by Captain Metaxa of the *Calypso*, Captain Sanderson of HMS *Wildfire* and various other naval officers.

Fully an hour passed before the German corvette *Victoria* and artillery training ship *Mars* hove into view, followed by the despatch vessel *Pfeil*. A further delay was caused by the low state of the tide which compelled the little flotilla to circumnavigate the island before anchoring off the north harbour. From the outset, navigation of the waters around Heligoland was proving trickier than the German Navy had anticipated. Once the ships were riding, they fired a 21-gun salute in honour of the British flag, a tribute that was acknowledged by a similar salute from the *Calypso*. Then there followed a salute of 17 guns in honour of the British Governor. Just after 3pm von Bötticher arrived by boat at a jetty richly decorated with flags, palms and garlands of flowers. With him was Privy Councillor Lindon, the new civil and naval governors, and a financial comptroller. As soon as they were safely ashore, a cordial greeting took place between this party and Arthur Barkly, who introduced Colonel Edward Whitehead, Professor Gätke, and a small knot of other British officials. The entire group then proceeded to Government House where Frances received them, accompanied by a large party of wives and daughters of the other officials, as well as many of the leading islanders, whom the Barklys had invited to witness the ceremony. Frances positioned herself in an upstairs window of Government House to gain the best view of the proceedings.

The guard of honour was stationed in the English-style garden. The officials and naval officers, all in full uniform, accompanied Arthur to a place close to the flagstaff, where he performed the brief but impressive ceremony of handing over the island to German control. The proceedings were simple and uncomplicated, consisting only of the reading of a clause from the Anglo-German Agreement. For the few Britons present it was a very sad and moving occasion, especially when the German flag was hoisted beside the Union Jack. This caused ecstatic cheers from the countless German trippers crowded along the esplanade, who burst into an impromptu chorus of the patriotic song *Deutschland über Alles*, which von Hoffmann had composed on the island many years earlier. The hoisting of the German flag was also greeted by a salute of 21 guns from both German and English warships in the harbour. Herr von Bötticher then called upon the excited crowd to give three 'Hochs' for Queen Victoria, which was done with great enthusiasm. The ceremony passed off without the slightest hitch, and with the utmost cordiality on both sides. The two flags were left to flutter side by side until sundown.[16]

Meanwhile, some 4,000 miles away in Africa, other pieces on the gigantic colonial chessboard Salisbury had devised with Bismarck's successors were being fitted into place. At the precise hour that the German flag was hoisted in the garden at Government House in Heligoland on 9 August, it was lowered for the last time in parts of East Africa, most notably in Zanzibar.

Barkly next proceeded down to the Conversation House in the Unterland where he held a farewell reception with forty of Heligoland's leading citizens, in the presence of the British naval officers, his official entourage and the German officials. Even there, as he had throughout the day, Arthur Barkly received telegrams from the Foreign and Colonial Offices in London, and was obliged to hurry off to deal with the special instructions they contained. When the lunch ended he was present to hear the final speech, made by von Bötticher. In the name of the inhabitants and all succeeding governors, he thanked Barkly 'For all the good seed he and his predecessors had sown; the fruit of which was now to be reaped.' For Arthur, it was almost too much. Deeply moved and struggling to keep his composure he responded in a low voice. The strain increased when an island dignitary, the Baths Director, stood up to express a few simple words: 'Our present rulers will not think ill of us if, in bidding farewell to the Queen of England, who has ruled us so kindly, we do so with heavy hearts.'

Soon it was time for the governor to go. By the late afternoon the Barklys' children and servants, together with Colonel and Mrs Whitehead and their family, had boarded the Admiralty yacht *Wildfire*. Shortly before 6pm, having made the final arrangements at Government House, Arthur sadly made his way down through the narrow streets to the landing stage, past the good-natured faces he had come to know so well. He was warmly cheered by the spectators, as everyone pressed forward to shake hands with the last of the English governors. At the pier he boarded the *Calypso*'s steam pinnace. Frances was overwhelmed by bouquets of flowers, tied with the Heligoland ribbon; there were so many she could not hold them all and they had to be accommodated in the pinnace. As the boat speedily puffed and hissed towards the warship, everyone shouted and waved their last farewells.[17]

Instantly Arthur set foot on HMS *Calypso* the corvette commenced firing a 17-gun salute. Each deafening boom of the cannon thudded like a quivering arrow into his breaking heart. As the tide ebbed further, at just after 7pm the 21ft draught *Calypso* shifted berth out to deeper water. There was one last duty to perform. At 11pm a party of six British coastguards, under Royal Naval command, made for Government House and lowered the Union Jack for the last time, before returning to the *Calypso*. They were the last British officials to leave the island.[18] At 11.40pm the Barklys stood solemnly on *Calypso*'s quarter-deck as the warship weighed anchor. Slowly she gathered steam, gracefully listing as she cleared the southern tip of the island. Then, in company with the *Seamew* and *Wildfire*, she headed for England. Large drinks in hand, the Barklys watched the twinkling lights of the island until they faded out of sight over the horizon.

Scarcely had Governor Barkly's party made ready to leave Heligoland that evening than thirteen warships of the German fleet appeared and took possession of the anchorage just vacated by the *Calypso*. Several admirals and other senior naval officers landed from the various ships, and strolled about the decorated narrow streets. All was again bustle and confusion, for there seemed to be no time even to make the preparations for the Kaiser's visit the next day. Government House had to be made ready for the reception and a banquet in the large drawing-rooms for sixty people, including Wilhelm II and his entourage and the chief personages of the mainland and insular governments. Few officials or people on the island slept that night, and most were still working hard at dawn.

At Osborne that week Queen Victoria's emotions must have been in turmoil. Displeased at being required by Salisbury to hand over a cherished colony, she was cool towards her mistrusted grandson, although she was obliged to treat him with respect as he was a head of state. Would she have been shocked that the Kaiser would so soon take her name in vain? For Wilhelm, the experience of reviewing his grandmother's impressive fleet at Spithead further fuelled his keenness to get to the North Sea to inspect his latest possession. Hurrying eastwards from the Isle of Wight on the night of 9 August Wilhelm was aboard the imperial yacht *Hohenzollern*, escorted by a fourteen-strong German torpedo-boat flotilla.

Later that week the satirical magazine *Punch* irreverently devised an 'unreported' incident that had occurred as the German Emperor approached the island:

> The new landlord . . . was most anxious to take possession. He was all impatience to appear before his recently acquired subjects, to show them the Military Uniform he has assumed after discarding the garb he loved so well – the *grande tenue* of an Honorary Admiral of the Fleet in the service of

> Victoria, Queen, Empress and Grandmother. There was a consultation on board the *Hohenzollern*, and then a subdued German cheer. The chief Naval Officer approached His Majesty. 'Sire', he said falling on one knee, 'all is now ready.' 'But why has there been this delay?' asked the Kaiser. 'Sire, we could not find the island. Unhappily we had had mislaid the, er,' paused the naval officer. 'Charts and field-glasses?' speculated His Majesty. 'No, Sire,' was the reply. After some hesitation, the chief of the German sailors continued. 'The fact is, Your Majesty, we had lost our microscope!'

Funnily enough, the *Hohenzollern* was actually involved in an impromptu encounter en route to the island, although the details were never revealed to Parliament. Only *The Times* picked up the story, erroneously claiming that the *Hohenzollern* had rendezvoused with a squadron of German ironclads on exercise manoeuvres in the North Sea.[19] What really happened is recorded in the log-book of HMS *Calypso*. At 5.40am on 10 August, just off the coast of Borkum, the westernmost of the German Frisian Islands, the Sheerness-bound cruiser, with the *Seamew* and *Wildfire*, sighted Wilhelm's steam yacht with its escort of torpedo-boats heading towards Heligoland. Such was the Kaiser's vanity that protocol had to be observed, even so far out at sea, and there ensued an exchange of masthead flag-hoisting and ceremonial gunfire.[20]

Brilliant weather greeted the Kaiser's arrival in Heligoland. The sun shone brightly on what for the visitors was a cheerful scene. The whole island was decorated with flowers and flags, and the streets were full of sailors in smart uniforms and Heligolander girls in their national costume. The stairs to the Oberland were crowded with people going up and down, and all was excitement and expectation. From the Oberland a rare naval sight was presented to view. All the warships were bedecked with brightly coloured signalling flags. The manoeuvring squadron had positioned itself 2 miles out to sea, anchored in two lines. The warship *Kaiser*, on the right of the outside line, was flanked by the *Deutschland*, the *Frederich de Grosse* and the *Prussen*. The inner line also rode at anchor, somewhat closer in shore, with the artillery training ship *Mars* nearby. Standing on the bridge of the *Hohenzollern*, the German monarch steamed up to the island, between 11am and noon. The imperial yacht approached the German warships from the south-west, and amid the thunder of salutes from the warships made its way between the two lines. Then it steamed round the island, to the delight of the German crowds watching from the Oberland.

The Heligolanders, having had no time to reflect on the British departure, began to feel apprehensive as the unfamiliar fleet lingered off their island like a shoal of hungry sharks. Their initial alarm was caused by the disembarkation of some three thousand German marines in full uniform. The prospect of seeing the Kaiser meant that throughout the morning more and more jubilant visitors arrived from the mainland. Never before had there been so many people on Heligoland. The Germans indulged in every possible form of rejoicing just before noon when Wilhelm jauntily stepped ashore at the landing stage.

He was greeted by von Bötticher, the two naval and civil governors of the island, and a variety of high-ranking military and official personages in full uniform. A souvenir was presented to him by a committee of Heligolanders, and a number of young Heligoland girls in national costume presented a tribute of flowers in the shape of an immense floral anchor in the Heligoland colours of green, red and white. Then a procession formed up and, walking at its head, the Kaiser paraded slowly through the densely crowded streets, from the Unterland to the Oberland, where a field service was to be performed near the Lighthouse tower. The imperial procession halted within a square formed by about three thousand sailors and marines drawn up in ranks. Wilhelm took his place a short distance in front of the field altar, which had been erected in the centre of the square between two flag-poles. The military chaplain spoke impressively of the day's events in his sermon, as the Kaiser and all his troops stood with their heads uncovered. At the close of the service, an imperial proclamation by the Emperor was read out by von Bötticher:

> The government of Heligoland and its surroundings has, in consequence of a treaty with her Majesty the Queen of Great Britain and Ireland, been transferred to myself. The former relationship to the German Empire is restored by peaceful means to the German Fatherland, to the annals of which it pertains both by position and circumstance. By community of language and interests you were hitherto related to your German brethren. Thanks to the wisdom of your previous rulers these features have sustained little alteration during the period of your loyalty to the powerful British Empire. With so much pleasure does every German subject, along with myself, welcome your reunion with the German people and the Fatherland. I reserve to myself according to treaty, to decide the immediate form of government,

> but as I now take possession of Heligoland gloriously and for ever for myself and my successors, I trust to the acknowledged prudence of all Heligolanders who wish to become German that they remain unbroken in loyalty to myself and the Fatherland. On the other hand, I promise my protection and my utmost care both for yourselves and your rights. I shall ensure that justice will be impartially administered to all, and that your local laws and customs shall, as far as possible, remain unaltered. A well-meaning and guarded policy will also be essayed in the future to promote your welfare and increase the economic value of the island. In order to ameliorate the transfer, with its new surroundings, all now living males will remain exempt from military or naval service, all rights of property which have been acquired either by private persons or corporations under the British rule in Heligoland will remain in force. The fulfilment of these promises will be the aim of myself and my government. The retention of the faith of your fathers, the care of your church and schools, will have my earnest attention. I receive with pleasure Heligoland into the wreath of German islands which surround the shores of the Fatherland. May the return to Germany, the participation in its glory, its independence, and freedom be the care of yourselves and your descendants!

The proclamation was received with loud cheering by the massed Germans present and affixed in public places later in the day. Just before the hoisting of his imperial standard and the German flag, the Kaiser was expected to address his new subjects directly. In sharp contrast to the reassuringly honeyed words from von Bötticher the previous day, Wilhelm's speech effectively disregarded the islanders as he barked with a rasping voice:

> Comrades of the Navy! Four days ago I celebrated the Battle of Wörth, at which my revered grandfather and my father gave the first hammer-stroke towards the formation of the German Empire. Now twenty years have gone by, and I, Wilhelm II, German Emperor, King of Prussia, reincorporate this island with the German Fatherland without war and without bloodshed, as the last piece of German earth. The island is chosen as a bulwark in the sea, a protection to German fisheries, a central point for my ships of war, a place and harbour of safety in the German Ocean against all enemies who may dare to show themselves upon it. I hereby take possession of this land, whose inhabitants I greet, and in token thereof I command that my standard be hoisted, and by its side that of my Navy.

When the older inhabitants of the island heard the Kaiser speak so fiercely for the first time many felt their eyes filling with tears. The Heligolanders huddled together, outnumbered on their own island. But it was too late now for them to feel maudlin towards Britain. Characteristically they had been too slow to act. For ever more they would probably have to pay the price for their complacence in not demanding a plebiscite on the cession. Their changed circumstances became still more apparent to them when the imperial flag was hoisted in the presence of their new monarch. At that moment a salute of 21 guns was taken up by all the German warships anchored offshore. After lunch at Government House the Emperor made a short tour through the little town. At 4pm he departed from

Heligoland on the *Hohenzollern*, amid the acclamation of the tourists and trippers, and yet another salute from the squadron.

That evening, when Wilhelm had triumphantly led his warships home to the German mainland, the chief Heligolanders had several reasons to be alarmed, not least because of the dishonest declarations made by their new monarch. Wilhelm's proclamation had claimed that Heligoland had been 'restored' to the German Fatherland: 'By community of language and interests you were hitherto related to your German brethren.' Yet the Heligolanders knew they had never been German, nor had their island; it had only ever been Danish or British. Similarly, at the lunch in Government House he had spoken of his delight that the island had come into his possession 'with the free will' of the islanders – although he must have known that the Heligolanders had not sought the cession; indeed, they had not even been consulted, much less given it their approval. The German public had been led to believe that the cession was a 'gracious gift' from Britain. At the luncheon Wilhelm had alluded to the 'friendly gift of the island from Her Majesty to myself'. The Heligolanders were in no position to know that Queen Victoria had personally opposed the cession, but Wilhelm had doubtless had several difficult conversations with his grandmother at Osborne and can have been in no doubt about her true feelings on the matter.

Meanwhile, by lunchtime on Monday 11 August HMS *Calypso* had conveyed the Barklys in fine weather to the edge of the Thames Estuary at Sheerness. She then chugged upstream to Chatham where her damaged cutter was to be replaced. The Barklys were taken by pinnace from the anchorage to

Sheerness pier, where they were reunited with the rest of their party, who had arrived on the *Wildfire* only an hour before. That weekend Arthur had been at the epicentre of an international event, but now he was no longer a governor and so there was no reception to mark his return. Later that evening the Barklys arrived by train in Kensington. Frances later recalled in her memoirs: 'We were thankful to rest quietly, after undergoing so much fatigue and excitement, not to speak of the very hard work of having to quit the island at such short notice.'[21]

The leading article about the hand-over in *The Times* that morning incorrectly stated that on 9 August: 'The imperial standard floated above the Union Jack until sundown, when both flags were hauled down.' It was at the very end of a long report, and it was only a minor slip, but Arthur was unable to resist the temptation of writing a corrective letter, which the paper published on 21 August.

> Sir,
> *The Times* report of 11 August is wrong. The two flags floated together on the same mast, at precisely the same height until sundown, when the Union Jack was hauled down by a naval detachment from HMS *Calypso* and brought home on that ship.
>
> Yours,
> Arthur Barkly

The letter had the effect of drawing the attention of the Colonial Office to the forgotten story. When staff scrutinised the article more closely, they found mention of a royal coat of arms still fixed to a wall in Government House when the Kaiser had lunched there. The finicky Colonial Office now demanded to know why Barkly had not had it removed, then wanted to check the inventory of artefacts brought home on the *Calypso*. Such was the ill-feeling that Arthur, now aged forty-seven, became anxious about his prospects of getting a further governorship. He was already depressed by the transfer of Heligoland to Germany, and this new worry seriously affected his health. During a visit to Stapleton Park, the country estate of Frances's brother in Pontefract, he was taken ill and died there on 27 September 1890, just seven weeks after the cession.

Circumstances were equally miserable for the large Whitehead family. The Colonel was given an annual salary of just £50 by the Colonial Office, and even that was on condition that he was not appointed to another post while receiving it.[22] Whitehead sought compensation and in April 1891 was asking the Colonial Office why his letters on the subject went unanswered. Eventually, in August that year, he was offered a one-off payment of just £200. Insulted and aghast, he complained to the Colonial Office that he regarded it as totally insufficient.

Aware that her late husband had only grudgingly been reimbursed his small expenses for the Berlin trip, the newly widowed Frances was now informed that the Colonial Office would pay him an imperial salary and lodging allowance of just £3 a week up to the date of his death.[23] There was worse to come. When Arthur died, she learnt that the only money she and her five children could expect from the Colonial Office for his years of service was a pension of just £50 a year. Letters in support of the Barklys were posted to *The Times* and the Colonial Office by Ernest Maxse and other influential figures. Publicly shamed into taking action, the Colonial Office increased the pension to £350.

To make ends meet Frances commenced a career as an author, producing *Among Boers and Basutos*, the story of her life in South Africa with Arthur, and then in 1898 *From the Tropics to the North Sea*, a dignified account, without a trace of bitterness, of their time on Heligoland. Although she achieved some literary success, in monetary terms it was not enough. She and her young family were still obliged to rely on the generosity of her father-in-law, Sir Henry Barkly. Queen Victoria herself became involved, to the extent that she granted Frances a grace and favour apartment at Hampton Court Palace. This was a very unusual step for a Colonial Service family, and perhaps indicates the sense of conscience Victoria appears to have suffered about abandoning Heligoland.

6

Riddle of the Rock

On 11 August 1897 a small cutter-rigged yacht hoisted sail, slipped quietly out of Dover harbour and headed southwards. At the helm of the 28ft *Vixen* was its owner, Erskine Childers. A cousin of Hugh Childers, a former Chancellor of the Exchequer and Secretary of State for War, who had been a member of the Carnarvon Commission on Imperial Defence, young Erskine was by profession a House of Lords committee clerk. He was intent on taking his converted ex-lifeboat on a leisurely summer voyage to the Mediterranean. But after crossing to France the *Vixen* was delayed in Boulogne by inclement winds blowing from the east. That chance patch of unseasonal weather caused Childers to make a highly momentous decision: abruptly abandoning his plans he set course instead for the Baltic. En route, during the next few weeks, the *Vixen* island-hopped between the many Frisian Islands along the Dutch and north-west German coasts. In response to what he discovered in those parts, Childers wrote his influential book *The Riddle of the Sands*, a semi-autobiographical thriller largely based on his 1897 voyage – though even a mind as wide-ranging as Childers's could scarcely grasp the magnitude of the consequences which the so-called Heligoland–Zanzibar swap was having in Africa.

However heartless, and indeed immoral, Salisbury's epic swap deal had been, its timing had been guided by pure genius. He had secured it at the precise high water mark of Britain's bargaining power with Germany. For a few weeks that summer the German newspapers reflected the German nation's romantic tide of goodwill towards Britain for ceding Heligoland. That mood soon changed, initially with some sympathy for the freelance coloniser Dr Karl Peters. In March 1890 he had induced Mwanga, King of Uganda, to sign a treaty placing his kingdom under German protection. When Peters reached the coast near Mombasa at Bagamoya on 16 July, after an arduous journey from Lake Victoria, he was astounded to hear that the territory he had just acquired for the Fatherland had been given to England. His emotions were running so high that – as he stated in his book *New Light on Dark Africa* – he needed to withdraw into a private room for two hours to regain his composure. He later furiously exclaimed that the kingdoms of Witu and Uganda had been sacrificed 'for a bath-tub in the North Sea'!

Ironically, the central figure in Germany's growing condemnation of the Heligoland swap was Prince Otto von Bismarck himself. Since his dismissal by Kaiser Wilhelm II in March 1890, the embittered former imperial Chancellor had turned against his successor, his former protégé Count Caprivi. Bismarck's devoted supporters could never accept his unfortunate successor. Everything Caprivi did they ridiculed and condemned, while the agrarian Conservatives despised his lack of landed property. Caprivi's difficulties were greatly exacerbated because Prince Bismarck entered the fight against him with all his characteristic energy. That summer he famously denounced the exchanging of so many African concessions for Heligoland as trading 'a whole suit of clothes for a trouser button'.

The wisdom of the swap, which had been one of the high-points of the German political year in 1890, became a significant factor in the demolition of Caprivi's credibility. Had Heligoland been acquired in the chancellorship of Prince Bismarck, it would probably have been valued very highly. Under Caprivi, it simply let loose a flood of criticism. Many years later Kaiser Wilhelm II glumly recalled in his memoirs:

> It was merely Caprivi, the usurper, who had the audacity to sit in Bismarck's chair, and the 'ungrateful' and 'impulsive' young master who had done such a thing! Had Bismarck only wished he could have had the old rock any day, but he never would have been so unskilful as to give up to the English for it the very promising African possessions, and he never would have allowed himself to be thus worsted. That was the sort of thing heard almost everywhere.

Curious, indeed, were the criticisms of the exchange, particularly the loss of Zanzibar and Witu, indulged in by the Bismarckian press, which had previously always explained that Bismarck had little belief in the value of colonies in themselves and looked upon them merely as objects of barter. His successor acted in accordance with these ideas in the matter of Heligoland – and was subsequently violently criticised and vilified. Supporters of Karl Peters and all manner of nationalists compared Caprivi to the simpleton in the fairy tale *Jack and the Beanstalk*, who naively exchanged a healthy cow for a few beans.

The deluge of criticism gathered in strength to such an extent that on 10 December 1890, when the Reichstag met to consider a somewhat belated bill concerning the incorporation of Heligoland into the Kingdom of Prussia, Bismarck himself publicly condemned the exchange. Late in 1891, at Friedrichsruhe, his country estate, he outlined his personal thinking on the question of Caprivi's East Africa policy and Heligoland during a private after-dinner conversation with his biographer, Dr Moritz Busch:

> Zanzibar ought not to have been left to the English. It would have been better to maintain the old arrangement. We could have had it some time later when England required our good offices against France or Russia. In the meantime our merchants, who are cleverer and satisfied with smaller profits, would have kept the upper hand in business. To regard Heligoland as an equivalent shows more imagination than sound calculation. In the event of war it would be better for us that it should be in the hands of a neutral power. It is difficult and most expensive to fortify.

Across the Atlantic the audacious Heligoland swap deal was commented on with amazement by the *New York Times*. In Paris publication of the Agreement aroused intense anti-British feeling. By strengthening the defences of the Fatherland it dealt another blow to French naval supremacy, by making a French blockade of the Elbe in any future conflict much more dangerous. Furthermore, as members of the French Chamber indignantly pointed out, by assuming a Protectorate over Zanzibar without first consulting France, the British government had violated the Anglo-French Declaration of 1862, whereby both countries had agreed to respect the independence of the Sultan.

They demanded compensation for this act of gross international discourtesy. The day after the news reached Paris, Alexander Ribot, the Foreign Minister, observed to the British ambassador that as Britain had given Heligoland to Germany, he supposed she would not now mind handing Jersey over to France!

In several important respects Salisbury's Anglo-German Agreement deal was successful. As he had intended, it had the knock-on effect of settling other crucial colonial spheres of interest arguments – but at a price. As Lord Salisbury admitted in conversation with the French Ambassador on 21 June, Britain and Germany had 'completely forgotten' about the 1862 Declaration, an oversight which gave the French government an excellent opportunity for seeking compensation in Africa. On 5 August – just four days before the cession of Heligoland – a new Anglo-French Convention was signed. Britain agreed to recognise French claims to a Protectorate over Madagascar, while France withdrew her opposition to the British Protectorate over Zanzibar. In the opinion of the French ambassador in London, his country had obtained considerable advantages from the bargain at a minimum sacrifice. The Anglo-German Agreement also generated enough diplomatic momentum for Salisbury to clear up a number of festering colonial disagreements with Portugal, by means of the Anglo-Portuguese Agreement signed that year.

These agreements amply fulfilled the purpose for which they were designed. The pacification proved a lasting settlement, as well as an immediate one. The stream of acrimonious disputes, which for years past had flowed between the African departments of the various Foreign Offices, dried up from 1890. Indeed, peace reigned in those regions both diplomatically and actually, until all peace was swept away in the cataclysm of 1914. According to Salisbury's daughter, the writer Lady Gwendolen Cecil, a year or two before his death in 1903 he dwelt with satisfaction on the presence of Germany in Africa: 'Britain could not be sufficiently grateful for it', he said. 'It was the best, indeed the only, guarantee that Britain possessed of South African loyalty.'

Another benefit of the Anglo-German Agreement was that countless thousands of indigenous peoples in East Africa came under the British flag and so were spared the cruelties of German rule. The details of Germany's harsh colonial practices were only belatedly made known to Parliament and the public at large in 1894, when the Foreign Office in Whitehall published their *Report on the German Colonies in Africa and the South Pacific*.[1] By then news was emerging that Dr Karl Peters, while at Kilimanjaro in January 1892, had hanged a native girl called Jayodja. She was one of his concubines (whom he called his 'princesses'), who had fled for protection to a neighbouring chief. Peters reputedly had the girl brutally flogged, day after day, until her back resembled 'minced meat'. He was brought before a disciplinary court at Potsdam in April 1897, six years later, and was sentenced to be dismissed from the service – not because of his actions but because he had made false reports. Yet owing to the pressure applied by the Colonial Party, Peters was granted a pension by the Emperor, and a statue of him was erected in his honour in Dar es Salaam. Another was later erected on the seawall near Heligoland's Biological Institute.

All the while, on their tiny island off the coast of Europe, the Heligolanders sacrificed for Salisbury's diplomatic triumphs were adjusting to their new overlords. Improvements were certainly made in terms of tangible facilities. Within weeks Heligoland joined the telephonic age, as a telephone cable was laid connecting Heligoland with Cuxhaven. It was also connected to Sandy Island. The resort facilities were improved, most significantly by an enhanced lift in the metal tower built alongside the old Pottchen steps linking the Unterland and the promenade on the Oberland. In 1892 the island's clean air conditions were justly rewarded with the founding near the harbour of a small scientific research centre, the Biological Institute Helgoland (BAH). All classes of island shopkeepers were soon enjoying more prosperity. The novelty of the Fatherland's newly acquired island meant the number of trippers and excursionists increased, although the vast numbers of proletarian three-day-eventers meant that the princes and higher nobility of Germany no longer went to Heligoland for the summer as they had done when it was in English hands.

The swiftness with which the Germans began the fortification of Heligoland far exceeded Barkly's most dismal prognosis. Within weeks of the cession a barracks arose in the Sapskuhlen area of the plateau. A small army of military engineers and Italian labourers built a light railway and constructed a fortified battery on the South Point. The island's shores were faced with granite to protect them against the ravages of the sea, and to reinforce a safe naval harbour. No Heligolanders were employed on these projects. Even the islanders who had welcomed the transfer of sovereignty, hoping for improvements in public facilities, were becoming despondent. Everything – including the islanders' well-being – was subordinated to militarisation. The ransacking of the

Grunen Wasser dance-hall by a gang of marines further soured relations. The Heligolanders were even more displeased when – for security purposes – iron gates were suddenly built on the Pottchen steps. Perhaps the first-ever 'Iron Curtain', they had a menacing presence which the locals resented, alarmed at the idea that their freedom of movement on their own island could be restricted. Under British administration, law and order had comfortably been maintained by three unarmed policemen; now there were ten armed German military policemen.

In early 1891, after the legislative process was complete and Heligoland's incorporation into Germany had been constitutionally settled, the interim governmental arrangements were stood down. The system of having separate civil and military governors was abandoned and the office of governor abolished; the senior representative was henceforth to be termed the Commandant of the island. Administratively, Heligoland remained *de facto* a colony but it was shifted from the German Colonial Office to a subsection of the province of Hamburg. Evidently Germany was resolved to assimilate the island into the mainland both culturally and administratively.

In social matters, it became evident that Germany was attempting to stamp out Heligoland's ancient laws and traditions, thus violating the letter and the spirit of the Treaty. The Heligolanders did not speak German. Their language was Frisian – a tongue far more closely related to English than to German or Dutch. Yet the Germans insisted that the islanders spoke German, and soon forbade the teaching of both English and Frisian in schools. The new colonial power also changed the official spelling of the island's name from Heligoland to Helgoland.

Nowhere did this drive for Germanisation affect the islanders more than on the question of nationality. Despite pleas for Heligoland to have a British consul to represent its British citizens after the cession, Whitehall refused. An ideal candidate would have been the former Government Secretary and ornithologist Heinrich Gätke. Danish interests on Heligoland were represented by an honorary Danish consul, even though Denmark had vacated the island eighty-three years earlier! The Germanisation of the island mattered because, under Article 12.2 of the Anglo-German Agreement, any islanders wanting to adopt British nationality had to do so before 1 January 1892. Somewhat arrogantly, the British government had handed over not only the island but *the nationality of its inhabitants as well.* During Sir Percy Anderson's negotiations in Berlin, between 21 July and 6 August, the rights of the islanders were reduced from electing to *remain* British to needing to opt *for* British nationality. In practical administrative terms this meant that in order to *regain* their British nationality every islander would individually have to go before a uniformed German official to make the necessary declarations. This was a highly intimidating procedure which many islanders found an insurmountable hurdle. In the absence of a consul no British representative was present on the appointed day to see that fairness was observed. As a matter of fact those who did choose to remain British very soon found themselves boycotted by the German authorities. One instance will suffice. It was declared that only German subjects were eligible for employment in ferry-boats and so, within a few months, to save their livelihood and live at peace with their new masters, *all* the men (some of whom had sons or brothers serving in the

Royal Navy) were bullied or cajoled into becoming German citizens, with a single exception.

Hardly surprisingly, Whitehall made no effort to bring this early breach of the spirit of the Anglo-German Agreement to the British public's attention. The writer William George Black had just returned from a visit to the island, where he was approached by the islanders who begged him to speak out on their behalf. On 25 September 1891 he succeeded in getting a letter published in *The Times*. Black also contacted Salisbury, requesting an investigation. This Salisbury agreed to, and the process even involved accepting evidence from high-ranking diplomats such as Sir Percy Anderson and Sir Edward Malet. However, its effectiveness was wrecked by a memo maliciously scribbled by a Foreign Office functionary. Without any foundation it dismissively referred to Black as 'discovering a mare's-nest'. The put-down cast a long shadow over the investigation – and in late 1891, quite unbelievably, it was reported to Salisbury that the islanders had no grounds for complaint in this regard!

Salisbury was a hard-nosed diplomatic strategist, and within a fortnight of achieving the Heligoland-East Africa swap in early August 1890 he ruthlessly poured cold water over Kaiser Wilhelm's next act of self-important posturing. Curiously impervious to the existence of antagonistic sentiment, the Kaiser was anxious that the transfer should be endorsed by the presence of British warships at the German naval manoeuvres at Kiel in September 1890. Lord George Hamilton made a tactful excuse, but the Kaiser persisted, refusing to take no for an answer. Count Paul von Hatzfeldt, the German ambassador, appealed earnestly to Lord Salisbury to overrule his First Sea Lord. The Kaiser, it was explained, had the matter closely at heart and would be bitterly disappointed at a final refusal. Salisbury was driven to candid explanations. The English people, he said, were and always had been particularly jealous of any foreign influence upon their government, and this year that jealousy was concentrated against Germany. On 22 August 1890 he informed Hatzfeldt:

> I do not think that it would be a wise thing to do . . . [in] the same year as that in which we have ceded Heligoland. The cession of Heligoland has not excited much open objection in England, but it is bitterly resented and will not soon be forgiven by a small political section. Unfortunately this section consists of men who are, or were, among our strongest supporters. We have, besides, plenty of opponents who are anxious to raise the cry that the German Emperor has too much influence over us. If that cry were raised and if an ignorant electorate were to echo it, our power of taking the right course in the greater game of politics in Europe would be very much hindered.[2]

But the Kaiser was an insecure character who just did not know where to stop. By the summer of 1891 it was no longer possible for Salisbury to further postpone Wilhelm's first state visit to Britain. (Hitherto Wilhelm had only come on private trips.) The previous year Salisbury had been able to delay the visit by telling Hatzfeldt that he feared the crowds would boo the Kaiser. This time he tried to keep him out of London by insisting it was 'full of socialists'. Even so, in July 1891 the visit went ahead. After a procession, a reception at the Opera, a speech at the Mansion House and another reception at Windsor, an enormous garden party was given for the Kaiser in the park at Hatfield, Salisbury's country house. There were sixty guests for dinner each night in the glittering banqueting hall. In commemoration of his visit the Kaiser gave Salisbury a gigantic oil painting. The picture was not a landscape or some such innocuous scene, but a 30ft x 10ft portrait of the Kaiser himself in the uniform of a British Admiral of the Fleet. The picture was so vast that it occupied one entire wall of Hatfield's drawing-room. Unimpressed by the picture and the dreadful foreign visitors, Salisbury retreated to his study – and wrote that he believed the Kaiser was 'a disturbing influence' on peace, 'mad enough for anything' and potentially 'the most dangerous enemy we have in Europe'. Given that he had probably held these opinions for some time, it reflects very badly on him that he willingly handed over the Heligolanders to someone he so distrusted.

In February 1891 Wilhelm had meddled in administrative matters concerning the Royal Navy, recommending some trivial procedural improvements. Salisbury's response was to ask the First Sea Lord to send a reply 'showing that in some directions we are adopting his recommendation. . . . It rather looks to me as if he was not "all there"!'[3] Within a year or so, there was another incident. 'One of the best days of my life', the Kaiser later remarked, 'which I shall never forget as long as I live, was the day when I inspected the Mediterranean Fleet when I was on board the *Dreadnought*, and my flag was hoisted for the first time.' Wilhelm at this time was enjoying a cruise in the Mediterranean, and visited Athens to attend the wedding of his sister to the Crown Prince of Greece. He decided that in his new role as an honorary British officer he would exercise command. Consequently the

Union flag, the emblem of the Admiral of the Fleet, was unfurled on the main-mast of the battleship *Dreadnought*. Nominally at least, as long as the flag was flying, the Kaiser was in command of the greatest of all the fighting squadrons of the British Empire.

Heligoland was to play a part in the development of Wilhelm's increasingly bizarre love–hate attitude towards Britain and the Royal Navy. He wanted to develop Kiel as a prestigious yachting centre to rival Cowes, and in 1891 founded the Imperial Yacht Club there, but as few Germans were interested in competitive sailing he needed to persuade British racing yachts to cross the North Sea. In 1892 he instigated the Dover–Heligoland yacht race. The winner received the Emperor's Cup, his gift, although every yacht entered was virtually guaranteed a prize. Staged every year until 1908 it became a prestigious event, and was the only regularly held ocean race in Europe in the early part of the century. Attracting overseas entries from the United States and France as well as Britain, it was the first truly international yacht race. Just how close to Heligoland those giant racing schooners dared to anchor when they completed the 300-mile course is not known. In this race, as in races at Cowes throughout the 1890s, competition was fiercest between Wilhelm's yacht *Meteor* and the Prince of Wales's *Britannia*. Such was the Kaiser's ludicrously compulsive need to be seen to be winning, he even entered *Meteor* for races in which the prize was the Meteor Shield – supplied by himself! It was a deadly game. In August 1898 the *Meteor* accidentally collided with the yacht *Isolde* in the Solent, killing Baron von Zedtwitz, its owner.[4]

From 1895 onwards the Dover–Heligoland races served their declared sporting purpose of attracting yachts to Kiel. On 20 June that year Wilhelm officially opened what came to be known as the Kiel Canal, entering it at Brunsbüttel on the Elbe aboard the imperial yacht *Hohenzollern* before ceremonially cruising through it. Present at Kiel were some three hundred yachts and eighty warships from fourteen nations. This international gathering was reputedly the most impressive assemblage of warships the world had ever seen. On 26 June, at Kiel, Wilhelm dined on board the visiting British flagship *Royal Sovereign*. Speeches and ceremonies emphasised the commercial benefits of linking the North Sea and the Baltic, and praised the Kiel Canal as an international waterway for the benefit of merchant shipping, but its real purpose – as had always been intended – was militarily strategic. With its opening the importance of Heligoland – as had been predicted since Bismarck's time – also increased considerably.

Events in the Solent that summer had a far-reaching impact on the development of the German Navy and on perceptions of Heligoland. Wilhelm was no longer satisfied with his usual escort of a dozen torpedo-boats. In 1895 he also brought with him four large battleships. These caused immense irritation to influential yachtsmen by obstructing the racing course, while their crews flooded the quiet town of Cowes. Further annoyance was caused by the firing from his warships of numerous salutes. To the bafflement of most British present these apparently boorish displays were in celebration of Germany's military triumphs – and the humiliation of her enemies – in the 1870 Battle of Wörth. The Emperor treated Cowes as though it were Kiel, and the Prince of Wales nicknamed him 'the boss of Cowes'. The Kaiser's psychological state was observed by a member of the crew of Erskine

Childers's sailing boat, which was close by when the Kaiser came ashore from the *Hohenzollern* at the Royal Yacht Squadron steps:

> A well-set-up little person and a little lop-sided owing to his left arm being shorter than the other. He was exceedingly dramatic and obviously very vain. He spoke English very well and took pride in picking up and making use of English slang expressions and the colloquial phrases that have become a habit to many English people. He would omit the 'g' in words like hunting and yachting, which was in him affected and grotesque, and in his anxiety to copy the colloquialisms of ourselves he would often get them wrong.[5]

Significantly, also present at the regatta was the American cruiser USS *Chicago*, commanded by the versatile Captain Alfred Mahan, who was much better known as the author of the thought-provoking work *The Influence of Sea Power upon History*. Over many months the Kaiser had read the book thoroughly from cover to cover, scribbling many annotations in its margins. It became his guide for an awesome expansion of the Germany Navy. The process was prepared for him by Admiral Alfred von Tirpitz, who took office in June 1897. His first memorandum was explicitly anti-British. It set down that the most dangerous naval enemy was England; that a shortage of German coaling stations outside Europe meant Germany should avoid a global war with England; and that Germany must build as many battleships as possible. Lastly, he insisted that: 'Our fleet must be so constructed that it can unfold its greatest military potential *between Helgoland and the Thames*'. These recommendations were destined to be put into effect in 1898 when the Reichstag approved Tirpitz's plan for a massive warship-building programme. It won the support of expansionists such as von Bülow, who famously remarked in the Reichstag that December: 'We don't want to put anyone in the shade, but we too demand our place in the sun.'

On 3 May 1897 the Kaiser ordered the High Command of the Navy to prepare an operational study for war against England. Ludwig Schröder, the Admiralty staff officer entrusted with the work, went so far as to advise the Kaiser that Germany should 'out-Copenhagen' the British by seizing neutral Antwerp and the mouth of the Schelde in a sudden *coup de main* before war had been declared, and mounting an invasion of England from the Belgian coast. This plan of Schröder's was dismissed as 'insane' by Tirpitz, who favoured the concentration of a powerful fleet of battleships in the North Sea, which might opportunistically wrong-foot a Royal Navy enfeebled by its world-wide commitments.[6]

Wilhelm later revealed in his autobiography *My Memoirs* (1922) that in February 1900, while he was with the German fleet on manoeuvres at Heligoland, he had received an astonishing telegram from Berlin. Russia and France had approached Germany with a proposal to make a joint attack on Britain now that she was involved elsewhere (the Boer War was in progress), and to cripple her sea traffic. Wilhelm objected and ordered that the proposal should be declined. Assuming that both Paris and St Petersburg would present the matter in London in such a way as to make it appear that the proposal had originated in Berlin, Wilhelm immediately telegraphed from Heligoland to Queen Victoria and the Prince of Wales, explaining the facts of the Russo-French proposal and his repudiation of it. Victoria answered, expressing her hearty thanks, while the Prince of Wales replied with an expression of astonishment. Later Victoria told Wilhelm confidentially that the false version of the story had indeed been told in London, just as he anticipated, and that thanks to his despatch she had been able to expose the intrigue to her government. Somewhat implausibly, Wilhelm also remembered, 'she added that she would not forget the service I had done England in troubled times'! And yet, only three years earlier, the Schröder plan had been devised on his orders.

Erskine Childers was busy writing his adventure novel *The Riddle of the Sands* at that time. It was the fictional tale of a patriotic English yachtsman, Arthur Davies, and his Foreign Office accomplice, Carruthers. While sailing the converted lifeboat *Dulcibella* around the Frisian Islands they discover a secret German plot to use the islands' remoteness to conceal an armada of barges for transporting troops to invade the east coast of England. Carruthers spies on the Kaiser's late-night inspection of the secret fleet, which proves the scheme is being formulated with the approval of the highest authority. Romantic interest is provided by Clara, the daughter of the scheme's fictional mastermind, Dollmann. The *Dulcibella* is safely towed through the Kiel Canal by a trading schooner, but not before Davies's heroic little yacht is nearly lured to destruction by Dollmann. The villain of the piece hoves to at the Elbe Outer Lightship, not far from Heligoland, and maliciously urges the *Dulcibella* to take a short cut to Cuxhaven and thence on to Brunsbüttel via the dangerous, semi-submerged maze of shoals between the Scharhorn sands and the shifting Knechtsands.

By coincidence the plot uncovered by the plucky yachtsman was remarkably similar to the audacious 1897 Schröder plan, and there has always been speculation as to where Childers obtained the elements for his 'fictitious' yarn. Heligoland now seems to provide the answer. His main invasion warning appears in the epilogue to *The Riddle of the Sands*, where Carruthers argues that the likely landing place for an invasion would be on the flats of the Essex coast, just north of the Thames estuary, 'between Foulness and Brightlingsea'. Such a shore, he hypothesised, 'would form an excellent roadstead for the covering squadron, whose guns would command the shore within easy range'. However, Carruthers insisted, the expedition would be doomed 'if by any mischance the British discovered what was afoot in good time and could send a swarm of light-draft boats, which could get amongst the flotillas while they were still in process of leaving the siels [shallows]'. Surprisingly, what has hitherto never been detected is that this was precisely the argument made by the anti-Heligoland cession campaigner Robert Heron-Fermor in a speech on 9 July 1890. That evening he had asked:

> What would be the consequence to England of the incorporation of Holland with the German Empire? Why, in the event of war, our whole East coast would be open to invasion. Because from the Thames to the Humber we have no harbours nor roadsteads where vessels could lie under the protection of guns. On the other hand the creeks and inlets of Holland swarm with places of refuge where fortifications could be thrown up, and an invading flotilla could lie concealed under their shelter in perfect safety.

As a clerk at Westminster, Childers would have had access to the House of Lords library, and it is not beyond the bounds of possibility that he came across Heron-Fermor's 1890 pamphlet there, and with it a full transcript of the speech. Perhaps it was Heron-Fermor's forewarnings of the folly of swapping Heligoland that supplied the strategic substance of *The Riddle of the Sands*.

The novel was published in London in May 1903 and rapidly became an enormous success, eventually selling some two million copies. It established Childers as a pioneering practical yachtsman, one of the few willing to venture so far in a small, makeshift, cruising yacht. *Vixen*'s cruise to the Frisian Islands and the Baltic did, however, have a precedent. In 1889 Edward Knight had published *The Falcon on the Baltic*, an obscure account of a cruising yacht's voyage from Hammersmith to Copenhagen. In it, Knight referred to the 'old enemy, the north-west wind'.

But it was Childers's book that caught the public imagination, with its thrilling combination of high adventure and nautical yarn. The sailing sequences in *The Riddle of the Sands* were some of the most beautiful ever written in the English language. Unfortunately for Heligoland, despite Childers's affection for the Frisian Islands, he set the novel's most memorable episodes among low-lying islands, either at night or in dull weather, in order to maximise the dramatic effect. This immensely popular novel certainly romanticised the Frisian Islands – and by association Heligoland – and brought them to public attention, but in the process unwittingly gave the lasting impression that such dismal conditions were usual there.

A shock naval defeat on the far side of the world just a year after the publication of Childers's novel utterly transformed Heligoland's strategic importance. As tensions mounted between Russia and Japan, on the night of 8 February 1904 Admiral Togo's battle squadron suddenly appeared at the outer harbour of Port Arthur and pounded Russia's powerful Pacific Squadron into smoking hulks. Caught entirely by surprise the Russian ships scarcely fired a shot.[7] This attack echoed Germany's 'Copenhagen complex' nightmare, especially because the shelling had occurred *before war had been declared*. That October the furious reaction of British public opinion to the Dogger Bank incident – when Russian warships fired on Hull fishing boats in the North Sea just 230 miles from Heligoland – frightened the Germans quite as much as the Russians. In fact German suspicions that influential decision-makers within the British naval establishment were calling for a *coup de main* against Germany's rapidly growing navy were partly justified. In early 1904 Sir John Fisher, the pugnacious First Sea Lord, *had* in fact suggested to King Edward VII that it would make sound sense to 'Copenhagen' the German fleet before it got too strong. The king replied: 'My God, Fisher, you must be mad!' The belief that 'Fisher was coming' actually caused a panic at Kiel at the beginning of 1907.[8]

The collapse of Russian military power in the Far East and the first stirrings of revolution at home threatened to remove the Russian Empire from the ranks of the great powers. As a result, Germany had much less to fear from the northern power on her eastern boundary. This meant that German naval planners came to regard the North Sea and not the Baltic as the principal German naval base. However, as Büchsel noted in a lengthy memorandum to Tirpitz in early 1906, the defences around the Elbe estuary would be totally inadequate in the event of a surprise British attack, hence there was a pressing need to turn Cuxhaven into a first-class fortress now that the High Seas Fleet was to be based on the Elbe. He suggested the development of a triangular system of fortresses to protect the mouth of the Elbe, using Heligoland and two other islands several miles offshore: Borkum, off Emden, and Sylt, just by the Schleswig-Holstein coast. All three islands would require fortifications, underwater defences, docks and communication systems.[9]

These strategic constructions seemingly justified the warnings in *The Riddle of the Sands*. Childers became ever more insistent that Whitehall should heed his advice and develop a North Sea base for major British warships, either on the Clyde or at Harwich. In early 1906 he sent a memorandum to the Cabinet's Committee of Imperial Defence entitled *Remarks on the German North Sea Coast in its Relation to War between Great Britain and Germany*, in which he advocated that officers should be sent to 'explore' the coast in order to gain practical personal knowledge for future operations and landings. Some yachtsmen volunteered to go as freelance agents; one such was Brigadier Gordon Shephard, who got himself arrested at Emden. In 1910 two characters were invited by Naval Intelligence to make a 'walking tour' of the newly fortified Frisian Islands. Marine Captain Barney Trench and Lieutenant Vivian Brandon spent three weeks that spring on their tour, visiting Heligoland, then Sylt, Cuxhaven, and each of the islands in the Frisian chain until they reached Borkum. In the course of their fact-finding tour they took photographs of secret installations and filled notebooks with technical observations. At Borkum they were arrested as spies before being transferred to Leipzig. At their celebrated show trial – well reported in British newspapers – they were sentenced to four years' imprisonment.

Tirpitz was more inclined to invest in effective warships than in fortresses, and was uneasy about allocating substantial capital resources for the fortification of Heligoland. He was not alone. Various other leading figures in Berlin thought so too; indeed, it was in connection with such work that – as Kaiser Wilhelm recalled in his memoirs – 'the Empire and Prussia fought like cat and dog'.[10] Tirpitz believed that if money was to be allocated for the fortification of the Frisian Islands, it ought to be spent on defending Heligoland which could assist in *offensive* sorties by the battle fleet.

That fateful decision having been taken, Heligoland became the subject of a huge new phase of military building intended to develop it into a formidable offshore base for torpedo-craft, gunboats and light cruisers. To the south-west, jutting out from the corner of the island where the high red cliffs of the Oberland joined the Unterland, a concrete mole was constructed, a protective arm projecting some 1,950ft out to sea. Another mole, 1,300ft long, was built to the east, and the area between the moles was ambitiously reclaimed from the sea by means of infilling with millions of tons of sand brought from the Elbe estuary. To this vast new diamond-shaped apron, known as the Südhafen (South Harbour), was attached an electric railway and jetties forming various specialist harbours. All the while the main island itself was coming to resemble a huge unsinkable battleship. Mounted high on the cliff-tops at the north and south ends of the island, the main armament consisted of groups of long-range guns with 12in-diameter barrels. The very contours of the Oberland, most of which had traditionally been used by the islanders as potato fields, were harshly altered when the north group of guns were installed on a miniature mountain, fashioned out of the material blasted out of the ground during the construction of the maze of subterranean stores and shelters. Indeed, most of the works were underground.

The guns were housed in four massive, heavily armoured steel turrets, which could be swivelled for all-round fire. These turrets, which the German Navy lightheartedly named 'Anna', 'Bertha', 'Caesar' and 'Dora', were so streamlined that they were almost flush with the ground and thus would have been especially difficult targets for British warships at sea. All maritime facilities on the island were upgraded to the very highest standard. By 1913 even the lighthouse had been specially modernised with the latest searchlight mirrors and arc lamps. Boasting 38 million candle-power, it became, or so it was claimed at the time, one of the most powerful lighthouses in the world. The present lighthouse keeper there now doubts the truth of that claim.

Less and less information about the islanders was reaching Britain each year. Spy-fever and the construction of the heavy-duty fortifications meant that the German authorities were in no mood for it to be otherwise. No doubt wishing to keep the island from the prying eyes of visiting British yachtsmen, in 1908 the Kaiser himself decreed that henceforth the Dover–Heligoland race was to be held every three years. Rather more worryingly, the German authorities banned British vessels from entering the island's waters *at any time*. This was in flagrant contravention of the 1890 Treaty of Cession's Article 7 – which had prominently guaranteed access for British fishing boats to Heligoland's anchorages in all weathers. The Foreign Office scarcely bothered to complain. Indeed, the only discernible voice in support of the British link with the island was that of William George Black, who twenty years earlier had been denigrated by the Foreign Office in its internal departmental memos.

Entirely at his own expense and on his own initiative, Black visited the island in June 1911. In the absence of any British consular representation there, he was the best (if not the only) person to report on the islanders' living conditions. Mindful of the spy-fever that had not so long before claimed Shephard, Trench and Brandon, and sensing he was being watched, he was most careful to avoid taking photographs or notes. He found that some five hundred Italian and East Prussian labourers had been toiling for three years in the construction of subterranean passages, chambers and galleries designed to allow the artillery secure and easy access to every part of the island. Apart from the barracks Germany had created for her own soldiers no provision had been made to house the greatly increased population. The foreign workmen were obliged to find lodgings with the Heligolanders, where they became more or less members of the family. Hitherto there had been little crime among the island's population of two thousand, and no door needed to be locked at night. The lodgers paid good rates for their accommodation, but their presence disturbed the islanders' close-knit way of life and the morale of their ancient nation was further eroded. Had the Heligolanders been able to continue with their proper occupation as fishermen they could have compelled the government to provide accommodation for the labourers, but the fishing industry, according to Black, had been wrecked, the nets torn apart by submarines and other vessels.

On returning to England in 1911 Black's observations were published in an article entitled 'From Heligoland to Helgoland' in the *National Review*. By chance the journal was edited by Leopold Maxse, the son-in-law of Lord Salisbury and the nephew of the island's most distinguished former governor, Ernest Maxse. Black's article described the military changes he had noticed. There was construction activity across the roads on Dune (formerly Sandy Island), although the outline of that dependency had been greatly diminished by recent storms. What used to be the healthy open Oberland was almost entirely occupied by buildings and fortifications. Peering through the barbed-wire fence overlooking the new dockland complex he had seen one of the specialist harbours being prepared for submarines. German warships were almost constantly employed in gun practice in the neighbourhood of Heligoland, sometimes by day, often by night, and the Heligolanders told him they could hit the mark at a distance of 7 miles.[11]

At about that stage in the maritime arms race Admiral von Tirpitz and Germany's naval planners anticipated that the threat of a pre-emptive attack by the Royal Navy would be removed by 1914 when the Heligoland fortifications were completed and the Kiel Canal widened. In contrast, on the other side of the North Sea, Lord Fisher, who was always looking ahead, believed that the threat of war would increase at that time. In a conversation with the Cabinet Secretary, Sir Maurice Hankey, he predicted that when the German programme of ship-building was completed, and their fleet able to match the Royal Navy, Germany would declare war. He expected that this would happen in September or October 1914, basing his forecast on a consideration of the date by which the alterations to the Kiel Canal would be finished and the German harvest safely gathered in.

7

Churchill Prepares to Invade

On 1 August 1914 a large German steamer anchored off Heligoland. It had come to expel the two thousand inhabitants. They were given just six hours to pack, and could take with them no more than they could carry by hand. Strict orders were issued by the island's Commandant that all keys to houses, rooms and cupboards were to be left in their locks, and the islanders were told that their household effects, bedding and furniture would all remain unattended until the war was won – in a few weeks. Several years earlier the Heligolanders had been warned that when the construction of the island's fortifications was complete many of them might need to be rehoused on the mainland, in a village on the Elbe, but nothing had happened. Even so, the cold abruptness of the deportation now was more unnerving than the fact of leaving. Some Heligolanders had lived on the island all their lives and had never set foot on mainland soil. Now many were sent to Altona, others to Blankenese, a suburb on the Elbe a few miles from the centre of Hamburg. There they were treated as semi-English. The only two British subjects resident on the island, one of them a sailor with twenty-three years' service in the Royal Navy, were arrested and flung into prison. And Britain had not yet declared war on Germany![1]

Germany was understandably eager to deport the Heligolanders. Berlin had good reason to suspect, but did not know for certain, that Britain was contemplating an invasion of the island. Since October 1911, when he was appointed First Sea Lord, Winston Churchill had been contemplating the islands in the Heligoland Bight with a view to establishing a British base on one of them in the event of a war with Germany. This would enable British blockading flotillas to be easily replenished.

Churchill well knew that the traditional war policy of the Admiralty had developed during the prolonged struggles with France. Immediately upon the outbreak of war, the procedure was to establish a blockade of the enemy's ports and naval bases by means of flotillas of small (but strong) craft supported by cruisers, with superior battle fleets in reserve. In recent years, although the potential enemy was no longer France but Germany, the fundamental principle of Britain's naval strategy – that 'the first line of defence is the enemy's ports' – held good. Yet now, instead of operating across the English Channel, with the supporting ships close at hand in safe harbours, the Royal Navy would need to operate in the Heligoland Bight, across some 240 miles of sea and with no bases suitable for their supporting battle fleet nearer than the Thames or the Forth. Evidently the Germans adhered rather to the French concept of the torpedo-boat as a means of attack, whereas Britain's destroyers were constructed principally for their sea-keeping qualities and firepower. But the great distances over the North Sea immensely reduced the Royal Navy's effectiveness, and it was reckoned that, in order to carry out its old strategic policy from British home bases, it would require flotillas at least three or four times as numerous as those of Germany.

Many years later Churchill revealed in his book *The World Crisis 1911–1918* that to begin to overcome this situation, with the concurrence of the principal British commanders afloat, he had set out a policy of distant blockade in the Admiralty War Orders of 1912. In 1913 Churchill instructed Admiral Lewis Bayly to examine the potential of such offensive actions, which he did with Sir Arthur Wilson and Lord 'Jacky' Fisher. He even went so far as to have plaster models made of the Heligoland Bight, with which an invasion could be planned.

At a meeting of the War Group in June 1914 Wilson advised that landings should be made on the Frisian Islands and on the German North Sea coast. He also proposed that one of the six army divisions available for such operations should cooperate with the Navy in the capture of Heligoland. A. Nicolson, an assistant secretary to the Committee of Imperial Defence, angrily rejected the suggestion as 'madness', because the island was heavily fortified.[2] However, Churchill was keen and so too, for a while, was Lord Fisher. Other senior figures at the Admiralty were more sceptical. In July 1913 Ballard, who had become Director of Operations, condemned as unacceptable gambles the schemes submitted by Bayly for the capture of Borkum, Sylt or Heligoland as an advance base. On the eve of war Churchill resurrected these plans and on 31 July he sent them to the Prime Minister, Herbert Asquith.

War broke out on 4 August 1914. On that day Churchill's private secretary, Sir Edward Marsh, who was a sailing associate of Erskine Childers, mentioned Childers to Churchill, suggesting that such unique local knowledge ought to be pressed into service. Already a member of the RNVR, Childers was summoned from Dublin by Admiral Sir Herbert Richmond, Assistant Director of Operations, who requested him to revise the remarks he had made on the German North Sea coast in his 1906 paper to the Hydrographic Office. Almost immediately Childers redrafted that earlier paper, this time presenting it as a plan for capturing a base for operations against Heligoland. It was entitled *The Seizure of Borkum and Juist.*

This plan doubtless came to the attention of Major Sir Hereward Wake, who was then preparing for Downing Street – albeit from the army's point of view – a consideration of the amphibious possibilities indicated by Churchill's plan. On 11 August 1914 Wake completed his assessment, which he called *A Report on Proposals to Occupy Certain Places as Temporary Naval Bases for Offensive Action against Germany*. He envisaged that British forces would suffer very high casualties, particularly in the event of an invasion of Heligoland, and his report was seized by Downing Street personages, who were sceptical of Churchill's audacious intentions, as the evidence they needed to damn the First Sea Lord's plans. Because of this criticism, and the distractions of the first three months of the war, Churchill did not revert in earnest to the theme of an advanced base until November 1914. On the 5th of that month a War Group consisting of Admiral of the Fleet Sir Henry Oliver, Lord Fisher and Sir Arthur Wilson met to discuss future operations. Churchill was now less enthusiastic about storming Heligoland, and instead wanted to land troops at Borkum to capture both that island and Emden. The others thought both islands would be impossible to hold if captured because Britain did not have the necessary land forces. Fisher wanted to send the Grand Fleet into the Baltic as part of a plan to convey a Russian army from Petrograd to land in northern Germany and take Berlin. Wilson suggested bombarding Heligoland with old pre-Dreadnought battleships, before troops were put ashore to capture it.

Human nature being what it is, as the War Group discussed these extraordinary schemes, two members were inevitably vigorously opposed to the third's plan. Although this meant the question of a landing on one of the German islands went unresolved, the War Group remained prepared to do so. To facilitate an armed landing on whichever island was eventually chosen, in December 1914 the monitors then under construction were hastily completed.[3] The shallow draft of these remarkable vessels enabled them to approach close to the shore and attack definite points on the coast. Typical examples were HMS *Mersey* and HMS *Severn*; each 267ft long, they carried 6in and 4.7in guns, but had a draft of only 4ft 9in. Later monitors were equipped with huge 11in and even 15in guns. Stationed off the coast of Belgium, they were pressed into service to harass the advancing German army and prevent the fall of Dunkirk and Calais. All the while Churchill was considering other possibilities for waging this kind of amphibious warfare. One consequence of his frustration at his inability to get approval for a landing on the Frisian Islands was that in 1915, when planning the Dardanelles campaign, he side-stepped consultations with his colleagues – with disastrous consequences. Perhaps the heavy losses the Allied forces suffered at Gallipoli, in terms of men and matériel, were an indication of the likely cost of such a landing on Heligoland.

From the moment war was declared, British submarines kept a constant watch on German shipping

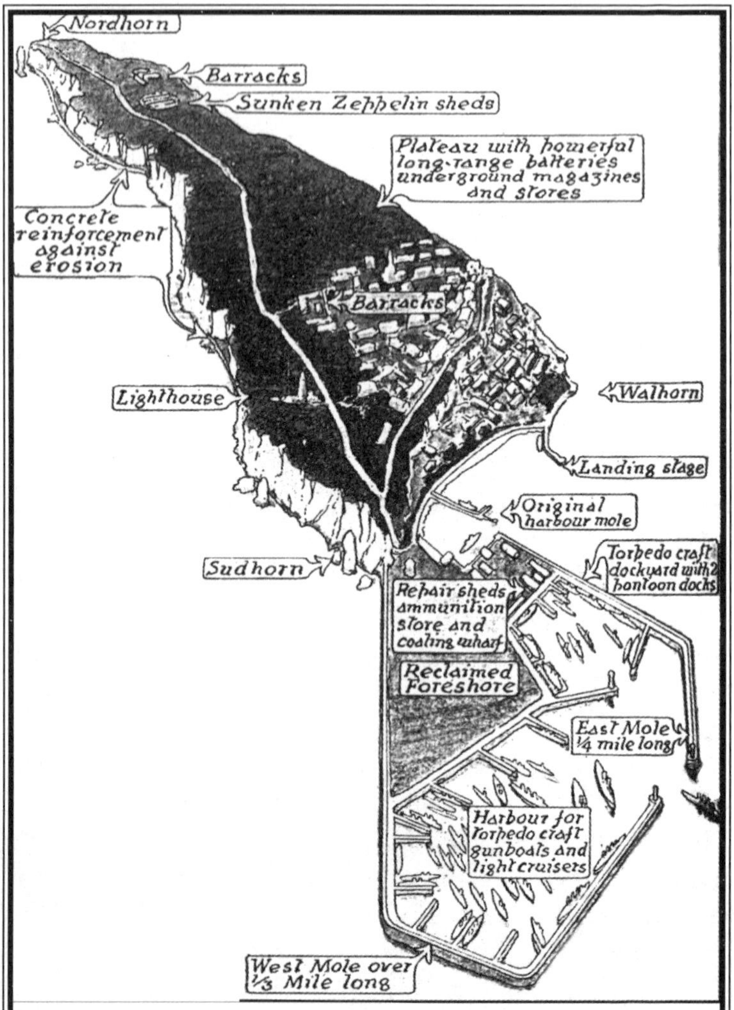

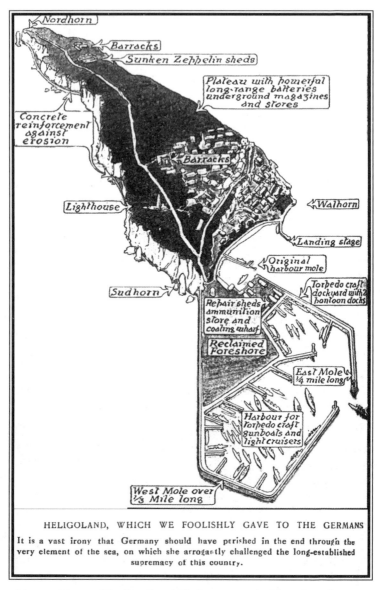

HELIGOLAND, WHICH WE FOOLISHLY GAVE TO THE GERMANS

It is a vast irony that Germany should have perished in the end through the very element of the sea, on which she arrogantly challenged the long-established supremacy of this country.

Map 5 In 1914, Winston Churchill, the First Lord of the Admiralty, was initially so keen to storm Heligoland's cliff-top fortifications and long-range guns, he had special bombardment ships constructed. Disastrously he opted instead to attack the Dardanelles. (The *Graphic*, 1918)

in the Heligoland Bight, venturing far into the protected area and noting the routine of the various units of the Kaiser's fleet. Justifiable worries about the risk posed by German submarines to British transport ships meant that during 15–17 August 1914, when the greater part of the BEF was shipped across the Channel, the Heligoland Bight was closely blockaded by Royal Navy submarines and destroyers. Their operation was a success, but at the time the British public was impatient for a glorious victory at sea.

As dawn broke on 28 August 1914 British light cruisers of the Harwich Force, under the command of Commodore Sir Reginald Tyrwhitt, were carrying out a sweep several miles west of the coast of Heligoland when they sighted dim shadows in the mist. These proved to be German destroyers, which scuttled back to the shelter of Heligoland at top speed as soon as they sighted the British cruisers. One German destroyer, the *Frauenhob*, failed to regain Heligoland and was sunk by the 6in guns of Tyrwhitt's own ship HMS *Arethusa*. Presumably the menacing guns of the fortress, atop the lofty red cliffs, could not see the British ships through the mist. For twenty-six years Germany had spent lavish amounts of money on constructing sophisticated state-of-the-art defences, and up-to-the-minute observation and communication systems, but it all proved worthless in the face of Heligoland's weather!

After this first contact the German light cruisers ventured forth from the island to look for their opponents. They were joined by the *Mainz*, which had dashed out from Emden, and the *Köln*, the torpedo-boat squadron's flagship, from Wilhelmshaven. The *Mainz* became separated from the other German vessels, but put up a good fight before she was sunk.

Admiral Sir David Beatty's battle cruiser squadron now appeared over the horizon and entered the fight. Up to this point the German naval units had been all in a muddle, largely because of the weather conditions; their headquarters at Heligoland had been unable to figure out exactly how many British ships were present, let alone identify them by class. As Beatty's squadron arrived, they tried to recall all their ships but it was now too late for them to run to safety. The German light cruiser *Ariadne* was sunk by Beatty's heavy cruisers and soon afterwards the *Köln* met the same fate. With the exception of one stoker, she sank with her entire crew – which included the newly appointed Admiral of Torpedo-Craft. As the *Köln* went down Beatty's heavy cruisers headed towards Britain, leaving Tyrwhitt's light cruisers to fight a rearguard action. By then the German battlecruisers had been alerted. One of these 'four-funnellers', the *Stralsund*, sighted Tyrwhitt's *Arethusa* and opened fire. Unable to match the German battlecruisers, all the British ships turned and fled, escaping with only minutes to spare.

Immediately dubbed the 'Battle of Heligoland Bight', the action was the first surface naval battle of the First World War. In Britain news of the sinking of three German light cruisers and a torpedo-boat sparked off much public elation. *The Times* hailed it as a 'great victory'; the *London Gazette* published an apparently full report of the action; and the famous military writer Lionel Cecil Jane celebrated it with a special Oxford Pamphlet. Commodore Tyrwhitt became something of a minor national hero and was soon venerated in the book *The Harwich Naval Forces*, written by the pioneering small boat yachtsman Edward Knight.

This British victory was both a psychological and a material blow to the German Navy, although it came as no surprise to those in authority, who were convinced their forces could not hold their own against the British. Reluctant to risk another surface action, they decided to reduce the British fleet by submarine and mine action.[4] The next major clash occurred six months later at the Dogger Bank, some 200 miles west of Heligoland. On 24 January 1915, having received intelligence that a German fleet under Admiral Hipper was approaching the Dogger Bank, Admiral Beatty prepared to intercept it. Hipper's intention was probably to pretend to flee in order to lure the British fleet on to the minefields he had laid off Heligoland. The first contact was made by Tyrwhitt's squadron, to whom Beatty again gave his support. In the ensuing fight Beatty's flagship, the *Lion*, was repeatedly hit, possibly by the German cruiser *Helgoland*, and he had to transfer his flag to another cruiser. As soon as Hipper saw Beatty's fleet he made for Heligoland and the battle developed into a chase. The German ships, a few of them severely battered, fled through their minefield. Thankful to gain shelter at the island, the German warships – as in 1864 – anchored there to lick their wounds. Subsequently the Admiralty published a telegraph report of the fight purportedly from Beatty but in fact amended to meet Admiralty views. Beatty was made to say that it was he who 'broke off the engagement owing to the presence of "submarines"'. As a result, he came in for a large amount of hostile press criticism for apparently allowing the Germans to escape.

Fed up with inaccurate newspaper stories derived from such distorted official reports, on 21 June 1916 Beatty wrote a furious private letter to the First Sea Lord Arthur Balfour (Churchill had resigned from that post after the Dardanelles fiasco). In those days senior public servants sometimes had enough character to speak out against ministers. In that letter, written aboard the *Lion*, Beatty revealed that his victory in the August 1914 Battle of Heligoland Bight had nearly been a catastrophe. Owing to faulty staff work at the Admiralty, he thundered, one portion of the force employed was unaware of the presence of the other – a fact that was never permitted to appear in print. As a result, the initial support for Commodore Tyrwhitt's squadron was

> drawn away in pursuit of our own destroyers and so prevented me from rendering the urgent support urgently required by Tyrwhitt. This made it necessary for me to use the battlecruisers to support him in a position close to Heligoland, where they ran a very considerable risk of mine and submarine damage. The end justified the means, but if I had lost a battlecruiser I should have been hanged, drawn and quartered. Yet it was necessary to run the risk to save two of our light cruisers and a large force of destroyers which otherwise would most certainly have been lost.

Beatty was by no means exaggerating the danger to British warships in that part of the North Sea. On 22 September 1914, just a month after the Battle of the Bight, three elderly British cruisers, *Aboukir*, *Cressy* and *Hogue*, had been swiftly sunk by a lone submarine, the *U-9*, just off the Dutch coast.

Air forces were soon to be employed to support naval operations in the Bight. Erskine Childers, who was respected within Naval Intelligence circles as something of an enthusiast for unconventional forms of warfare in the Heligoland Bight area, unexpectedly found himself embroiled in this new, and totally untried, form of fighting. It was, after all, only five years earlier, in 1909, that Louis Blériot had made the first powered cross-Channel flight. Since then the Royal Navy, one of the earliest fighting forces to recognise the military potential of aircraft, had founded the Royal Naval Air Service (RNAS), a fledgling dare-devil unit. Like any RNVR officer, when war broke out Childers would have expected to be called up to serve in ships or perhaps submarines. Yet although he knew nothing about aircraft – indeed, he had never even flown – he was immediately assigned to the RNAS. Within a week of updating his paper on the German coast and the Frisian Islands for Admiral Richmond, on 18 August 1914 Childers was sent to Chatham as a commissioned RNAS officer to join HMS *Engadine*, the world's first seaplane carrier.

As a naval observer his duties would be to assist with seaplane navigation and dropping bombs. *Engadine* had not been designed for her new carrier role, operating three Short 135 seaplanes. Initially a Channel ferry, like her sister ships *Empress* and *Riviera*, she had no proper flight-deck and could only launch and recover her aircraft by precariously craning them to and from the sea. At about the time of the Battle of Heligoland Bight, Childers was informed that *Engadine*'s forthcoming secret mission would be to attack the Zeppelin hangars just south of Cuxhaven. In addition to his task of instructing the seaplane pilots in the art of navigation, he had been selected to go along for the ride on account of his unique local knowledge of the North Sea islands. Zeppelins were a serious threat which somehow had to be tackled. With their magnificent cruising range and ability to fly at altitudes beyond the accurate range of British guns, they were the 'eyes' of the German fleet; later they would also become a menace to civilians – the first Zeppelin appeared over the British coast on 20 December 1914.

Having spent the summer months on the North Sea close to the mouth of the Tyne spotting for mines *Engadine* sailed to Harwich to join Tyrwhitt's Harwich Force. On 11 October a force was readied to attack Heligoland itself with the seaplanes, but the following day it was deemed 'too risky', and called off. However, a fortnight later the seaplane group, escorted by the Harwich Force, put to sea and headed for Heligoland. Childers's task had been to prepare charts for the pilots. The intention was to close to within 15 miles of the island, then launch the aircraft, which would fly 50 miles to the target at Cuxhaven. However, various mechanical mishaps with the seaplanes led to the cancellation of the raid in the early hours and soon *Engadine* was back in port. Undeterred, the Admiralty decided to rerun the scheme, but with rather more thoughtful planning and a greater sense of purpose.[5]

Churchill, having read intelligence reports that German battleships were gathering in the Weser and Elbe estuaries, wrote to Jellicoe, the Commander-in-Chief of the Grand Fleet, advising that 'the aerial attack on the Cuxhaven shed, which we had previously thought desirable in itself, might easily bring on a considerable action in which your battle-cruisers and the Grand Fleet might take part without undue risk'. Churchill's idea was to lure the Germans into what might turn out to be a decisive naval battle. Childers, having for some time wondered how seaplanes might be navigated more accurately in the Heligoland Bight, hastily prepared air charts showing every sea-mark he could recollect. The operation was planned to start on

25 December 1914, and for the first time in history aircraft, surface ships and submarines were deployed together in a combined operation. Having been transferred from the *Engadine* to a sister ship, the *Riviera*, he was selected at the last minute to be the observer in the leading seaplane, and early that Christmas morning Childers was rowed in a dinghy through a heavy swell from the *Riviera* to seaplane no. 136, his designated flying machine. As before, the planes were readied for action something like a dozen miles from Heligoland.

What became known as the 'Cuxhaven Raid' started well. Seven seaplanes took off and headed towards Heligoland. The weather was clear and Childers could see what he described as Heligoland's 'grim cliffs'. As the aircraft approached the mouth of the Elbe estuary he ought to have been able to make out the Scharhorn and Knechtsands, where the *Dulcibella* nearly came to grief in *The Riddle of the Sands*, but the seaplanes were now encountering thick weather and were compelled to fly low. This was no fictitious adventure but the real thing – and very dangerous. At lower altitude the aircraft were exposed to heavy fire at short range from ships and shore batteries. A few machines were hit, but most remained airborne. As his seaplane circled Cappel, near Cuxhaven, Childers prepared to hand-release the Hales bombs on to the Zeppelin hangars they were aiming for, but a misfire caused by extreme moisture in the seaplane's 200hp motor forced them to seek open water. As they struggled towards the *Riviera* they spotted fourteen large German warships anchored in the Schilling Roads, in the Jade estuary just off Wilhelmshaven, which acknowledged their presence with anti-aircraft fire. Bursting shrapnel shells severed some wing wires and damaged a chassis strut.

At about that time, realising an attack was on, the Heligoland garrison belatedly launched a defence with such aircraft as it had at its disposal. As yet, no means had been found by which the limited space on the island could be utilised for operating Zeppelins or land-based aircraft. The only flying machines to hand were a squadron of military float-planes kept ready in a neat line alongside the inner harbour. A few of these roared off into the air and scattered in search of the fourteen British warships involved in the raid. They too carried bombs, but when these were dropped on the British vessels they either failed to explode or simply bounced off. As a consequence of the British seaplanes' reconnaissance a part of the German fleet was moved from Cuxhaven to various places further along the Elbe and the Kiel Canal.

By eleven o'clock Childers was back on board the *Riviera*, refreshing himself with Bovril, sherry and a biscuit in the wardroom. His views must have been mixed. The raid had not been an unqualified success: only four of the British planes had returned; the Zeppelin shed had been neither located nor destroyed; and the German fleet had not been lured into action. Nevertheless, a precedent for combined operations had been set and valuable information regarding the disposition of German ships and defences had been obtained. The Admiralty honoured Childers's participation by sending a copy of *The Riddle of the Sands* to every ship in the navy. Churchill regarded the exercise as an invaluable experience and personally thanked Childers for having displayed 'daring against the Germans on the Cuxhaven Raid'.[6] For Erskine, the adventure had confirmed the need for accurate maps of the Heligoland Bight. In 1916, by which time he was serving with Coastal Motor Boats, he persuaded the Admiralty's Hydrographic Department to produce an improved quality chart covering Heligoland, the Elbe and the entrance of the Kiel Canal at Brunsbüttel, to be used for planning raids in that area, as he had done in seaplanes near Heligoland on 28 September and 22 October 1916. A limited number of these revised charts were produced, and became known as the 'Childers Charts'.

All the while the two thousand Heligolanders, virtually interned in what should have been only a temporary settlement near the Elbe, were pining for their homeland. Although the men were not required to join the German armed forces, they knew too much about the coast and the fortifications to be allowed the smallest chance of escaping abroad. It was hard for them, especially the veterans, to be herded into internment camps, and many of the elderly did not survive the experience. This was the dark period for the island when no Heligolander remained to hoist and salute the island's tricolour. It broke a continuous thread of civilian occupation that was said to have begun before the time of Christ.

On Heligoland itself the morale of the 4,300-strong garrison had been dented by the fortress's lack of effective involvement in the Battle of Heligoland Bight and the Cuxhaven Raid. Indeed, having so far only succeeded in getting the main armament to fire one shot, the senior gunnery officer was severely reprimanded. The troops there became disillusioned and bored, and for consolation they allegedly turned to the wine cellars of the absent islanders and helped themselves. On the Oberland they wandered about with their hands in their pockets, staring out to sea and wondering if the British might be plotting an invasion. Even a visit to Heligoland by Kaiser Wilhelm in the summer of 1917 (suggested by Paul von Hindenburg, chief of the army general staff) did little to improve morale.

The aftermath of the Battle of Jutland on 31 May 1916 provided an opportunity to reflect on the wisdom of allowing Germany to fortify Heligoland, which lay just 100 miles south of the battle area. The battle itself had ended in stalemate, although the British claimed the victory as the German ships sailed away. In a way it was a tremendous victory for Germany too – three decades earlier it had effectively had no navy to speak of, but now its navy had equalled, if not bettered, the world's greatest naval force. Fourteen British and eleven German ships had been lost off Jutland Bank, and the British ships had proved to be inferior in armour and guns. In Germany the clash was, for a time, the subject of much pride. Kaiser Wilhelm in his memoirs described it as a 'great victory'. And indeed it might have been an overwhelming victory for Germany if just a few more German warships had been present at the battle. This could have been achieved had not Germany's leaders – encouraged by Wilhelm – squandered millions in pointlessly widening the Kiel Canal. But the greatest single distraction of naval funds away from warship building had been Heligoland itself. Between 1890 and 1914 the German Exchequer had been required to supply a massive £35 million for the construction of the island's harbours and fortifications.

However, in Britain the indecisive Battle of Jutland stunned public opinion, which had been expecting an outright triumph, and prompted questions as to whether the outcome would have been more favourable if the Royal Navy had been better resourced. Did this not show, newspapers wondered, that Salisbury should have been stopped from handing over Heligoland to Germany twenty-six years earlier? Sensing the possibility of a future public demand for the return of Heligoland to Britain, on 16 September 1916 Arthur Balfour, the First Sea Lord, circulated to his Cabinet colleagues a confidential memorandum on the pros and cons of retroceding Heligoland in future peace negotiations with Germany. Balfour, who was – perhaps significantly – Lord Salisbury's nephew, was himself not much in favour of altering the status quo.

'The man in the street', he informed his colleagues, 'whether the street be in London or Berlin, undoubtedly holds the view that the possession of Heligoland has been a great naval strength to Germany and that whether Great Britain was right or wrong to cede it under the settlement made in 1890, modern developments both in sea power and air power have proved that she made a very bad bargain.'[7] Balfour, rather unconvincingly, went on to claim: 'It is clear from such informal conversation as I have had on this subject with high naval authorities, that this is not their view at all.' In order to 'clear this matter up' he drew up a series of questions whose answers, he hinted, might provide a foundation for any decision which Britain might be called upon to take. Having initially asked if Germany's possession of Heligoland was helpful to the German fleet, he moved on to wonder if Britain's possession of the island would help the British fleet.

Typically, it was the unpredictably grim weather of the Heligoland Bight which appeared to demonstrate how strategically important Heligoland had become to Germany. During the winter of 1916/17, when the Elbe and other main German rivers were frozen over, sixty-six submarines used Heligoland as a base. During the two months of that severe frost their sallies from the island reputedly did a massive £30 million-worth of damage to Allied shipping. Heligoland's significance as a submarine base increased further on 1 February 1917 when Germany committed itself to a strategy of unrestricted submarine warfare. Suspiciously quickly, Kaiser Wilhelm seized upon the island's new worth, citing it as belated proof of the wisdom of his enthusiasm for the 1890 Heligoland–Zanzibar swap. Having been so closely associated with the deal, he inevitably felt personally aggrieved, even many years later, when it was criticised. In his memoirs he revealed that 'Not until the World War was on did I see articles in the German press which unreservedly admitted the acquisition of Heligoland to have been an act of far-sighted statesmanship.'[8] On 21 September 1917 *The Times* quoted Herr Engel as claiming, 'The German submarine war would be almost an impossibility if Germany did not hold Heligoland'; three days later that newspaper published a despatch from Amsterdam authoritatively quoting the Kaiser as commenting of the island: 'Today this trouser button holds our whole suit together.'

In response to pressure from President Woodrow Wilson to seal off Germany's main U-boat bases, in May 1917 the Admiralty's operations division devised an audacious plan to jam the Elbe and Weser by sinking hundreds of Allied concrete blockade ships. First, Heligoland would need to be quickly captured – by means of poisoning the garrison with clouds of 'Blue Star' chlorosulphic gas released from specially fitted submarines. Preparations were made in consultation with the Army's gas expert, Brigadier Charles Foulkes. But Churchill – who had now returned to office – was less keen on capturing

Heligoland than the island of Borkum. The entire scheme was abandoned that autumn because the US Navy Department, and then Admiral Jellicoe and the Naval Staff, believed the invasions to be impracticable. In May 1918 also dismissed was another secret Admiralty plan, to temporarily occupy a West Frisian island of the neutral Netherlands for use as an advance base from which to bomb Heligoland's fortifications with two hundred RNAS aircraft.

A consequence of the drubbing received at the Battle of Jutland was that Germany's heaviest battleships were not allowed to put to sea in wartime again. Such evasion caused resentment among the crews of the capital warships, especially as they were being deprived of resources in favour of the upstart submarine fleet. With the end of the war in sight, on 21 October 1918 Admiral Scheer recalled all U-boats from their war on merchant ship convoys 'in order', he claimed, 'to avoid anything that might make the attainment of peace more difficult'.[9] Rather oddly, at the same time he issued another order 'to make the High Seas Fleet ready for an attack on, and battle with, the English Fleet'. The venue for this clash, as envisaged in 'Operation Plan 19' devised by the naval staff at Wilhelmshaven, was to be off the Dutch Frisian Island of Terschelling. Now the disgruntled battleship crews really smelt a rat: they suspected that Kaiser Wilhelm, foreseeing that Germany was going to lose the war, had ordered this last-ditch sortie so he could sacrifice his beloved battle squadrons gloriously and thus avoid having to surrender them. So unhappy were the crews that they could not be relied upon to obey orders, and on 29 October 1918 the plan had to be abandoned just before the battle-cruisers put to sea. Admiral Franz von Hipper ruefully noted in his journal: 'Our men have rebelled. I could not have carried out the operation even if the weather conditions had permitted it.'[10]

Ironically the mighty battleship *Helgoland*, whose name ought to have symbolised an expanded, unified Germany, played a part in the country's capitulation. In late October 1918, while she was anchored in the Schillig Roads off the Jade estuary, just north of Wilhelmshaven, her crew mutinied. Arming themselves with guns, wrenches and even meat cleavers, they mounted attacks on officers and petty officers. The mutiny spread to other capital ships of the High Seas Fleet at Wilhelmshaven and thence to other bases, notably Kiel, which by 4 November was in the hands of revolutionaries, with every battleship there flying the Red Flag. Although the large surface warships had fallen to the mutineers, throughout the fleet the lesser ones had, almost without exception, remained loyal. Hoping to separate some units of the High Seas Fleet from the corrupting tidal wave of mutiny von Hipper ordered all submarines and torpedo-boats – nearly a hundred of them in total – out of Kiel and Wilhelmshaven. Some sailed westwards to Borkum, many others for the sanctuary of Heligoland.

But on Heligoland the garrison's sense of boredom had evolved into rebellion. Control of the island had been seized by a Soldiers' Council, which was in no mood to give shelter to the loyalists' little ships. They refused them entry by closing down the U-boat and torpedo-boat harbours. Symbolically the great iron gates on the Pottchen, installed to thwart a British invasion, and loathed in peacetime by the islanders as a shadow on their liberty, were now barred in the face of the naval loyalists. 'We were without a refuge', von Hipper later recalled, 'ships without a port. The

Flying Dutchmen, ja?' On Saturday 9 November the squadrons were ordered back. They had no choice but to capitulate to the mutineers.[11] On that day too Kaiser Wilhelm abdicated and fled to exile in Holland. The war in Europe was over. For the fleet that had been his pride and joy there seemed to be no end of shame. Rounded up by the Allies, a fortnight later, on 21 November, the German Fleet sailed out from its harbours, past Heligoland for the last time, and across the North Sea to be interned at Scapa Flow. There Admiral Beatty obtained a souvenir from the battleship *Helgoland*: a piece of metal which he transformed into a simple inkwell for his desk at his country house in Buckinghamshire.

On 5 December 1918 the Heligolanders returned to their island. From the foredeck of the ship carrying them came sobs and cries of joy from the weary and emotional people as the deep red cliffs of their island home appeared: 'Ach, Helgoland! Unser Heim! Schön Helgoland!' On arrival they found their little homes were in a terrible condition. The storms of the last four years had damaged many of the old-fashioned, red-tiled roofs. Salt was encrusted upon the inner walls. The wallpaper hung in shreds. The floors were green and rotten, and fungi flourished in the damp rooms. The gardens were choked with weeds, the white palings blown down, the paving tiles lifted by grass. Penniless and hungry, the islanders set to work to put their houses in order, to paint and distemper, to polish the silver and brass name-plates which were the pride of every cottage, to prop up fences and cultivate their gardens.[12] Soon they had their fishing smacks seaworthy again, and moored them inside the war harbour, from where such craft had been rigorously excluded in former times.

The refurbishment work they had partly expected, but they were totally shocked to find that some houses had been occupied by German naval officers who had brought their families to the island with them. Worse still, virtually all other homes had been ransacked by the unruly garrison. At nights the island folk sat by their stoves amid their belongings, which had been trashed by the German military, and in their own Frisian-type tongue emotionally agreed that such actions would never have been allowed to occur when Heligoland was a British colony. Benignly neglectful though Britain certainly had been of the island, its governors had always been protectively mindful of the islanders' basic rights. The contrast between British and German rule was now sharper than ever before. Combined with the shock of the German vandalism, it suddenly made many islanders wistful for what now, more than ever, seemed to have been the golden age of British suzerainty.

It was a fundamentally defining moment, and has remained so: because not only do the Heligolanders know their history well, but they have long memories. A favourite maritime hymn, which the islanders love to sing in church at Christmas, is 'I saw three ships go sailing by'. They gathered in December 2000, at their Nordseehalle, to witness a pageant re-enacting their predecessors' first Christmas on the island after the First World War. When the appearance of the British Navy was depicted they all sang 'I saw three ships go sailing by', and it was quite noticeable that many of the older islanders had tears in their eyes.

After the war the military aspects of the island came under temporary British control. The members of the Royal Navy landing party that arrived on the island in late 1918 were surprised to find so many visible remains of the earlier British rule. Especially outstanding was Government House, the residence vacated by Governor Arthur Barkly and his family twenty-eight years earlier; there were also English street names and the bronze tablet on the church tower, with the English inscription commemorating its installation. A search in the churchyard revealed a tombstone with English wording, erected in memory of a drowned sailor. What astonished them most was that the first inhabitant to meet them was a pensioner of the Royal Navy. He had been unable to collect his pension for some years and was anxious to receive it! With him was a party of islanders who asked for it to be known that they wanted Heligoland to revert to being a British territory again.

Sensing the prospect that Britain might be about to recover its long-lost North Sea colony, on 16 November 1918 *The Times* ran a headline story headed 'The Man who hauled down the British Flag'. In a remarkable piece of popular investigative journalism that would not disgrace a tabloid today the newspaper had tracked down Henry Hedger, the coastguard who just before midnight on 9 August 1890 had lowered the British flag at Government House for the last time and had been the last Englishman to leave Heligoland. Now in his sixties and a verger of a parish church at Herne Bay, overlooking the Thames estuary, he was living in a house with many photos and other small mementoes of his four years' service in Heligoland. Among the most interesting was a picture of the coastguard group showing six bearded Englishmen, the English officer and fifteen Heligolanders. 'If it should', *The Times* helpfully ventured, 'become necessary to hoist the Union Jack again over Heligoland, Mr Hedger might be fittingly employed to do it.'

It became apparent that other influential institutions and people were calling for Heligoland to be readmitted to the British colonial fold. As early as 21 October 1918, Lord Fisher, in his capacity as a former Admiral of the Fleet, had written to Downing Street in response to an inquiry from Sir Maurice Hankey, the Secretary to the War Cabinet, about requests to be presented at future peace talks. Fisher informed him he had just five simple, if draconian, peace points to offer: that 'no spot of German territory in the wide world be permitted; that the German Fleet be delivered up intact; and ditto every German submarine. Fourth and fifthly: Heligoland be delivered up; and also the two flanking islands of Sylt and Borkum'.[13] These sentiments were reinforced on 6 November in a letter to *The Times* by yet another Admiral of the Fleet, Sir Culm Seymour, who claimed: 'I have been to Heligoland and knew it when it was ours. Now the war is drawing to its end I, as a naval officer, desire to express my opinion that it should be returned to us, and I think that many of my brother-sailors agree with me.' On 23 November there appeared another letter calling for Germany to be deprived of further use of the island, this time by the ingenious means of neutralising it by 'making it an international aerodrome for commercial aircraft'.

That letter was mysteriously signed 'G.F.W.' It could have been from the tenacious and faithful William George Black. So keen to write to *The Times* again on the subject of Heligoland he had perhaps sent two letters! The other, which the paper also printed on 23 November, he had written from the Carlton Club, and characteristically expressed concern for the well-being of the islanders. He called for the island to be recolonised by Britain on the grounds that: 'We could

1 The 'Gibraltar of the North Sea'. Stormy wave conditions, except during the summer, meant that for many months of the year Heligoland was virtually closed to visitors – which increased its allure. (*Schensky*)

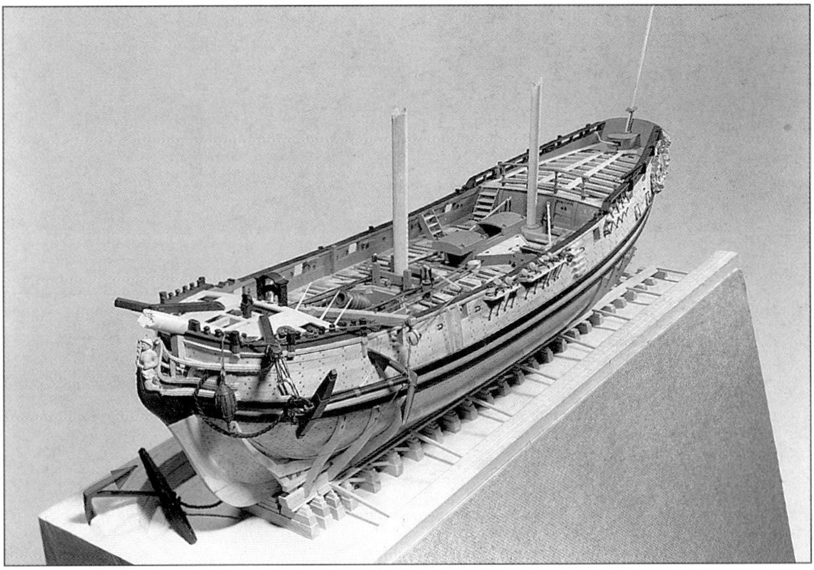

2 A heavily armed mortar ketch, similar to the one that arrived off the island in August 1807 to support the British invasion by bombarding urban areas, HMS *Explosion* was wrecked on a reef. The Foreign Office never revealed that when the islanders launched their boats to save her crew and armaments, Admiral Russell had gratefully expressed a hope that Heligoland would 'always remain British'. (*National Maritime Museum*)

3 Admiral Sir Thomas Russell was a humane leader who, when he appointed the first Governor in 1807, unwittingly established a tradition of British governors fearlessly protecting the islanders' interests against British governmental insensitivities. (*Christie's*)

4 Sir Edward Thornton, ambassador to the Hanse towns, and one of the very few Britons who knew something of Heligoland before the 1807 capture. Crucially he advised that the islanders' freedoms be respected. (*Scottish National Portrait* Gallery)

5 On 9 August 1890, Arthur Barkly, the last British Governor of Heligoland, handed over sovereignty of the island to Germany in the garden of Government House. The next morning Kaiser Wilhelm II arrived to inspect the North Sea island which had just been exchanged for much of East Africa. (*Helgoland Regierung*)

6 The perilously rocky shoreline exposed at low tide. An aerial view of the 12-inch guns at Heligoland's northern tip, which would have been observed by *Riddle of the Sands* author, yachtsman Erskine Childers RNVR, during a seaplane reconnaissance mission there on 22 October 1916. (*Imperial War Museum – Q36407-20*)

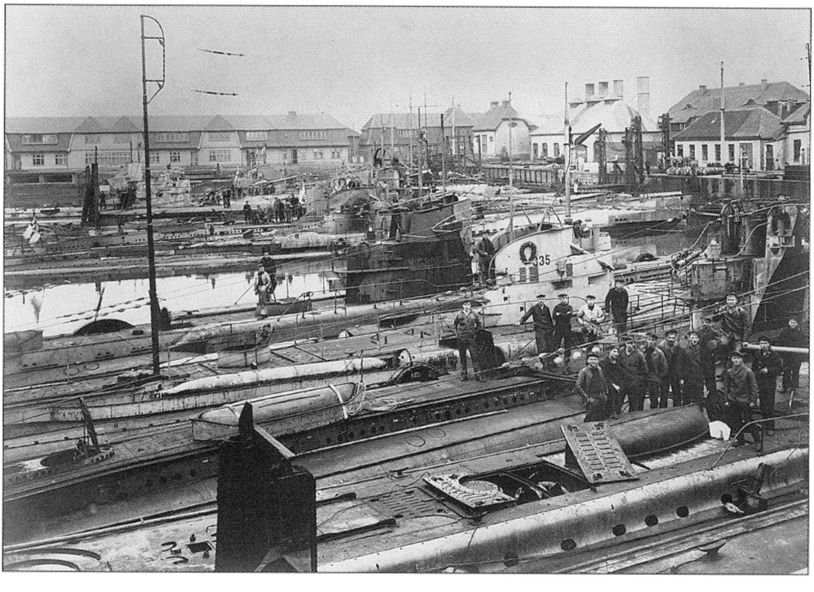

7 When the Elbe estuary froze in the winter of 1916–17 Germany based nearly seventy submarines in Heligoland's inner harbour, from where they sailed to inflict £30 million-worth of damage to British and Allied shipping. (*Imperial War Museum – Q36407-38*)

8 Tirpitz's harbour complex nearing completion in 1905. The terms of the 1919 Versailles peace treaty having required this and all the fortifications to be dismantled, between 1920 and 1922 Heligoland temporarily came under the rule of a British naval commission of control. The luxurious Empress of India hotel, in the foreground, was their headquarters. (*Imperial War Museum – Q36407-24*)

9 An audacious reconnaissance photo of ice-fringed Heligoland in February 1942, revealing aircraft detection masts and a gigantic U-boat shelter. The uncompleted sea walls of Germany's own Scapa Flow – Project Hummerschere – extend northwards at the top of the picture. (*Public Record Office, Kew*)

10 August 1940: on the fiftieth anniversary of the transfer of sovereignty, the islanders were forced to listen to the Commandant of Heligoland in the garden of Government House. They had never sought the refortification of their homeland in the 1930s, and those who secretly plotted a surrender in April 1945 were executed by the Gestapo. (*Helgoland Regierung*)

11 The seas of Heligoland Bight became a killing area in both world wars. Here high-speed RAF Beaufighters strafe an armed picket ship, 17 September 1944. (*Imperial War Museum – C4639*)

12 In the interwar years Heligoland prospered as a sophisticated duty-free holiday resort. (*Schensky*)

13 Three weeks before the war ended, a controversial RAF 1,000-bomber raid destroyed virtually every building on Heligoland. Inspecting the cliffside tourist elevator, built by a British Governor in the 1880s, Admiral Muirhead Gould RN accepts the shattered 140-acre island's surrender on 11 May 1945. (*Imperial War Museum – A28581*)

14 'Grand Slam' 10-ton earthquake bombs were dropped by the RAF's Dam Buster Squadron on 19 April 1945 to silence Heligoland's heavy guns. But the bombing continued for 7 years after the war ended as part of a secret test programme to develop a similarly streamlined airframe for Britain's 'Blue Danube' atomic bomb. (*Imperial War Museum – CH15369*)

15 The largest non-nuclear explosion in history: Operation 'Big Bang' on 18 April 1947 produced an 8,000-foot smoke column, but ought only to have demolished the wartime fortifications. Thousands of tons of depth charges having been shipped in beforehand, the evacuated Heligolanders accused Britain of attempted geographical genocide. Film of the explosion was used in the film *The Guns of Navarone.* (*Helgoland Regierung*)

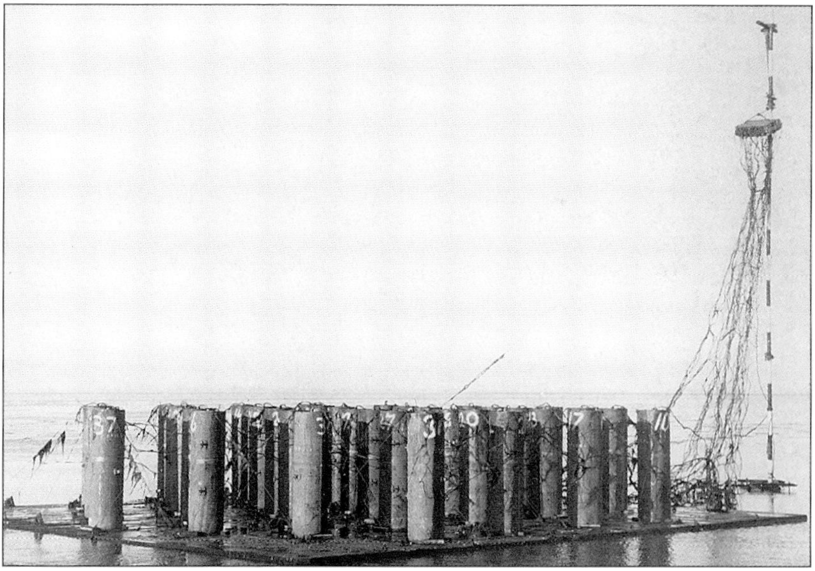

16 Initially, Heligoland's Sandy Island was the designated test site for the 'Charybdis' project: a scheme in 1947 to study the near-nuclear explosion characteristics of a base surge column of water, by detonating a hexagonal pattern of 10 tons of depth charges in shallow water. The Atomic Weapons Research Establishment instead exploded this particular apparatus off Shoeburyness in the Thames Estuary. (*Public Record Office, Kew*)

17 Prior to the creation of the V-bombers, British aircrews trained for precision operations with B-29A Washingtons identical to those of the USAF's Strategic Air Command. On camera the RAF's 115 Squadron are caught dropping practice bombs over Heligoland on 12 December 1950. (© *Crown Copyright 1950/MOD. Reproduced with the permission of the Controller of Her Majesty's Stationery Office*)

18 Protests meant the bombing of Heligoland ceased in 1952 when Britain's postwar control ended. By 1960 all the islanders had returned, and although the 300-foot 'Big Bang' crater still scarred the high cliffs, the island was rebuilt as a successful German holiday resort. Yet this enchanting island just 300 miles across the North Sea remains virtually undiscovered. (*Helgoland Regierung*)

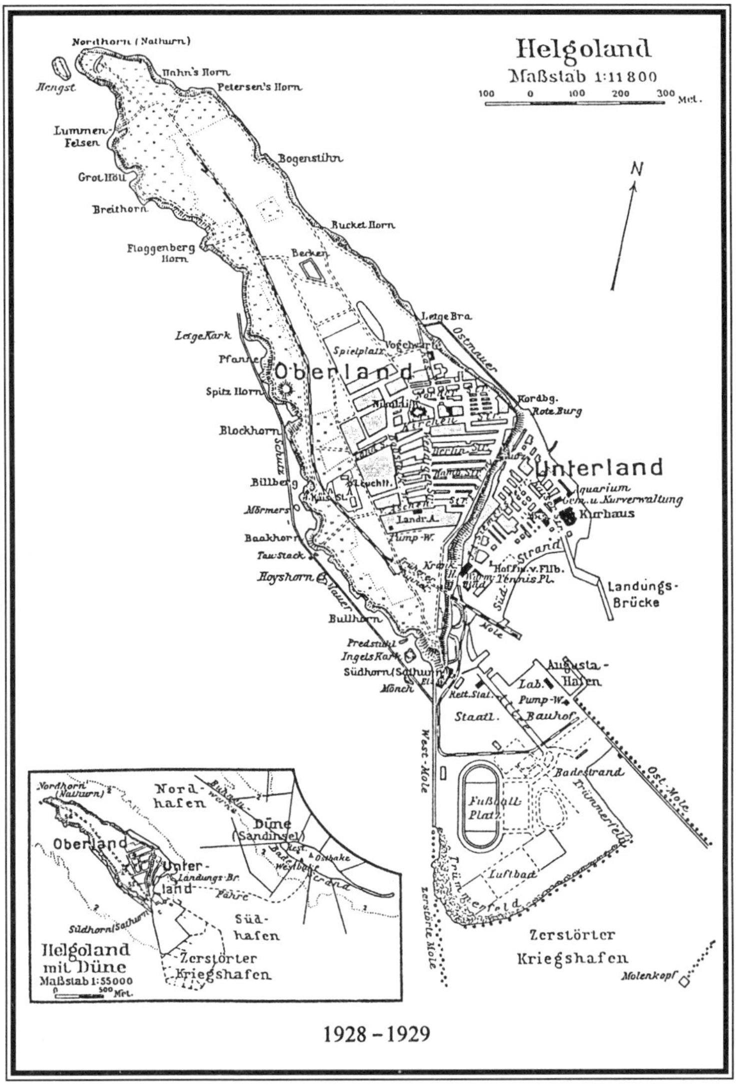

Map 6 Regardless of the breached sea walls of its southern harbour, because of the 1919 Versailles peace agreement, during the interwar years Heligoland regained its place as a stylish tourist resort. (*Helgoland Regierung*)

not have defended Heligoland had we retained it, but an unfortified Heligoland would have been little use to Germany; therefore, had we kept it there would have been no system of German coastal defence.' Additionally he called for Sylt to be given back to Denmark.

Irrespective of all the busy house-proud Heligolanders' make-and-mend efforts, conditions on the island were not much improved. Germany's own economic plight became ever more dismal, so that those islanders who had the heart to claim compensation for lost business and damaged property were reminded that people could scarcely buy a loaf of bread, so low had the Reichsmark fallen. This was an important factor in the agitation that swept the island in October 1919 demanding separation from Germany and union with Britain. Having watched the decline in Germany, they saw British rule as a haven in contrast. Understandably frustrated that their views were not being heeded in London they took matters into their own hands and petitioned the Supreme Council at the Versailles peace talks. Begging that the 'many injustices of the Prussian regime may be examined and abolished', they stated that 'under the long and blissful administration of the great British nation, all our rights and customs were always most loyally upheld'. The quaint concluding phrases of the petition bear repetition:

> We Heligolanders, on our little island in the middle of the seas, far from all the world's commotion, form the very smallest nation which has for centuries maintained its independence and its local customs. We seek neither wealth nor ostentation, but desire and hope to live in our lonely home upon the rocks,

> in peace and contentment, as our forefathers did before us.

Were Heligoland to be returned to Britain as part of a postwar agreement, the diplomatic means by which such a move could be facilitated were available at the Versailles peace conference. However, the tide was beginning to turn and there seemed to be too few influential British statesmen willing to endorse those pleas. Winston Churchill, who had returned to government as Secretary of State for Munitions, and at the time of the Armistice was Secretary of State for War and Air, happened to speak on the subject of Heligoland at a well-reported public meeting in Dundee on 4 December 1918, when he was asked whether he was in favour of the island being returned to Britain. He replied: 'Admiralty experts had come to the conclusion that it was not necessary to demand it. There had always been two views as to whether it would have been of use to us during the war.' By then he had probably received intelligence reports detailing the newly discovered German defences found on the island: camouflaged emplacements; concrete trenches hidden beneath sand and soil; and an apparently plain dwelling house at the head of the Pottchen stairs, which concealed a strongpoint commanding the Unterland. It all showed that his Heligoland invasion scheme, had he persevered with it, could have been disastrous.

The Foreign Office's response to the revanchist urgings was to produce, somewhat half-heartedly, a pamphlet entitled *Heligoland and the Kiel Canal*, which conspicuously made not the slightest mention of the islanders' requests. Unfortunately for Heligoland, a leading British representative at Versailles was the Foreign Secretary Arthur Balfour, the nephew of the deceased Lord Salisbury, who had already shown himself none too keen to reclaim Heligoland.

At Versailles almost any future for the island seemed possible. Perhaps it would be 'internationalised', as had happened to several other strategic places just a few miles distant, such as the Kiel Canal and the mighty Elbe. The question of the disposal of Heligoland was discussed on 17 March 1919 in connection with proposals by the Allied naval authorities that the military facilities on the island be dismantled. The US President, Woodrow Wilson, was sceptical. Although acknowledging that the harbours had been constructed solely for warlike purposes, he objected to their destruction, on the grounds that they might be used as a refuge by merchant shipping in bad weather. The Prime Minister, David Lloyd George, recognising that Heligoland was currently a subject of popular interest in Britain and there might be public disappointment there if the island remained German, telegraphed London that afternoon calling for the War Cabinet to convene and formulate an opinion. Meeting urgently in Downing Street the next day they were profoundly influenced by an Admiralty memo which feared that the fall of a British-held Heligoland would be an unnecessary national humiliation. Uniquely, the memo argued the most crucial part of the island was the harbour complex, because it was only through that could Heligoland's heavy fortifications – if razed – be rebuilt. Winston Churchill endorsed that view, scribbling with red ink in the paper's margins: 'I agree that it should be destroyed – let me see.' Accordingly the delegation were telegraphed on 21 March: 'From a practical point of view it is most desirable that the island should not be taken possession of by Great

Britain: from a sentimental point of view it is desirable that it should not be returned to Germany.' And thus, the message concluded: 'It is urged that either: 1. The island be razed to the high water mark, making re-fortification impossible, in which case the harbour might be retained; or 2. That the fortifications and the harbour be destroyed.' Lloyd George's delegation accepted the latter option.

On all such matters the views of the islanders were never taken into account. As a consequence of the Versailles conference even the question of whether or not Schleswig should be returned to Denmark was to be decided by the people of that province in a plebiscite. However, for the Heligolanders there was to be no such choice, and no voting opportunities were to be made available. Not long before, Balfour had issued his famous declaration of the rights of Palestinians to choose to be associated with their special homeland. To add insult to injury, Britain deliberately chose not to renew the 1890 Heligoland–Zanzibar Treaty, even though it was listed as Article 289 at Versailles. This meant that Britain would no longer have any legal status with regard to the Heligolanders' conditions. There were even some rumours that Britain might agree to cede Gibraltar to the League of Nations. But for the 'Gibraltar of the North Sea' there would be no change.

No one was more damning of the Foreign Office's refusal to regain Heligoland for Britain than the gung-ho Lord Fisher, who wrote in his memoirs: 'Through some extraordinary claim of reasoning, absolutely incomprehensible, the islands of Heligoland, Sylt and Borkum were not claimed or occupied. In view of the prodigious development of aircraft it was imperative that these islands should be in the possession of

England.' Later Fisher claimed: 'All this to me is absolutely astounding. The British Fleet won the war, and the British Fleet didn't get a single thing it ought to have, excepting the everlasting stigma amongst our allies of being fools in allowing the German Fleet to be sunk under our noses.'[14]

8

Project Hummerschere

Thousands of miles away in East Africa the First World War was still going on. Elsewhere on the planet the guns fell silent on Armistice Day, 11 November 1918, but in Tanganyika a defiant German guerrilla force under Colonel Tafel continued fighting. Throughout the war the Allies had been unable to entirely conquer the vast territory known as German East Africa, nor did they succeed in doing so until 25 November 1918. Tanganyika's borders had been secured as part of the 1890 Heligoland–Zanzibar swap agreement but even Lord Salisbury could not have predicted the extent to which the fates of those three possessions would be linked. In 1915 the German raiding cruiser *Königsberg*, having destroyed a dozen merchant ships in the Indian Ocean, became trapped in the shallow waters of the sinuous Tanganyikan Rufiji river, where she was discovered by British seaplanes. However, someone at the Admiralty happened to remember the two monitors HMS *Mersey* and HMS *Severn* which Churchill had insisted on building in 1913, despite the unremitting protests of the 'battle-cruiser gang', as part of the planned invasion of Heligoland. Such was the low draft of those vessels that their designers claimed they could be 'sailed in the Round Pond at Kensington Gardens'. Sent via the Suez Canal and Aden to Zanzibar, the monitors edged upriver for the kill, and eventually destroyed the *Königsberg* – at last they had a target worthy of their guns.

At Versailles, Germany was stripped of all her colonies, but her humiliation was not total. She was allowed to keep her smallest and nearest colonial-style island, Heligoland. What subsequently happened at the peace conference shows how curious was Britain's attitude to various colonial possessions. The strategically important but tiny island of Heligoland she cast aside, while eagerly taking responsibility for the strategically and economically unimportant Tanganyika – all 373,000 square miles of it – to be run as a League of Nations trusteeship. Effectively it was a new British colony.

For the Heligolanders any remaining hope that Britain might take their little island back as one of its colonies ought to have come to an end on 28 June 1919 when the Treaty of Versailles was signed. Arthur Balfour had successfully seen to it that the Heligolanders' pleas for recolonisation fell on deaf ears. But still they did not give up. Even in October 1919 reports were reaching London, and published in *The Times*, of agitation for separation from Germany and union with the United Kingdom. In November there were further stories of the islanders' resentment of German injustice. They were still disgusted by the way their houses had been vandalised by the German military, and to add insult to injury those who had received compensation payments found the money virtually worthless.

They now had other anxieties, too. What particularly concerned them was that in the impending demolition of all the German-built fortifications on the island, a few structures that were relevant to their way of life might also be mindlessly destroyed. Attention focused on the plan to destroy the small boat harbour formed by the old marine mole and the northern wall of the New Harbour works. On 15 August 1919 the Heligolanders put together a petition calling for the retention of the small area known as the north-east harbour. When the request reached London on 1 September 1919 it was dealt with by the Admiralty, rather than the Foreign Office, because the island had long since ceased to be a British colony. That their Lordships were sympathetic to the islanders' plight was evident from a comment an Admiralty official scribbled four days later in the margins of a file hastily put together on this very subject: 'It is considered the islanders' views on this matter are deserving of consideration.' The petition was passed to the Head of the Naval Section at the British Delegation in Paris, who forwarded it on to the Naval Inter-Allied Commission of Control (Heligoland Sub-Committee). It was practically the first issue considered when the latter began work. So favourably disposed were they towards the islanders that on 7 October 1919 the Head of the Naval Section was able to report to the Admiralty that the Commission on Heligoland had decided the small boat harbour should be retained.

Fortunately for the Heligolanders, although nobody in the Foreign Office seemed to care about them, there were various influential people within the Royal Navy who were concerned. One such was Andrew Cunningham, a talented naval officer destined for flag rank, who in 1919 was appointed commander of the team preparing to dismantle the fortifications on Heligoland. One factor in favour of the retention of the fishing boat harbour was derived from the naval authorities' view that some redress was due to the

British-based commercial fishermen who had campaigned – as unsuccessfully as all the other non-governmental lobbyists in Britain – for the island to be retroceded. In 1918 the *Grimsby News* had even produced a special pamphlet urging that the harbour be kept, as it would thus ensure that the island could offer a safe haven to British fishing boats in the event of stormy weather in the Bight. (Many years later it was claimed that the appeal to save the harbour element of the dockland on Heligoland had been secretly inspired by the German Navy.)

The Versailles Treaty was finally ratified on 10 January 1920 and the task of defortifying Heligoland could formally begin. Cunningham's Heligoland Sub-Commission, consisting of seventeen Royal Engineers, travelled to the island on HMS *Coventry* in February 1920, to superintend the business of demolition. Perhaps appropriately, they were to make their headquarters in the Empress of India hotel by the foreshore, which had been named by Governor O'Brien in the 1880s. It was a peculiar experience for them to be in effective military control of this German-owned island, some thirty years after it had ceased to be a British colony. In anticipation of their arrival someone had scribbled on a wall an old Heligoland proverb: *Liewar duad es Skloaw* ('Better dead than a slave'). But the crews of the German minesweeping vessels which used the harbour as a base had quite different views and blatantly showed their disapproval of the British presence by assembling outside the Empress of India singing *Deutschland über Alles* and throwing stones at the building. However, that soon stopped and an apology was tendered by the officer commanding the minesweepers. Interestingly, although the singing took place round the statue of

Heinrich Hoffmann von Fallersleben, it took some time for Cunningham's party to realise the anthem had been composed on the island.

A meeting was arranged with the German Commission to agree a procedure for the dismantling of the fortifications. Bizarrely, the Commission included both the former chief engineer, who had spent some time on the island during the war, and also the man who had constructed the war harbour – and now had to assist in its destruction, surely a unique record. They were dignified, hurt, and not inclined to forgive or forget. They had lived there year by year, had built all those fortifications and designed the intricate machinery – and now had to watch as it was all smashed up and scrapped! They claimed that it was unfair to enforce the dismantlement of Heligoland. Germany, they felt, had not been truly vanquished and now was being miserably treated. The German technicians originally stated that the dismantling would take seven years to complete, but pressure was brought to bear and a few plans altered until that estimate was whittled down to two years. The work of demolition then began, carried out by some 500–600 German labourers under the supervision of the Sub-Commission. They worked well and gave little trouble. The operation seemed set to be a reverse of the building process.[1]

In fact, in the preceding months some minor dismantling had already taken place. Instruments, gun-sights and fittings of all kinds had been taken as souvenirs by the departing naval garrison. Hitherto working at a rather leisurely pace, they had removed light guns, anti-aircraft batteries and searchlights, leaving stores of timber and metal littered about the Oberland. Now the Allied dismantlers were in charge and they concentrated their attention on the main armament. At the north and south groups of twin 12in gun turrets, the workers began their task, laboriously slicing the huge gun barrels of Anna, Bertha, Caesar and Dora into sections with oxy-hydrogen cutters. Similarly cut up were the eight coastal defence 11in howitzers and four single-turret 21cm guns in the centre of the island. Next they turned their attention to the secondary armament: batteries of 15cm and 8.8cm quick-firing guns mounted on the cliff edge overlooking the harbour, and numerous 3.7cm anti-aircraft guns. On the main island an ingenious wooden extractor mechanism was devised for pulling out sections of gun mountings, and various impromptu branch lines were added to the existing light railway in order to move the dismembered pieces of weaponry to the diagonal funicular railway tunnel and down to the harbour. With the remains of the guns went trolley-loads of live ammunition. All the cut-up metal was taken to Wilhelmshaven and sold, and the proceeds divided among the Allies. Where concrete emplacements proved resistant to pneumatic drills they were shattered with dynamite demolition charges. A highly significant discovery – which certainly ought to have been known many years later – was that only 1½lb of explosive was needed to break up a ton of chilled cast-iron around the turret beds. Some of the main tunnels connecting the north group to the howitzer batteries and south group, and the cable and pipe tunnels at a lower level, could not be destroyed even by this means and instead were bricked up.

While the dismantling was in progress a considerable friendship developed between the islanders and the British officers. To the British, the islanders seemed Scandinavian in appearance, pleasant and courteous in manner, and devoted to their island home. Cunningham's superior, Admiral Sir Edward Charlton, visited Heligoland and asked the local people he met what they did in winter. The reply was: count the money they had made in the summer! The islanders were particularly impressed that when off duty the officers mingled informally with the local people, even donning traditional fishermen's attire. The Heligolanders, it seems, were appreciative that although extensive dynamiting work needed to be done the British engineers were always careful to minimise the inconvenience caused. They even put steel netting around the sites being blown up to protect the islanders' property from flying shards of metal and concrete.

Spreading their activities down to the water's edge the dismantlers then flattened the seaplane base, including its hangars and stranded aircraft. By July 1920 they were hard at work preparing to demolish the dry dock and the west mole. The sides of the dry dock were blown up and the foundations of the moles were destroyed by explosives, and the winter gales, always heavy, soon made them little more than a mass of ruins. The main harbour entrance was sealed by huge 2-ton blocks dropped from a floating crane. The retaining walls around the reclaimed ground created by Tirpitz, on which stood the dockyard building, were pierced to allow the sea to suck out the millions of tons of sand brought from the Elbe for its formation. Thus the whole place appeared to have been wrecked in such a manner that no new harbour could be constructed on the site. Over at Dune a battery of anti-aircraft guns, a signal station and searchlight were similarly destroyed. Eventually, on 1 June 1922, the entire work of orderly destruction was completed, the last act being the immobilisation of the diagonal tunnel from the Unterland to the Oberland. All the while, conscious that they would need to be able to prove to the Inter-Allied Commission and the outside world that the fortifications had been razed, the Royal Engineers had been accumulating an impressive photographic record of their demolition activities. This was gathered into a vast leather-bound album which they took with them when the Commission departed in 1922.[2] It seemed that British interest in the island could henceforth surely be only sentimental and historical.

No sooner had the British departed than it became apparent that the destruction of the sea walls could already be having a potentially devastating effect on the island. The moles and port installations had been razed below the level of low water. The sole exception was part of the long west mole. Some 300 metres of this, nearest the Sudhorn – the southernmost rocky tip of the island – was spared to protect the weather side of the fishing-boat harbour. However, the rest of the unprotected areas of Tirpitz's reclaimed dockyard land were visibly being gnawed away by the sea. If the sea walls were not restored, in just a few years as much as a quarter of the island could be washed away. Even the lifeboat station was at risk. Somehow the islanders managed to patch up enough of the vulnerable deconstructed remains to stem the depletion.

The islanders did what they could to attract visitors back to Heligoland, building a football pitch for soccer enthusiasts, a public swimming pool and, for more discerning visitors, a tennis court on the Strand promenade. Ugly stumps of steel and concrete – the scars left by the Allies' heavy-handed demilitarisation – remained, but even so the tourists started to return.

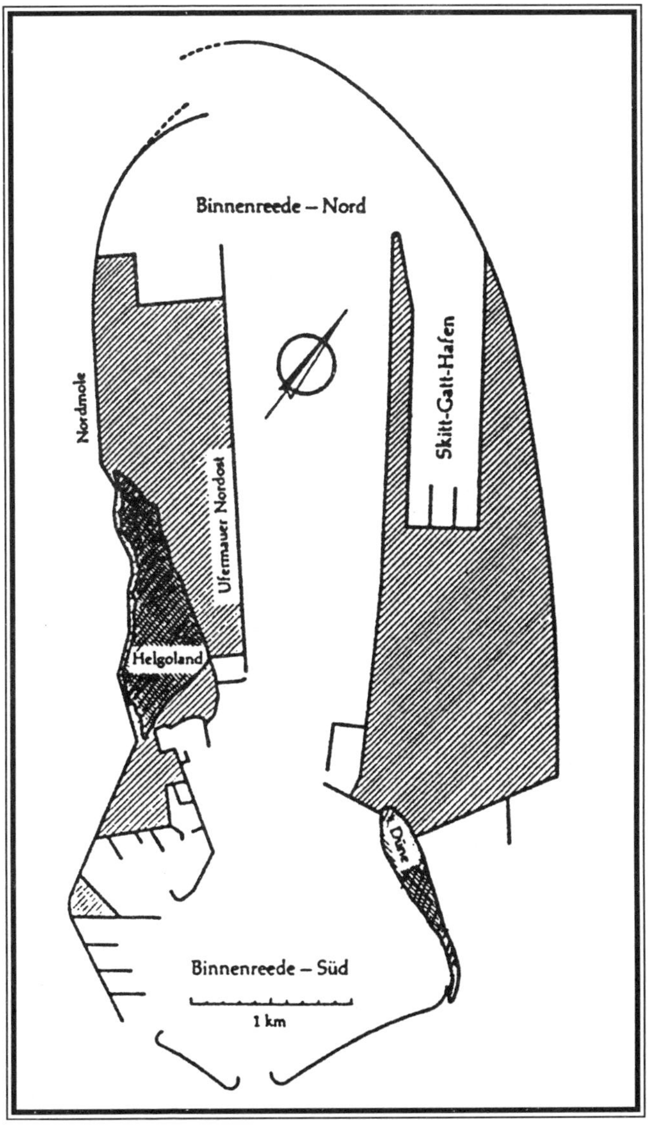

Map 7 In contravention of the Versailles treaty, during the 1930s Germany commenced Project 'Hummerschere' (lobster claws): an ambitious scheme to create a German Scapa Flow by building on Heligoland's 1729 shallows. In 1938 Hitler himself visited Heligoland to see how work was progressing – and even walked down the High Street – but the project was never completed. (*Helgoland Regierung*)

The reintroduction of the Dover–Heligoland yacht races also helped to put a shine on the island's tarnished kudos. Gradually the numbers of trippers grew and by the early 1930s Heligoland was welcoming some 30,000 visitors a year – more than before the First World War. Fewer than ever were British, but such was the lingering affection for England in the island that visitors could still stay in the Hotel Victoria or the Hotel Queen Victoria, and enjoy an evening's entertainment at the Queen Victoria-Bierhalle.

In the midst of all this, there was also a revival of the nineteenth-century tradition of intellectuals gaining exceptional flashes of inspiration on Heligoland; this happened when the German scientist Werner Heisenberg visited the island in June 1925 to do some research and recover from flu. One night he had an idea and he went for a stroll along the Oberland cliff-tops overlooking the Lower Town to consider it further. Not far from the grounds of Government House, where Arthur Barkly had handed over the island thirty-five years earlier, he developed the brilliant mathematical theory that became known as the uncertainty principle. It explained the structure of the hydrogen atom and although he was only twenty-four at the time of the discovery it eventually won him the Nobel Prize for Physics.

The initial impact on Heligoland of the rise to power of Adolf Hitler and his Nazi party was economic. In Hamburg alone there had been 173,000 unemployed as recently as 1932. But in 1933 Hitler's efforts to ease the economic crisis meant increased affluence on the German mainland and tourism on the island flourished. This time the visitors were more affluent than ever, eager to spend their new-found wealth in the island's numerous drinking places and in the expensive gift shops that lined the Lung Wai, the main street leading up from the landing stage. In the Kaiserstrade trippers could purchase collectable pictures by the Heligolander Franz Schensky, an internationally renowned underwater photographer who specialised in beautifully dramatic pictures of the island in rough weather. Other scenes he depicted were of traditional fishing boats, such as the elegantly functional shallow schooners and ketches favoured by the islanders, irrespective of the sophistication of the tourists.

During a celebrated speech on 21 May 1935 Hitler unilaterally repudiated the clauses demanding the disarmament of Germany in the Treaty of Versailles. It was he who alleged that agents of the German Navy at Versailles had tricked the Allies into sparing the fishing-boat harbour at Heligoland – and thus the demilitarisation had never really been carried out. The commencement of the refortification of the island meant the islanders' peaceful existence was shattered. Soon the German Navy uncovered the funicular railway tunnel leading from the harbour to the Oberland, and set about rebuilding the fortifications that had been there in 1918. To establish beyond doubt Germany's command of the seas around the island, and thus of the outer estuaries of the Weser and Elbe, huge 12in and 6in guns were mounted in turrets on the cliff-tops. Those large naval weapons, situated some 200ft above sea-level, were capable of firing shells some 40,000 yards. Impressive though they were, in fact the island was actually *less* well armed now than it had been in the First World War. Instead of eight 12in guns, it had only three, mounted in single turrets in what was called Batterie Schröder at the northern end of the island.

Hitler's next step was to implement an epic plan to use the newly fortified Heligoland not just as an anti-aircraft fortress, but as a centre for the creation of a gigantic new naval base to rival Scapa Flow, the Royal Navy's strategic anchorage in the Orkneys. Codenamed 'Project Hummerschere', the scheme was the brainchild of Admiral 'Dr' Erich Raeder, the commander of the German Navy (1928–43), who was already achieving some renown as the strategic rebuilder of Germany's naval might. In effect Raeder was trying to recreate Heligoland as it had been in 1629, according to the famous map. In the seventeenth century the two halves of the island, called Rock Island and White Cliff, were linked by a natural causeway which had been swept away in a ferocious storm in 1721. Instead of building another causeway, Raeder intended to create a giant lagoon, some 4 miles long and 2 wide, with huge claw-shaped areas of land on either side – hence the name of the project, as Hummerschere means 'lobster claws'. The eastern arm, to be developed by extending Sandy Island northwards, would also serve as a Luftwaffe air base.

By 1937 Raeder's plan had been approved and construction work was in progress. The building of tunnels and underground chambers, by dynamiting and drilling, at the southern tip of Heligoland's Oberland produced many thousands of tons of excavated rock spoil. This appears to have been carted to the north-west corner of the main island and used for land reclamation. Dumped behind a sea wall it began to enlarge the area of the island by several hectares. Extending north from the 'Lange Anna', the northernmost tip of the main island, was built a kilometre-long mole which would, Raeder planned, serve as the west sea wall of the north dockyard. Over at Sandy Island a parallel mole, the Dünendamm West, was also extended northwards. Into the segments behind the breakwater were brought thousands of tons of sand dredged from the Loreley Bank several miles offshore. According to the legend of Atlantis, many centuries earlier this had formed part of the once huge island of greater Heligoland. Bizarrely, history was now being reversed. Enchanted by this scheme, Hitler visited Heligoland to inspect the huge construction works. He landed at the edge of the Unterland, just as the Kaiser had done, and walked along the main street. The date of this visit was 23 August 1938 – just a month before the Munich Crisis.

Under the Treaty of Versailles Germany was forbidden to rearm Heligoland. Article 115 clearly stated: 'These fortifications . . . shall not be reconstructed, nor shall any similar works be constructed in future.' Hitler, however, had no intention of abiding by the Treaty. In 1936 MPs at Westminster started asking parliamentary questions about the rumoured refortification. The first shot in what was to become an increasingly intense assault on the Conservative government's policy of appeasement with regard to Heligoland was fired on 13 July by the relatively unknown Commander Locker-Lampson MP. He sought to discover from the Foreign Secretary whether Britain had any right to inspect the island or whether that had been waived. He received a vague response from a junior Foreign Minister, Viscount Cranbourne. Astonishingly, Cranbourne, like Arthur Balfour, was also a relative of the late Premier, Lord Salisbury.[3] Far from reassured by the reply, just two weeks later other MPs pressed further, wanting to know details of Germany's apparent contravention of the terms of the Treaty: 'What representation has been made to Germany on the matter and what reply has been received?' Determined not to be lured into a position of picking a diplomatic fight with Germany on the question of the island, this time Anthony Eden himself answered. He acknowledged that the action of the German government was unilateral, but said that he did not propose to deal with this question separately since to do so might prejudice the negotiations which had just been set in train for a western pact.

The clouds of war were already gathering in March 1939 when the Prime Minister received a letter from Somerset Maxwell MP, wanting to know what reports he had received about the rearmament of the island. A polite reply, sent from the Foreign Office on Neville Chamberlain's behalf, stated that Britain's position had not altered from that set down by Eden in 1936, and went on: 'Subsequent developments have shown clearly that no useful purpose would be served by taking up this matter with the German Government.' Official documents now prove that considerable attention was given to the drafting of that reply, even the Admiralty being asked for its opinion.[4] The file on this matter shows that: 'According to a secret report which the Admiralty would not wish to be quoted, "Certain alterations" are now being made in the fortifications and they understand heavier guns are being installed. Some British Naval officers had been there last summer for regattas and had been able to see the position for themselves.'

Although the Admiralty knew what was happening on the island, scarcely anyone else in Britain did. There were several reasons why Heligoland had faded from public view. After the death of William George Black, the mantle of the island's champion ought to have fallen to Erskine Childers, the yachtsman-author who knew those waters so well. But, quite unbeknown to the Royal Navy, just before the Cuxhaven Raid he had become passionately involved with Irish republicanism. Although he had fought for the British in the Boer War as an enthusiastic imperialist, Erskine's lurch towards Irish republicanism was largely the work of his glamorous new American wife Molly Osgood, a prominent Boston-society Anglophile. In July 1914 the couple had smuggled a huge cache of rifles from the Flemish coast to Ireland in their sleek ketch-rigged yacht *Asgard*, which Molly's parents had given to them as a wedding present. Amazingly, within a month of that gun-running episode Britain was at war, and Childers soon found himself sent to the German Bight for the raid on Cuxhaven in December 1914. In 1922 he was executed by the British for treasonable activities, which made him something of a hero in southern Ireland, but his death deprived Heligoland of a potentially influential benefactor. Heligoland's tenuous links with Ireland have never been wholly severed. *Asgard*, somewhat implausibly described by an Irish minister as 'the most influential vessel in Irish history', survived – reverentially kept in a Dublin prison yard – and has now been restored to sailing condition.

One crucial consequence of the timing of the handover of Heligoland to Germany, many years before the modern British Commonwealth of former colonial nations began to take shape in the late 1920s, was that from that time on colonial history books almost invariably omitted to mention that Heligoland had ever been a British possession. A clear example of this can be found in the works of Professor Somervell, who was at that time a most popular historian of the British

Empire. His works were read by a generation of students and other educated people who went on to become influential in public life. Highly significantly, in 1930 the first edition of his best-selling book *The British Empire* referred to Heligoland as an 'uninhabited sandbar'. Subsequently, as the book went through several editions and reprints during the next few years, mention of Heligoland was gradually phased out, until by the fifth and final edition in 1942 it had ceased to be mentioned at all. It was as if there had never been any British involvement with Heligoland.

The question of why the island should have been swapped at all in 1890 was fleetingly considered in the 1920s by Lady Gwendolen Cecil, Salisbury's daughter, who published a selection of his letters. Intriguingly, despite her privileged access, she claimed that there were no clues to his innermost thoughts on that matter. Also getting into print at this time were edited selections of Queen Victoria's letters; these certainly mentioned her opposition to the swap, but no British historian thought to use this as a basis to question Britain's record on the island.

Once the Versailles Treaty had been signed, and Heligoland's political future thereby put beyond Westminster's influence, parliamentary interest in Heligoland had virtually come to an end. From the mid-1920s, and for many years thereafter, almost no questions regarding the island – except on the subject of rearmament – were asked in either the House of Commons or the House of Lords. Once the fortifications were dismantled, the island and the activities of its inhabitants ceased to receive any attention in the British national newspapers. It would be many years before *The Times* mentioned it at all.

Nazi intimidation meant that even in 1935 a reporter sent to the island by the American journal *National Geographic* had to be careful not to be caught taking photographs. The last Englishman to write about a visit to Heligoland was the pioneering naturalist Ronald Lockley, who landed there in October 1936 to see the famous migratory bird-trapping centre which had originally been created by the controversial ornithologist Heinrich Gätke. In his book *I Know an Island* (1938), Lockley produced an account of that pre-war trip, eerily redolent of William George Black's 1911 article for the *National Review*. He reported that when not ringing birds at the Fanggarten (he tagged an astonishing 752 birds of many species in just a day) he did what he could to explore the island, but found huge areas, most notably the fortress and the docks, fenced off with wire and 'Verboten' notices. Indeed, the non-military space had become so restricted that on fine summer days, when the ferries arrived and discharged thousands of sightseers, there could be as many as nine thousand people thronging the narrow streets. As the ferries docked, the crowds were so thick that no one could move one way or the other. Walking room was limited to the streets and the promenade around the island.

In such circumstances, most locals either remained at home or struggled to the 400-seater cinema. The films, which were changed weekly, usually included a newsreel and perhaps two or three propaganda films proclaiming the Nazi cause. Outside there would occasionally be demonstrations by some political organisation, which all young people had to attend. Almost every day a new 'thought' would appear on the notice-boards on the staircase joining the Upper and Lower Towns. 'Bolshevism' and 'Return our Colonies' were the most burning themes. There would also be entreaties to 'Fly your Swastika' and obey patriotic laws and etiquette.

But such exhortations were meaningless against the power of the sea. On 27 October 1936 Lockley witnessed a great gale approaching from the west. The waves leapt in clouds over the naval base and swept into the streets of the Lower Town. No steamer could approach the island. In the space of just a few hours nearly half of Sandy Island was swept away; many people watched through telescopes as the buildings upon it crumbled and slid into the sea. Finally came the news that the lightship *Elbe 3*, positioned between Heligoland and Hamburg, had capsized and sunk with all hands. Lockley, a seasoned mariner, chillingly noted: 'The whole shallow sea was perfectly white, as I have never seen in the white water of the Atlantic in its worst mood.' Later, when the storm had subsided, he took a ferry to Cuxhaven. As it passed the isolated anchorage where the lightship had gone down, preparations were already being made to install a new vessel. Poignantly, the Heligoland ferry paused for a moment and lowered its ensign in honour of those who had died.

At the outbreak of the Second World War in early September 1939 Britain's approach to fighting in the Heligoland Bight differed markedly from its conduct there in the First World War. Now the main weapon against German forces were aircraft not ships, but their activities were restricted by Neville Chamberlain's insistence that they operate within the terms of the 1923 Hague Convention insofar as they should not attack civilian targets. Heligoland might otherwise have been attacked on the last day of the war by Hampden light bombers which overflew it that very afternoon. On 29 September 1939, eleven Hampdens in two formations were sent to search for naval targets. Six aircraft bombed two destroyers, but without scoring any hits. The second formation of five aircraft did not return. A German radio broadcast later declared they had been set upon by a 'hornet's nest' of fighters and all the Hampdens had been shot down, killing eighteen of their twenty-four crew, including the squadron commander. The RAF eventually came to realise that the bombers' movements had been detected by 'Freya' radar installations on Wangerooge island and Heligoland.[5]

The massacre of the Hampdens, and other losses in subsequent weeks in raids against German shipping, prompted the RAF to opt for a change of tactics. On 20 February 1940 twenty Wellington bombers (known affectionately to their crews as 'Wimpys') were despatched on an experimental raid with the object of finding and bombing German warships in the Bight at night-time, in an effort to avoid the heavy casualties of recent daylight raids. Two served as reconnaissance planes and eighteen as the bombing force; but a recall signal was sent because of fog, in which one Wellington crashed in England and another was lost at sea. The strategy was not instantly repeated, but that sortie became historically important for being Britain's first mass night-time raid of the war.

Another RAF raid against German shipping in the Bight, on 3 December 1939, was also claimed to represent a historic milestone. Twenty-four Wellingtons were attacked by Me109s and Me110s and in the ensuing combat the Wellington formations survived undamaged, while one Me109 was shot down. The bombers had been returning from a raid on German warships in which they apparently hit two cruisers;

they dropped their 500lb bombs from 7,000–10,000ft to give them a better chance of penetrating the decks. One Wellington of 115 Squadron, which apparently suffered a bomb hang-up on its bombing run, flew back over Heligoland and despite fierce flak 'accidentally' dropped the bomb on the island. This was the very first bomb dropped by the RAF on German soil during the war – or so it has been claimed by RAF historians. In fact the islanders, who seem never to have been consulted on this matter, have entirely different recollections. Eyewitnesses who were fishermen at the time remember that the very first RAF bomb dropped over Heligoland fell not on the island but in the harbour, completely destroying a naval ammunition supply vessel.

For British planes to approach the Heligoland 'hornet's nest' required great daring. High on the cliffs was a 'Freya' radar installation, with a range of 130km. It stood near the lofty six-storey, anti-aircraft artillery observation centre known as the Red Tower. The highest point on the island, it even overshadowed the lighthouse, and directed the fire of the anti-aircraft batteries, including those on Sandy Island, called the 'Hermann-Goering-flak'. To the Germans it had always seemed likely that air raids would come from the west. But on 21 May 1941 there occurred an audacious attack which the islanders still speak of with awe. Utterly unexpectedly, six Blenheim bombers escorted by fighters in search of warships in the harbour approached Heligoland from the north, the island's 'blind' side. Racing towards the island at wave-top height, under the radar, they reached it undetected. At the last moment they climbed just enough to soar over the cliffs at the Lange Anna and then roared low over the astonished anti-aircraft positions and on to the harbour. Hitting three small ships and some jetties there they also reportedly machine-gunned the town.

A daring combined forces plan was formulated at the Admiralty in early February 1940 to send a naval force of four destroyers and three motor torpedo boats (MTBs), based in Harwich, to undertake offensive operations against enemy destroyers in Heligoland's anchorages and the south-west part of the Bight at a suitable time during 8–15 February 1940. Operation 'JB' was intended to involve an air cover escort of Blenheims flying from Martlesham Heath, but as they could only be guaranteed to be present some of the time, the vulnerability of the MTBs to German air attack led to the scheme being cancelled on the advice of the RAF.

By 1943 aircraft of the US 8th Air Force, stationed in Norfolk, were carrying out high-altitude daylight raids against Heligoland. Flying at around 26,000ft, out of range of the anti-aircraft guns, the aircraft involved were from the 91st and 303rd Bombardment Groups. Serving with the latter on one such raid was the celebrated B-17 'Memphis Belle', about which William Wyler made a documentary and Harry Connick jnr starred in an award-winning movie. One objective of these attacks was assumed to be the three huge U-boat shelters which had appeared in the harbour. They were some 485ft long, with reinforced flat concrete roofs 14ft thick, and aerial reconnaissance photographs had shown that their construction was already in progress in 1940. By autumn of the following year they were complete, and painted with contrasting tones and shapes in order to break up the appearance of the flat surfaces. However, a confidential Air Ministry report entitled *Heligoland: Submarine Basin*, written on 30

October 1944, stated that: 'Since the port was first photographed on 5.9.40 no U-boats have been seen in the harbour.' This message is repeated in its conclusion: 'No U-boats have ever been photographed in the harbour, but E/R boats have been seen on several occasions.'[6]

Thus it is all the more surprising that the decision was taken to make a quite extraordinary top-secret attack on these apparently unused facilities. The means to do so had been devised by an American Air Force officer, General Carl 'Tooey' Spaatz. Desperate to find a way to attack the underground bunkers where Hitler's V-1 rockets were being produced, he evolved a method of flying large military aircraft, in effect crude guided missiles, by remote control. His technique, codenamed 'Project Aphrodite', involved two aircraft, one of them pilotless. Packed with explosives, this would be crashed into the target. The second aircraft would fly nearby and control the 'bomber' by radio. A television camera in the aircraft's nose enabled the 'bomber' to be directed accurately to its target. The 'bomber' plane took off conventionally, the pilot baling out long before it crashed. The US Army and Air Force favoured using radio-controlled B-17 planes, and started using them on 4 August 1944. The US Navy favoured using B-24s, but with two pilots; their very first US Aphrodite bomber pilot was Lt Joseph Kennedy jnr, the elder brother of John F. Kennedy.

Joseph Kennedy's assigned target has usually been assumed to have been the Heligoland U-boat shelter, the three entrances to which were only 65ft wide and just 45ft high, with heavy torpedo nets at water level. At 6pm on 12 August 1944 his converted B-24, 'Zootsuit Black', took to the air from Dunkeswell airfield in East Anglia. As the plane headed towards

Heligoland, Kennedy prepared to bale out but first he needed to activate the remote control mechanism. Reportedly, as he did so the B-24, packed with 18,435lb of Torpex high explosive, accidentally detonated, blowing itself to smithereens. Kennedy was killed instantly. There are some doubts as to where this explosion took place, whether it was over England, the North Sea or near the island itself. Even now there are Heligolander eyewitnesses who emphatically recall, although they are unclear as to the date, a huge explosion when a lone Allied bomber inexplicably hit the waters of the harbour.

Undeterred, the US Navy made at least two other Aphrodite attacks. One took place in September 1944 near the airfield barracks on the tiny Sandy Island and was carefully analysed by British Air Intelligence. It devastated a massive area – some 72,700 sq. yards. The other occurred on 15 October 1944 when a pilotless bomber laden with an 18,435lb Torpex charge was crashed into the Lower Town, causing the destruction of an estimated 24,600 sq. yards of non-military property. The effects of the explosion were of much interest to the Armaments Department of Britain's Ministry of Home Security, which soon put together a detailed and highly classified report entitled *Incident at Heligoland.*[7] There were certain indications that the explosion in the town was not the consequence of an overshoot of the U-boat shelters but a deliberate experiment (on the entirely domestic and commercial buildings of the Heligolanders) and the report concluded: 'It is noted that no existing High Explosive load on an existing aircraft could demolish more than about half this area.' Another intriguing possibility is that the real target of this attack, and of that which Joseph Kennedy had embarked upon, was the

Biological Institute of Heligoland (BAH), the laboratories of which were severely damaged in the 15 October attack. It was near here that Werner Heisenberg had formulated his Nobel Prize-winning uncertainty principle – and having created a mathematical system known as matrix mechanics to explain the structure of the hydrogen atom, he was now busy in an underground bunker on the mainland as the head of Germany's secret mission to develop an atomic bomb.

At this time there were already some who were turning their thoughts to the island's future. In London one such character was barrister Dr W. Regendanz, who appears to have been acting on his own initiative. Most of his private research papers on the history of the island were destroyed in an air raid, but he was allowed to gather more information at the Foreign Office's library and the Royal Geographical Society. On 8 September 1943 he wrote to the Under-Secretary of State at the Foreign Office, Anthony Eden, suggesting that in a postwar peace settlement Britain should, for strategic reasons, seek to annexe Heligoland and the island of Sylt. These, he claimed, were in a similar position: an air force based on Sylt would command the Skagerrak and Kattegat, just as Heligoland dominated the Kiel Canal; and should Russia in the future become master of the Baltic Sea it would be important for British policy to close the only exits to the North Sea – namely the Skagerrak and the Kaiser Wilhelm Canal.[8] Significantly the reply from the Foreign Office thanking Regendanz for his letter was made on behalf of Eden by Frank Roberts, an official who would become prominent in the Heligoland story a few years hence. But in 1943 the Foreign Office wanted to keep Britain's options open regarding the island, and when in parliament Lt Cdr Hutchinson MP asked Eden if Heligoland ought to revert to British sovereignty he was curtly put down with the excuse that 'it was more a matter to be discussed at the Peace Conference than at Question Time in the House'.

However, at around this time, Barnes Wallis, the co-designer of the Wellington bomber, was seeking to develop an idea he had had in 1941 for a weapon powerful enough to put out of action the underground V-1 plants as well as U-boat shelters such as those at Heligoland. Although he had figured that it could best be done with very large bombs weighing 10 tons which would have a *camouflet* (earthquake) effect, for a while his proposals were rejected. They were revived in 1943 and a smaller version of the 10-ton design, weighing 12,000lb, was built. Known as the 'Tallboy', it was test-detonated at Shoeburyness in what was probably the largest explosion ever touched off at that range. It was heard 40 miles away at Chislehurst in Kent.[9] The men entrusted to use these weapons in anger were from the famous 617 'Dam Buster' Squadron, whose Lancaster bombers were converted to carry them (as later were those of 9 Squadron). An early success was their use to wreck the V-1 underground plant at St Leu d'Esserent, just north of Paris, where flying bombs were made. Another attack effectively demolished the major part of a massive concrete structure in northern France designed to house, underground, a number of 9-metre gun barrels set at a fixed elevation. This was one of Hitler's secret weapons, intended to drench London with hundreds of tons of high explosive every week.

By February 1945 the full 10-ton version, known as the 'Grand Slam', had been developed. Although the new weapon arrived untested from the manufacturers, it was successfully used by 617 Squadron to destroy the Bielefeld Viaduct near Hanover, a hitherto almost impossible target. Another success had been the attack on the battleship *Tirpitz*, which was sunk in Altenfjord by Lancasters of 9 and 617 Squadrons dropping Tallboys on 12 November 1944. As their ship capsized and the icy waters rose, the doomed crew inside were heard singing *Deutschland über Alles* – the anthem composed under British occupation in Heligoland.

By mid-April 1945 the war in Europe was only three weeks from ending. Canadian troops had overrun Friesland on 12 April 1945, and the British were advancing on Berlin. The strategic high command organisation, SHAEF, assumed that as the Allied forces would want to enter the Elbe and Weser estuaries the heavy guns of Heligoland would need to be put out of action. They had been alerted to that possibility by Field Marshal Bernard Montgomery, who on 23 March 1945, with regard to the German Bight islands, had written to the planning staff of his 21 Army Group: 'By far the most important island is Heligoland which dominates the entrance to all the north-west German ports from Emden to Hamburg.' Initially Montgomery wondered if the island might be starved into surrendering: 'If Heligoland continues to hold out it appears that we shall have to starve it out (meaning delays in opening Hamburg for British maintenance, and Bremenhaven for US maintenance, and Cuxhaven for minesweeping).' But wondering if an air attack might bring about the required result sooner he told the planning staff: 'It would be appreciated if you could examine the possibility of reducing Heligoland from the air, should the island continue to hold and after the rest of North Germany has been overrun.'

Another alternative considered had been the immobilisation of Heligoland's heavy weaponry by means of naval gunfire. However in late March the Admiralty formed the view that the emplacement of artillery there was such, in its present form, that the island was impregnable to attack by the sea. But was it really necessary now for the Allies to bother with the island at all? This is highly questionable because the maximum range of the 12in guns, the heaviest on the island, was only 12 miles, meaning there was just enough sea-room to allow safe access to the estuaries without needing to attack Heligoland. Moreover, it was never considered that it had not been necessary to invade or bomb any of the German-occupied Channel Islands, either before, during or since the Normandy landings.

On 31 March Bomber Command were asked by SHAEF to formulate a plan for 'neutralising' the guns of Heligoland. Sir Arthur 'Bomber' Harris and his colleagues, notably the Chief of the Air Staff Sir Charles Portal, had reason to relish an opportunity to attack Heligoland. After all, the tiny island had brought down the Hampdens and subsequently countless other Allied planes in its capacity as a fighter base. British Intelligence believed the island was an outstation of the 'X system' network that guided German military aircraft, and it had also given many warnings of imminent Allied raids on the mainland. Even now islanders recall how the German military used to look up in the sky, note the number and altitude of Allied bombers, and report where they were heading. On 4 April Bomber Command recommended a two-phase attack, initially using masses of conventional bombs to knock out the forty or so flak guns, then dropping Tallboys and Grand

Slams to destroy the big guns. Accepting Bomber Command's plan on 16 April, SHAEF ordered that the mission should make ready to proceed.

Unusually, word from the Allies reached the island that some intensive bombing was due to begin. The message from London was that if the garrison surrendered, Heligoland would be spared. The islanders certainly did not want their island to be extensively bombed and two men in particular, hotelier Eric Friedirics and roofer Georg Braun, wished to make sure of it. There were a number of German soldiers on the island who also reckoned the time had come to put a halt to the fighting. Four of them met with Friedirics and Braun to consider how to proceed. Should the surrender be forced by means of a rebellion and mutiny? Unfortunately these events coincided with the arrival of an SS detachment, sent to the island to halt any faltering in the garrison's resolve to battle on. According to various Heligolanders who were there at the time, the conspirators were in the course of making their views known throughout the garrison when the plot came to the attention of the Gestapo and the island's unpopular Military Commandant, Kapitan Roeggeler, an ardent Nazi. Action was swift and brutal. The six ringleaders were rounded up and arrested, then taken across to the coastal fortifications at Cuxhaven. There, after a summary interrogation, all of them were condemned to be executed, and were then shot.

Thus the white flag that the British had ordered to be hoisted over Heligoland by noon on 18 April never did appear. Readying themselves for the expected attack, the islanders made for the deep underground air-raid shelters set aside for civilians near the cliff-side staircase on the eastern side of the Oberland.

Early that afternoon the sirens sounded a warning, as they had done many times before during the war. But never had they foretold a raid more terrifying than this.

The sky was cloudless, clear and bright, as a vast armada of nearly 1,000 aircraft – mostly Lancaster and Halifax bombers – approached the island at 18,000ft, accompanied by squadrons of long-range Spitfire and Mustang fighters. The first to strike were twenty Mosquito pathfinders, which swooped in at low level to drop coloured smoke marker flares indicating the three aiming points: the North and South batteries on the main island and the Dune airfield. The RAF had sent 618 Lancasters and 332 Halifaxes to obliterate Heligoland and they rained down 4,953 tons of bombs on the island. Although fierce resistance was put up by the flak guns, which brought down three Halifaxes, it was remorselessly overwhelmed. Long before the later waves of bombers arrived, RAF crews could see huge columns of smoke rising from various parts of the island. A huge oil fire was burning at the south end, and elsewhere great fires were raging under clouds of smoke which drifted across the plateau.

The bombs fell relentlessly for an hour and a quarter, and even now older islanders can vividly recall the horror of that raid. Even deep in the shelters the noise was tremendous. The bombs fell in systematic patterns, like giants' footsteps getting closer and closer. As they approached, those who were not speechless with horror were screaming in terror. At one point the generators failed and all the lights went out, leaving them in total darkness. Almost without exception the Heligolanders thought they were going to die.

When the civilians finally emerged from their refuge that afternoon, blinking in the sunshine, they could hardly take in the scene of total devastation. Their island was a crater-pitted moonscape. Virtually every building was so utterly destroyed that there was scarcely one stone left standing on another. Historic places such as the Villa Hoffman von Fallersleben were utterly wrecked, as were all the buildings for so long associated with British rule: the church with the model ship presented by a former governor; the Empress of India; Government House; and even the streets with English names. By a supreme irony the only building effectively unscathed was the highest structure on the island – the anti-aircraft control centre, the Red Tower. Its survival became a prominent new addition to the island's aura of indestructibility against the odds.

But the firestorm had not yet ended. The next afternoon the RAF returned, officially to destroy the 12in and 6in guns – although many had already been put out of action. This time the escorting Spitfires and Mustangs nearly outnumbered the bombers – there were just thirty-three of them. But these were special aircraft: Lancasters of 617 and 9 Squadrons carrying Tallboy and Grand Slam bombs, as well as a camera crew filming events. No attempt was made to attack the U-boat shelters. The targets were the heavy gun positions. For the 'earthquake' bombs to be effective, they needed to be dropped within a radius of 60–90ft of the target. The bombs were delivered from 13,000ft, the six 22,000-pounders from the north and the twenty-seven 12,000-pounders from the west. For the islanders this attack could have been even more deadly than that of the previous afternoon if an earthquake bomb had reached their shelters. An Air Ministry assessment of the 18–19 April raids subsequently concluded: 'Damage by 500lb and

1,000lb bombs was very serious in that gun positions and, in particular, radar installations were affected. The damage to military and naval installations on the island by Tallboy was very small.'[10]

All the Lancasters returned home to Britain safely. Such was the gratuitous callousness of the attack that it was described in one newspaper as making Heligoland look 'like a stale cake crumbling under a knife', and in Paul Brickhill's famous book *The Dam Busters* (1951) it was noted as having been done for the purpose of 'plastering' the island fortress.[11] This raid on Heligoland was the Dam Busters' penultimate attack of the war, the very last being the notoriously absurd bombing of Hitler's mountain hideaway at Berchtesgaden in the Bavarian Alps. Unable to distinguish the Führer's Eagle's Nest from the snow-covered mountains, they bombed the staff barracks.

Hitler's suicide that very day, 28 April, and the meeting of American and Russian troops on the Elbe on the 26th, meant the end of the war could not be far off. It came on 4 May, after a surrender document was signed in a small tent on Luneburg Heath. The following morning *The Times* reported the German capitulation with the headline 'Biggest Mass Surrender'. Astonishingly, in this historic report of the war's end in Europe, Heligoland was apparently regarded as being of such noteworthy significance that it had its own piece titled 'Heligoland's War Ends'. Field Marshal Montgomery had insisted in his ultimatum to the Germans at Luneburg that they 'must surrender to me unconditionally all German forces in Holland, Friesland, and the Frisian Islands, and in *Heligoland*'.[12] Subsequently puzzled by what to do with the captured island, Montgomery's headquarters wrote on 22 May 1945 to the Supreme Allied

Commander, General Eisenhower, to sound out his views on the prospect of Heligoland being utilised by the British Army as a concentration camp. Eisenhower immediately considered the idea, but the British Army declined the opportunity to use Heligoland for such a purpose.

Even on the very day of the Luneberg signing the Admiralty was taking no chances that the RAF had finally accomplished the silencing of Heligoland's huge guns. It stood ready to bring into action monitors similar to the pugnacious HMS *Mersey* and HMS *Severn*, which Churchill had ordered to be constructed in 1913 in anticipation of a British invasion of the island. On 4 May the English admiral in command of naval forces in the Heligoland Bight issued a memo concerning the monitors, which 'have been brought to 4 hours' notice to steam and I consider these should accompany the minesweeping force to provide retaliatory action against Heligoland, should interference be experienced'.[13]

9

'Big Bang'

Given the severity of the bombing of Heligoland on 18–19 April 1945, German military losses there were surprisingly light: just over one hundred men were killed, mostly at the flak guns. Miraculously, all but three Heligolanders had survived unscathed, deep in their air-raid shelter. But for all of them, life was to change dramatically. With every house in the Oberland and Unterland either destroyed or rendered uninhabitable, the entire population was now homeless. The only protection afforded them from the elements were the air-raid shelters, but those cramped spaces could only realistically serve to provide a few hours' refuge. Apparently there was not enough space for them in the labyrinth of military underground tunnels, either. It seemed to the British naval authorities that the only alternative was for them to be deported to the mainland. This immediately meant a few new and entirely unexpected worries: where would they go, how long would they be gone, and what would happen to their beloved island in their absence? By the evening of 12 May four confiscated German steamers had taken the islanders across the dangerous waters of the Bight – during which journey they were at risk of being sunk by Allied submarines or aircraft – to the mainland to begin their uncertain future.

Victorious though Britain was, she struggled to muster enough of her own warships for the purpose of communicating with Heligoland. Astonishingly, the British occupation of the island began when an English admiral and an infantry company of Scots Guards were conveyed there in captured enemy warships. On 11 May 1945 Rear-Admiral Muirhead Gould, the naval commander in north-west Germany, travelled to Heligoland with a staff of gunnery and disarmament experts in a German R-boat (a small but powerfully armed coastal escort vessel), with a German crew. Before the admiral was piped aboard, the breech-blocks of the guns were removed and the scuttling charges disarmed. During the voyage the German crew gathered aft, except for the commanding officer who remained on the bridge. As they approached the island this officer, proudly wearing the Iron Cross, respectfully addressed the Admiral: 'Heligoland in sight, Sir.'

At that stage there appeared five ships of the 7th German Minesweeping Flotilla, ships of the famous M-class which had given the Royal Navy so much trouble during the war. These ships carried the Scots Guards detachment who were to form the temporary garrison under the command of Major Raeburn. As they steamed into the dock at Heligoland they passed two merchant ships full of some 2,500 German soldiers. These men had made up the island's garrison and manned its guns: not just the great guns of the fortress, which had never been fired in anger, but also the flak guns, which had been very busy throughout the war. Admiral Muirhead Gould stepped ashore on a jetty still strewn with debris from the last RAF raid. One member of his staff produced a document by which the Germans bound themselves to keep the surrender terms faithfully and in detail. Kapitan Roeggeler, the most senior German officer present, signed at once, using an overturned water-tank as a table.

The British personnel soon began to explore the island, their main concern being to see how many guns had been put out of action in the two RAF raids. Several big ones had been knocked sideways, with great gaping holes in their turrets. One gun turret was pointing skyward – but little was left of it apart from the barrel. It seemed evident that no emplacement could withstand a direct hit from the earthquake bombs.

Just outside the submarine harbour were seven sleek black U-boats. Whether or not they had been stationed at Heligoland was not apparent. Close inspection showed that – in contrast to the turrets – the huge, long U-boat shelters with three pens had suffered no damage, except that bits of concrete had been chipped off the roof. Inside, the 14ft thick roof showed no sign of even a crack and all the apparatus for repair and maintenance was in good condition. Outside, the spring sun blazed strongly down on the wreckage of homes and gun batteries, but inside the U-boat shelter it was cool and refreshing.[1]

The surviving fortifications at that time were mainly centred on the island's south-east corner. Beneath the gun emplacements lay a honeycomb of underground shelters, vaults and passages. They contained machines and other items worth millions of pounds which might serve the cause of peaceful reconstruction – modern machines, a completely equipped power station, diesel trains all ready to take to the rails, plus materials and tools of all kinds. What has never been brought to light is that Lt-Commander C. Aylwin, who had been left in charge by Muirhead Gould, between

11 and 17 May 1945 (when the island was finally abandoned) gradually discovered the island's defences, contrary to what had been assumed, were anything but formidable. In a secret memo to the Admiralty,[2] Aylwin soon reported that a minefield against Aphrodite radio-controlled bomber attackers had been found at the harbour entrance; although in all other respects the fortress's remaining armaments were astonishingly out of date. The sighting and control systems in the red flak tower were pre-war; throughout the island all the guns were only fired by percussion; the daunting 12inch guns at the Schröder battery had originally come from the elderly German ship *Derflinger*; while the 170mm guns at the southern battery, which had come from the heavy cruiser *Alsace*, had been made in 1901. Other than some barbed wire there were so few defences against a landing taking place the island could have been captured from the sea had an assault been made a few hours after the 1,000-bomber raid. Three German officers, having been quizzed as to why most of the gun equipment was so old, said: 'First came the Luftwaffe, then the Navy, then the West Wall, then the Eastern Front, then everything else, and finally Heligoland.' They regarded themselves as the fifth front.

During the interrogation of Kapitan Leutnant Deckert, a specialist in torpedo work, Aylwin was astonished to learn that the island had *not* been used as a U-boat base, and no U-boat had ever drawn any torpedoes or mines from the huge stockpiles there. Orders had been received from the German Admiralty, in conformity with the general scorched earth policy, to blow up the military installations; but this was never done. But also, as the war neared its end there had evidently been an intention to turn Heligoland into a supply base as part of a wider German scheme to establish a northern redoubt. Accordingly, Aylwin was able to report, he had uncovered a huge intact store of food on the island – enough for 5,000 people for three months. The significance of that, which was never publicly disclosed, was that those foodstocks were of such quantity that the means were available to enable the Heligolanders to survive on the island. Yet the mass deportation of civilians had gone ahead.

Britain's formal need to bring about the destruction of all of these defences resulted from the terms of the 1945 Potsdam Agreement, which established the political and economic principles governing the treatment of Germany in the initial period of Allied control. It was held that Potsdam required the *complete* disarmament of the German armed forces and the destruction of *all* German fortifications and military installations surplus to Allied requirements. In the process of calculating what would be required to destroy the fortifications on each of the Frisian Islands, in 1945 Field Marshal Montgomery's planners carefully estimated that the effort needed to accomplish that on Heligoland would be 48,400 hours of labour, and 730 tons of explosives.

In July 1945 a naval party, NP 1746, under the command of Commander F.W. Sandwich RN, came ashore and started work on primary disarmament. Some 4,300 tons of machinery, equipment and all the food were transferred to Cuxhaven and 500 tons of ammunition were dumped in the sea, just a few hundred yards due north of the roadstead between Heligoland and Dune. A careful glance at the latest Admiralty chart shows that the remains of those bombs are still there. Significantly, this clearance operation was already in progress *before* the Potsdam Conference, which took place on 17 July and 2 August 1945.

The Heligolanders suspected at the time that Britain's overriding wish was to destroy the island itself. When they had been compelled to leave their island they had been allowed to take with them only what they could carry. It was for this reason that, in addition to the German naval and military officers who had awaited Muirhead Gould's arrival on the island, there stood an anxious crowd of fishermen, many of them hoping that the order to evacuate the island might be postponed. It was a forlorn hope. The islanders' suspicions of British motives were well founded. At the Potsdam Conference British negotiators evidently made no effort to spare some of the island's fortified facilities for the peaceful use of the Heligolanders. The diplomatic process rolled on and soon the term 'fortification' was defined for the purpose of Potsdam in Control Council Directive no. 22. That scheduled the Heligoland U-boat shelters as a Priority One target, due for destruction by June 1947; the remainder of the fortifications were Priority Two, to be destroyed by December 1948.

Soon after the Potsdam Conference, Sandwich's naval party was withdrawn. This was to enable the RAF to do special bomb trials with the submarine shelters as the target, for the next few months. By 1946 the most curious aspect of Britain's handling of this postwar bombing activity against Heligoland was that no one seemed to be in overall charge. And yet, almost by a hidden hand, various military activities were being arranged to take place there. It was almost as if someone, or some secretive small group, had reason to be especially careful not to be seen to be associated with such activities. Whatever it was, it was a dangerous game because the consequences were becoming lethal. On 19 July 1946 a team of Royal Marine demolition experts had just arrived by boat to reconnoitre the island when they realised something was very wrong. Overhead there was the roar of approaching heavy aircraft and RAF bombers passed over on their final sortie to drop experimental bombs on the island. Furious messages were sent between the differing forces as the bombs were already falling. By sheer chance there were no casualties. Heading the reconnaissance party was Captain L.P. Skipwith RN, the naval officer in command at Cuxhaven. He was furious as he stormed about the already badly cratered island. On completing his inspection he turned to a subordinate, Frank Woosnam, who was to supervise the implementation of the Potsdam directives, and instructed him to arrange to 'blow the bloody place up'.

It was to be a historic act of demolition, perhaps the greatest the Royal Navy had ever performed. Preparations for Operation 'Big Bang', the purpose of which was to destroy the fortifications in one massive explosion, commenced on 15 August 1946 when the Royal Navy took to the island the accommodation hulk *Royal Prince*, aboard which was a demolition team consisting of a Royal Marine captain, 3 officers, 3 petty officers, 12 German technicians and 70 German labourers. Some of the explosive power was already there in the form of many hundreds of torpedo warheads and depth-charges, tens of thousands of shells and grenades, and hundreds of thousands of rounds of small arms ammunition. The problem was how to make absolutely sure it all exploded simultaneously. The simple answer to this puzzle unexpectedly came to Woosnam while he was having a bath: he would rig the detonator wires like the ring main-type arrangement of a battleship. Thus if some of them were fractured at the moment of explosion the necessary current to the other detonators would reach them by other wires.

It was less clear what he would need to import from the mainland to be sure of achieving such a massive explosion. Wanting to be sure that all the munitions exploded, Woosnam sent a request to the British authorities in Germany for appropriate-quality explosive detonators. Inexplicably he was ordered to accept a massive consignment of TNT – 455,591 boxes! Also being sent from the mainland were many hundreds of tons of old munitions. Notionally these were also to be used to enhance the explosion in more inaccessible quarters of the fortifications. The transportation of these unsuitable and unwanted explosives to the island was a perilous operation. That winter was bitterly cold; the Elbe froze solid and conditions on Heligoland itself were bleak indeed. Bad weather and storms in the Bight greatly hampered the process of transferring the astonishing number of boxes of TNT to the island in the unseaworthy, shallow-draft landing-craft supplied.[3]

Seeing the red danger flags fluttering at the mastheads of those busy supply vessels carrying explosives across the Bight could only mean one thing to the Heligolandish lobster fishermen who witnessed it – Britain was intent on destroying their island. Like the rest of the islanders the fishermen had been exiled to the mainland, but so rich with sealife were the coastal waters off Heligoland that a few often ventured into the Bight to fish just offshore of their homeland – on which they were forbidden to land. A few of those fishermen still have vivid memories of what they saw and heard, and even now can readily quote a phrase they believe was used by one of the officers in charge at the time, about being intent on 'making Heligoland only fit for inhabitation by seagulls'. They are quite right. A check through some old copies of the Paris edition of the *New York Herald Tribune* reveals that on 6 January 1947 a virtually identical form of words was clearly used by a senior naval officer (believed to have been the NIOC at Cuxhaven, Captain Skipwith): 'When we have finished, it will be only a beautiful bird sanctuary, nothing but a pile of rocks.' He added that the island would not completely disappear, but considered it would 'never again be fit for human habitation'.

On the shelves of the Public Record Office at Kew there is an apparently innocuous archive file from the Air Ministry's Meteorological Office. Hitherto unnoticed it is entitled: *Seismology, Heligoland Explosion on 18.4.47 (including explosions in Germany, Bikini, etc).* The file was begun on 26 July 1946, just three days before Captain Skipwith's reconnaissance team landed on the island. Contained within the file is a letter from an organisation called the Armament Research Department, based at Fort Halstead near Sevenoaks in Kent. It is a detailed reply to a letter dated 20 August 1947 from Dr William Penney, who had been checking on the accuracy of the seismic equipment used at the Kew Observatory to monitor a recent huge explosion in Europe.[4]

Superficially, William Penney was a simple seismologist – but he also happened to be the Chief Superintendent of Armament Research. What no one knew at the time was that he had recently taken on other responsibilities. On 30 June 1946 he was one of the two British scientists present at Bikini Atoll in the

Marshall Islands in the Pacific to monitor Operation 'Crossroads' – the detonation of an experimental atomic bomb. On 24 July another device was exploded at Bikini, except this time it was done underwater. In February 1946 American officials, having informed the inhabitants of Bikini that their idyllic homeland was needed temporarily 'for the good of mankind to end all world wars', unceremoniously deported them to an inferior distant atoll. Dr Penney had been the coordinator of the blast-measuring instruments at Bikini, and on his return to England wrote a confidential fourteen-volume report on the explosions and the test equipment which had monitored them.[5]

The decision to research and develop a British atomic bomb was taken by a small inner circle of ministers, and in early 1946 Clement Attlee, the British Prime Minister, personally persuaded the semi-retired Viscount Portal of Hungerford to take the post of Controller of Production, Atomic Energy, and to assemble an appropriate team. Portal duly set up his headquarters in central London within the Ministry of Supply's Atomic Energy Directorate, in a wired-in enclosure on the fourth floor of Shell-Mex House. Ironically, this dour building in the Strand stood on a site owned long before by the politically powerful Salisbury dynasty! From there Portal recruited his senior personnel. These included Wing Commander (later Air Vice-Marshal) John 'Archie' Rowlands, who would be closely involved with the ballistic design of the weapon, and William Penney, who knew more than any other British scientist about the methods used to develop the American bomb.

Uncharacteristically for a scientist, William Penney had a talent for devising brilliantly innovative administrative structures. An opportunity to put that into effect occurred as a consequence of an inner-circle Cabinet meeting on 8 January 1947 at which the momentous decision was taken to proceed with the building of a British atomic bomb which could be test-exploded before summer 1952. The select few ministers present endorsed a memo sent by Portal, but based on Penney's ideas, describing how secrecy might best be maintained during this crucial development stage.[6] The recommendation accepted was that rather than building an atomic weapon through the ordinary agencies in the Ministry of Supply it should be developed under special arrangements conducive to the utmost secrecy. Penney's brilliant idea was that the facilities for the necessary research and development could be 'camouflaged' as Basic High Explosive Research – a subject for which he was actually responsible but on which no work was being done. It was agreed that just as had been done at Shell-Mex House, at Fort Halstead and Woolwich Arsenal special fenced-off enclaves should be formed within the main establishment.

The camouflage concept meant basing the work on a section within the Armaments Research Establishment, to form a cell there and subcontract bits of work to other parts of the government machine. To coordinate this subcontracted atomic bomb work, in November 1948 the High Explosives Research Operational Distribution Committee (HEROD) was established. Although in almost all respects the farming-out practice was ideal, even for the ballistics elements, there were a couple of components – the fusing system and radioactive parts of the bomb – which Penney's High Explosive Research (HER) boffins at Fort Halstead would need to do themselves. This decision necessitated taking on many more staff, and resulted in a move in early 1950 to a disused airfield site at Aldermaston in Berkshire, which subsequently became the Atomic Weapons Research Establishment (AWRE). No wonder Heligoland's links with the development of the atomic bomb remained hidden for so long.

No nuclear bomb was ever actually exploded on Heligoland, although it is quite probable that such a fate might have been contemplated for the island, however fleetingly. It appears that in five distinct respects – seismic measuring, blast effect, ballistic shape, crew training and USAF involvement – the island was used in the development of techniques, and in the collection of data required for the eventual testing of an atomic bomb elsewhere in the world.

'The greatest non-atomic explosion in history' was how *The Times* described the 'Big Bang' which occurred on 18 April 1947. There was an eerie sense of persecution about the entire operation. It happened at noon, precisely two years after the island's failure to surrender led to its initial devastation in a gratuitous RAF raid. And now the Royal Navy was all ready to finish it off. Safely aboard HMS *Lassco*, anchored 9 miles offshore, the moment the fourth pip in the BBC's time signal sounded Frank Woosnam pressed a firing button and detonated the 7,000 tons of munitions in the island's labyrinth of deep tunnels.

According to the *Daily Express*, 'From the island's centre, like a Bikini mushroom, rose a massing cauliflower of smoke as the blast from the deepest tunnels of the fortress 180 feet down in the rock surged to the surface.' The *New York Times* said 'the island seemed to rise out of the sea in a spectacular red and black explosive flame. In seconds, the cloud was twice the size of the island. As these layers moved off, one could see and feel the articles of red sandstone that gave the cloud its reddish tint.' Reporting an eyewitness from an observation plane describing the island as seeming to 'take off into the air', the Associated Press also claimed the blast was 'the biggest man-made explosion since the American Navy's atom bomb tests at Bikini'. The explosion had sent the tall Monk rock, one of the sandstone pillars carved by the seas, crashing into the waves. But when the 8,000ft column of smoke cleared it was evident that only about 14 per cent of the island's surface had fallen into the sea. All the rest stood firm, enhancing Heligoland's reputation for defiance.

According to the *New York Times* British newscasters to Germany were reported to have been 'asked to play down' coverage of the Big Bang. But some intriguing accounts did slip out, such as the *Daily Telegraph*'s showing that inexplicably, on an RAF Mosquito and a destroyer, HMS *Dunkirk*, there had been microphones to record the explosion.[7] Declassified confidential guest lists done at the time, of the numerous VIPs invited to witness the event from a safe distance on Royal Navy ships, make rather curious reading because they now appear to have noticeably refrained from mentioning the names of any important scientists there. Yet stories which appeared in the *New York Times* on 18 and 19 April 1947 stated that there were present senior American boffins from the acoustics department of the United States Naval Ordinance Laboratories. That ten-strong delegation had been headed by Dr John Atanasoff and Commander Beauregard Perkins who had also – the newspaper revealed – 'observed the Bikini explosions'. Important though they were, the absence of any mention in British official records indicates that the

British government was being careful not to draw attention to them. Yet, unexpectedly, a glimmer of their presence accidentally did slip out. On 18 April 1947 the *Daily Telegraph* happened to report that on the morning prior to the Big Bang the destroyer *Nepal* had arrived from the Forth and anchored off Heligoland. Intriguingly the article also noted the ship had brought 'a party of scientists. They have a seismograph and other apparatus with which to record the effects of the explosion.' Seemingly arriving among that party of scientists were members of William Penney's team. According to US Naval Intelligence records of Commonwealth warships the *Nepal* certainly existed then – it was a Royal Australian Navy destroyer stationed in British waters. That is why the Public Record Office has no incriminatory ship's log of such a Royal Navy vessel at that time.

The explosion was so powerful that it registered on over a hundred seismographs in seismic stations in various parts of Europe – notably in Germany, France and Britain (at Kew). However, what use was that to Penney's boffins at the HER if they could not be sure exactly what quantity of explosives produced such shock waves? The Hiroshima bomb had been equal to 12,500 tons of TNT – a yield of 12.5 kilotons. It was envisaged that the Heligoland 'Big Bang' explosion would be just over half of that at 7 kilotons – but it was not.

The event had long been stated by the Admiralty as being 'the greatest demolition operation ever performed by the Royal Navy', and officially their declared view of 'Big Bang' was that it had been 'A 100% successful operation'. They even publicly announced that all members of the demolition team would be recommended for decorations. In reality, to the consternation of senior naval officers, a significant proportion of the explosives had failed to go off. This was 62 tons of the mysteriously late-arrival TNT which had stubbornly refused to explode on the Heligoland quayside. Instructed to return to the island without publicity (including radio silence) and finish the job, Woosnam's team secretly arrived there on 22 April 1947 in an R-boat and a captured German submarine. Fresh cordex-linked charges having been laid, firing wires were led to the Red Tower. The ML 150 and the U-boat having been put to sea to ensure there were no other craft in the vicinity, that night Woosnam set off the detonation.

That so-called 'Little Bang' took the form of a bright flash, and because the cloud cover was low, the loud detonation report even rattled doors and windows in Cuxhaven.[8] Woosnam's superiors, who had wanted the 'Little Bang' explosion to be discreet, were again furious. Uninformed by him, because of the radio silence, as to when the explosion would take place, they despatched a British destroyer from Cuxhaven to investigate the bright flash. Unusually, in the absence of any official account, these events were chronicled in a file Woosnam himself deposited in the Public Record Office in March 1950. And so the story remained hidden until January 1980, when – still not having received his medal – Woosnam found an Admiralty note in the newly opened PRO file accusing him of having made 'an error of judgement'. Indignant at being so besmirched he privately deposited a fuller chronicle, which significantly noted there had been no reprimand for any officer for the, still unexplained, despatch of the superfluous TNT to Heligoland.

The rest of the world must have assumed that once the almighty 'Big Bang' had been carried out there could be no need for further static explosions on the island. In fact during the summer of 1947 Penney's HER's interest in extracting seismic data from Heligoland became more focused. Released official papers show that on 30 May 1946 a special meeting was held at the Ministry of Works. In response to 'the advent of the atomic bomb', an urgent need was expressed by Sir Geoffrey Taylor, the Chairman of the Civil Defence Research Committee, to obtain seismic records by which to have a better knowledge of the propagation of blast in air-raid tunnels and other confined spaces. Taylor, a British scientist earlier assigned to the Manhattan Project, had made a name for himself as an expert in blast waves caused by high explosives. Penney was present at that meeting whose minutes show that, in terms of tunnels to be used for test explosions supervised by the Directorate of Armament Research, 'It was agreed that the most suitable tunnels were those on Heligoland'. Inexplicably that Civil Defence Committee gathering had before it a memo by their Chief Defence Advisers hypothetically noting that: 'If an atomic bomb equivalent to 20,000 tons of TNT were exploded 100 feet below ground there would result a crater estimated to contain, initially, about ten million tons of soil.'[9] Then on 22 April 1947, just three days after the 'Big Bang' the Committee – still including Penney – met again, this time at the Ministry of Supply, and agreed that 'part of the tunnel system at Heligoland should be used' in specialist trial explosions to determine the effect of shock waves.

The person selected to obtain readings was Major F. Taggart of the innocuous-sounding 'Explosive Storage and Transport Committee', based at Woolwich in an enclave codenamed B43. Contrary to press claims, not quite all of Heligoland's tunnels had been blown up in April 1947. One area remained: the only civilian air-raid shelter, known as the Spirale. Situated in the centre of the western side of the rock, it was a deep double spiral tunnel which led up to the surface of the Oberland. The tunnels were fitted with three tiers of bunks all the way up, and there the whole civilian population used to shelter when the island was bombed. A now declassified (but hitherto unopened) Foreign Office document (FO 371, German General Economic, 1947) reveals that on 5 November 1947 Taggart wrote a letter in which he clearly stated that it was desirous 'to obtain detailed information about the area covered by a radius of 200 yards from the Spirale which is adjacent to the north-east harbour'. He then went on to request a large-scale map, '25 inches to the mile at least'.

During the summer of 1947 the Explosive Storage and Transport Committee (which seems to have been an integral part of Penney's HER) became determined to keep this new seismic data from other scientists. The 'Big Bang' on 18 April had been a fairly high-profile event, and the Royal Society had been allowed to take its own seismic observations (as they had at some other large demolitions at Soltan on the German mainland). Their agent, in that respect, which had obtained permission for them, was the Department of Geodesy and Geophysics at the University of Cambridge. That department's Dr Edward Bullard had also attended the April 'Big Bang'. Having heard that Major Taggart was intending to conduct some unusual experiments on Heligoland in early September 1947, both the Royal Society and Dr Bullard wrote to the Foreign Office in London to ask them to forward their request to attend that autumn's test explosion. The letter of recommendation, dated 14 August 1947, from the Foreign Office's London headquarters to the German Section, is particularly illuminating because it revealed for the first time that German experts under Allied protection were cooperating in these test activities in Heligoland.[10] It stated: 'You will remember that valuable scientific observations were made on Heligoland early this year by British scientists from the Royal Society, with the cooperation of Research Branch CCG and German experts.' With regard to the demolitions which it understood were due to take place in September 1947 it said that the Royal Society again wished to be present to undertake extensive seismological observations of its own: 'We presume the Research Branch will make the necessary arrangements as before. Please ensure that the British and German scientists engaged in this operation receive all the facilities necessary to make that a success.'

However, in sharp contrast to their cooperativeness earlier in the year, the Research Branch were now utterly unwilling to encourage witnesses to the unusual explosions that Major Taggart was preparing to conduct. In a rather disgruntled letter of 29 August 1947, responding to the Foreign Office request, it refused to cooperate, claiming that such visitors could not be allowed because there was an acute shortage of rations. The author of this letter was clearly harassed, and in the course of his annoyed ramblings let slip that the department already had enough to do with other 'Matchbox' projects on which German boffins were employed. These were technicians who were brought over to the British side immediately after the end of the war. Some of them were atomic scientists who became involved in Britain's own atomic bomb-making project.

Sir Geoffrey Taylor, chairman of the Civil Defence Research Committee, had been influential in another respect. It was he who, having realised how invaluable was Penney's special knowledge of the behaviour of shock waves, earlier recommended he be appointed Chief Superintendent of Armament Research; and so, in effect, the head of Britain's A-bomb programme. Penney was fascinated by a phenomenon called 'base surge' which he had witnessed at Bikini Atoll. In an Atomic Weapons Research Establishment report, written in January 1948, he defined it as: 'When a column of spray and mist is thrown into the air by an underwater explosion it subsequently collapses under gravity and spreads over the water surface, giving a so-called Base Surge.'[11] In the early years of Britain's A-bomb research development Penney envisaged the most likely targets for such a weapon in wartime as being estuaries and harbours full of enemy shipping. With that in mind on 19 May 1948 he had written to Vice-Admiral Daniel, the Controller of the Navy: 'Recently I have been trying to work out the minimum depth of water which will give a base surge for an atomic bomb of present design.' Describing the need for the research, he had admitted in his January report: 'It is of importance to know the laws governing the collapse and spread of the column, and for this reason Trial Charybdis was devised.'

A released Foreign Office paper, FO 371, indicates that Heligoland's Dune isle was the first choice of site for the experiment. On 13 August 1947 it stated that 'Major Taggart is conducting experiments on Dune in September of this year'. That was confirmed in a September 1947 Atomic Weapons Research Establishment report of the 'Charybdis' trial, the stated purpose of which was to monitor the outward movement of a falling vertical column of water which had been ‘formed by atomisation’. This AWRE report, now available, clearly states: ‘It was considered that the trial might be carried out with surplus naval depth charges and the possibility was examined of carrying one or more experiments on the 20,000lb scale near the island of Heligoland during the progress of other trials for the Explosive Storage and Transport Committee.’ But instead, for undisclosed reasons, it was decided to do the test detonation in shallow waters 1,800 yards off Foulness Island on the northern edge of the Thames estuary. The apparatus used in the first Charybdis detonation consisted of conventional naval torpex depth charges together with cordex fuse-wire (for instantaneous detonation), elements of which – other than the precise hexagonal lattice pattern in which they were closely packed – were most similar to those used by Woosnam on Heligoland just a few months earlier. The first such test explosion occurred at Foulness on 3 October 1947.

Although notionally just an ‘enclave’ within the Army’s Shoeburyness range, as early as November 1945 the Foulness range adjacent to that had been prepared for Penney’s HER team to use for experimental work on bombs and shells. By 1947 Foulness was effectively an AWRE range with its own blast measurement group. In 1950 actual radiation explosions were being carried out there. On 2 May of that year the Superintendent of Armament Research at Foulness wrote a letter to the Admiralty’s Director of Physical Research, claiming ‘we would be happy to agree’ to it being used for the Admiralty’s ‘next series of radiation measurement experiments’. Heligoland seems to have be lucky, insofar as it was never used for actual radiation tests.

Irrespective of whether or not Britain was contemplating using Dune as a shallow-water site for a base surge test explosion, there is no doubt that on at least two occasions after the war chemical weapons tests were carried out on Heligoland. One type was white phosphorus, which was dropped at low level by RAF bombers. The evidence for this comes from Heligoland fishermen. One night rough seas in the Bight forced several Heligoland lobster boats to seek shelter in the harbour there – although the island was deserted and access to it forbidden. The fishermen heard the drone of approaching aircraft, and then several waves of bombers roared overhead at low level. As the first wave passed they heard a whistling sound as bombs fell through the air on to the already ruined Unterland. Then the pitch-black night sky was suddenly illuminated by numerous interlocking flashes of blinding light as the phosphorus bombs exploded, throwing off enormous heat and showers of cascading offshoots which fell all around the open, wooden lobster boats. Even now the surviving fishermen can readily recall their fear during that bombing trial. One, Karl Bloch, claims: 'When the next wave of bombers came in they were flying so low, and the light was so intense, I could actually clearly see the face of the pilot of one of them as it approached and sped over.' It seemed the Air Ministry was prepared to try out almost any type of weapon on the defenceless island.

Another hitherto unknown incident recalled by some older islanders occurred in the late 1940s. They make the astonishing claim that Britain had planned to explode a 100-ton ammonium nitrate bomb on the island. This scheme came to light when the ship carrying the chemicals for that trial exploded in the

English Channel. Even so, they believe, some chemicals were saved and did reach Heligoland. Far-fetched it might seem but in fact compelling written evidence does exist in the Public Record Office in Kew, verifying the truth of their account. The declassified document AVIA 6/18589, written in February 1949, shows in words, diagrams and photographs that a huge chemical apparatus *was* assembled and burnt off on the island by British technicians. Since the early 1930s, when it became known that ammonium nitrate exploded when rapidly heated, it had been used as a constituent of various explosives. It was often described as a 'fertiliser bomb', but it had rarely been exploded on a large scale by itself. This February 1949 Royal Aircraft Establishment report, *Analysis of Gas Samples from the Heligoland Nitrate Trials of Ammonium Nitrate*, shows that a working party had been sent to the island to use specially constructed instruments to obtain gas samples of the atmosphere around fires burning in a bunker.

In April 1947 the fortifications and U-boat shelters had been destroyed and thus the Potsdam terms fulfilled. This then was surely the time for Britain to stop all its military activity on Heligoland. Yet in some respects its involvement with the island was increasing. A memo in the secret Foreign Office file FO 371 (German General Economic), dated 1 December 1947, reported that: 'The Explosive Storage and Transport Committee's *series of explosives trials* [author's emphasis] on Heligoland and Dune has now been completed and all naval and military personnel and equipment were evacuated to Cuxhaven on 27 November 1947. The islands are required by the Air Ministry for bombing practice from 1 December 1947.'

The public were never informed that the RAF's 10-ton Grand Slam bombs only achieved spectacular successes against a few U-boat shelters; on others where the concrete was thicker – as at Heligoland, Farge and Bergen – they had virtually no effect. With a perceived need to urgently develop a better and 'tropicalised' version of this weapon against Japan, the war in Europe having been won, the Chiefs of Staff initially met on 3 June 1945 to consider an RAF proposal for using Heligoland as a live bombing range at which to improve it. Seemingly Heligoland's U-boat pens were of interest because they were the first Germany built with the especially heavy roofs. For the Air Force the unfortunately named Sir Douglas Evill said use of the island as a bombing range was urgently required until the defeat of Japan. Discussing the matter again on 14 June the Chiefs were persuaded by Sir Charles Portal to accept their argument on the grounds that there were 'increasing difficulties in retaining existing ranges, and of obtaining new ones'. Two days later the Prime Minister, Winston Churchill, informed the Air Ministry that he had no objection to the island being used as a live bombing range.

Peace had already been declared in the Far East when Project 'Harken' went ahead. Poor visibility over the Bight prevented it commencing until 1 January 1946. Modified Lancasters of 15 Squadron flew from Suffolk to drop various types of 12,000lb Tallboys from various heights.[12] In 1945 it involved American forces based in Britain: the 8th Army Air Force using B-17s. In March 1946 Project 'Ruby', their name for dropping experimental earthquake bombs on Heligoland, was joined by B-29 aircraft which had just arrived in the UK and were stationed at Mildenhall – the same base as 15 Squadron. Declassified photos now show that even if dropped from 20,000ft the earthquake bombs scarcely had any effect on the U-boat shelter. Nevertheless the Anglo-American trials continued until July 1946, and it was during the course of the last of them that Captain Skipworth's reconnaissance team was nearly wiped out.

The Chiefs of Staff had become so keen on Heligoland during the summer of 1946 that they had put in a secret request to the Cabinet's Foreign Affairs and Defence Committee for assurances that it could be used as a bombing range for the next ten to fifteen years! To them it seemed the ideal solution, and in the course of time it would also put the island beyond all prospect of being reinhabited – and thus refortified. This view was reiterated as late as 1950 in a secret paper the Air Ministry sent to the Chiefs of Staff Committee. Written on 2 February of that year, it stated quite categorically: 'the use of Heligoland as a bombing range had the additional considerable advantage of effectively demilitarising the island while the practice bombing continues.'

On 9 August 1946, just a fortnight after the Heligoland trials ended, the Air Ministry sent Penney detailed specifications for Britain's envisaged free-fall atomic bomb – which was to be called 'Blue Danube'. Those design requirements were much influenced by the capacity of the Lincolns (modified Lancasters) which might need to convey the bombs until June 1953, when the V-bombers were expected to enter service. Thus Penney was told: 'The bomb should not exceed 290 inches in height, 60 in diameter; its weight must not exceed 10,000lb; and it must be suitable for release between 20,000ft and 50,000ft, at 150–500 knots.' In October 1947 it was added that, in order to produce an effective underwater explosion, the bomb would need to withstand the shock of impact with water.[13]

William Penney knew there were advantages to be gained from replicating, in some respects, the United States' experiences with evolving the Hiroshima-type bomb, called 'Little Boy'. Dropped by a B-29 Superfortress over Japan on 6 August 1945 from a height of 31,600ft, the 9,000lb Little Boy bomb was some 28in in diameter and 120in long (a ratio of 7:30).[14] He would also have known that Britain already had a suitable bomb casing to deliver an atomic weapon, in the form of the Tallboy earthquake bomb. Weighing 12,000lb, it was 38in in diameter and 252in long (a not too dissimilar ratio of 19:126). Moreover, it was widely known that however blunt an instrument the atomic weapon seemed to be, to make the fullest use of its destructive power it needed to reach the target with pinpoint accuracy. The Tallboy could achieve exactly that. Precision-built, its aerodynamic fuselage caused the bomb to spin faster and hence allowed greater accuracy. However, it was also perceived that the RAF needed to be able to drop such a bomb accurately from an altitude of some 35,000ft and this, as yet, it had not perfected.

Meanwhile, despite the bombing range being temporarily closed while Woosnam rigged Heligoland for the 'Big Bang', the development of the Tallboy bomb continued. By September 1946 15 Squadron had been switched to dropping trial versions of it on the U-boat assembly shelter at Farge, near Bremen. At the Shoeburyness experimental establishment ballistic trials were conducted on models of the fuselage; and static conventional explosions of the Tallboy were done on the mudflats there, near the AWRE's Foulness range. Design and prototype production was now shifting away from Tallboy's originators, Vickers-Armstrong, towards the Royal Aircraft Establishment

(RAE) working on an agency basis for Penney's team. This meant that even Barnes Wallis, the inventor of the Grand Slam, was largely sidelined, although his views were sought. His diaries – now open at Imperial College, London – reveal that on 19–21 July 1945 he visited bomb-damaged Cuxhaven, and might have gone to Heligoland; on 26 October 1945 he had a 'Meeting at Thames House – official introduction to the [Secret Intelligence] Service'; on 30 October 1945 he attended a 'Tallboy Panel (Experiments)'; and as late as 7 February 1952 he was corresponding with the RAE at Farnborough who had requested Tallboy and Grand Slam technical data from him.[15]

Codenamed Project 'Emulsion', a 1,000lb streamlined bomb was the simple evolutionary link by which the Tallboy was recognisably developed into the casing for Britain's atomic bomb. A secret report on 'Emulsion' acknowledged this as early as May 1948: 'The bomb shape chosen was similar to Tallboy, which experience had shown to behave well ballistically from medium altitude and a 1,000lb size was used for convenience in trials. The first step in the stabilisation of bombs at transonic and supersonic speeds was made by choosing the Tallboy shape of body and fitting five different types of tail to it. It was found that a fine spin 1.4 x bomb diameter was adequate to stabilise this bomb at the speeds reached with release at *35,000 feet* and 350 mph.'[16]

Emulsion was initially tested in the United States at the USAF's Aberdeen proving ground at Atomic City, Idaho. Then, in 1949, the trial drops were focused on at the Orfordness bombing range on the Suffolk coast. Orfordness – where Penney's AWRE had established another of their characteristic enclaves – was serviced by a secret RAE airfield nearby, called Martlesham

Heath. Struggling along with a special flight of four fatigued bombers (two Lincolns and two Mosquitos), the RAE were required to complete the series of Emulsion drop tests for the AWRE. However, because of unserviceable aircraft and inclement weather, during the winter of 1949/50 they fell behind schedule. Martlesham's declassified operations record book discloses that in May pressure was increased by the delivery of unarmed prototypes of the Blue Danube: 'A new task has been added, and the particular stores have been received and dropping has commenced. For this purpose a specially modified Lincoln has been received.'[17] The number of sorties flown leapt in May, and the next month reached 33. Indeed, by June 1950 Penney and his scientists at Fort Halstead had put together a mock-up of the as yet untested British atomic bomb, codenamed 'Blue Danube', for members of the HEROD Committee to inspect. Was it at this crucial time that Martlesham's secret AWRE flight bombed Heligoland?

Inexplicably it was then that a specialist metal recovery programme, from early 1950 to early 1951, was instigated for the island. Every fortnight teams of metal collectors were to land on Heligoland to gather strategically valuable scrap. Somewhat intriguingly its codename was Operation 'Top Hat' – the confidential name used on the mainland to identify key physicists working for the occupying Allies.[18] To this day Heligoland fishermen who happened to witness the postwar test bombings insist that the heavy bombs dropped had mostly concrete centre sections. This is not surprising because the use of concrete would have enabled the HER scientists to experiment cheaply and easily with various shapes. The fin and tail were presumably made of distinctively shiny blue chrome molybdenum steel.

In the postwar years the British government never publicly revealed just how vital Heligoland was considered to be by a small miscellaneous group of influential officials. On 2 February 1950 the Chiefs of Staff Committee sent a paper to the Cabinet's Defence and Overseas Policy Committee, which at the time was considering the future of Heligoland. In no uncertain terms the Chiefs insisted: 'We consider it possible that if bombing-range facilities of the type provided in Heligoland were withdrawn the USAF might reconsider the basing of bombers in this country in peacetime.' Heligoland clearly represented a valuable card to play in the crucial game of keeping the United States involved in Europe. Only when NATO was formed in April 1949 was there a binding commitment from the United States to help defend Western Europe against a possible threat from the East.[19]

The USAF's Strategic Air Command deployment in Britain of B-29A Superfortresses, which had an A-bomb carrying capacity, began in July 1948 in response to the Berlin Crisis. Until bombing ranges for the B-29As were opened in Iceland and West Africa they mostly practised their nuclear targeting skills with conventional weapons against Heligoland, where in September 1948 they jointly participated in Exercise 'Dagger' with the RAF. To keep the strength of the SAC's presence in Britain obscure, various USAF B-29A squadrons were rotated on three-month tours of duty; while the UK airfields from which they operated were made to seem to be still entirely RAF bases.

This is evident from a paper issued by the Chiefs of Staff on 2 February 1950, which twice refers, very clearly, to the range having been used by both the RAF and the USAF since 1946, and later mentions its being 'also in continual use by the USAF bombers based in

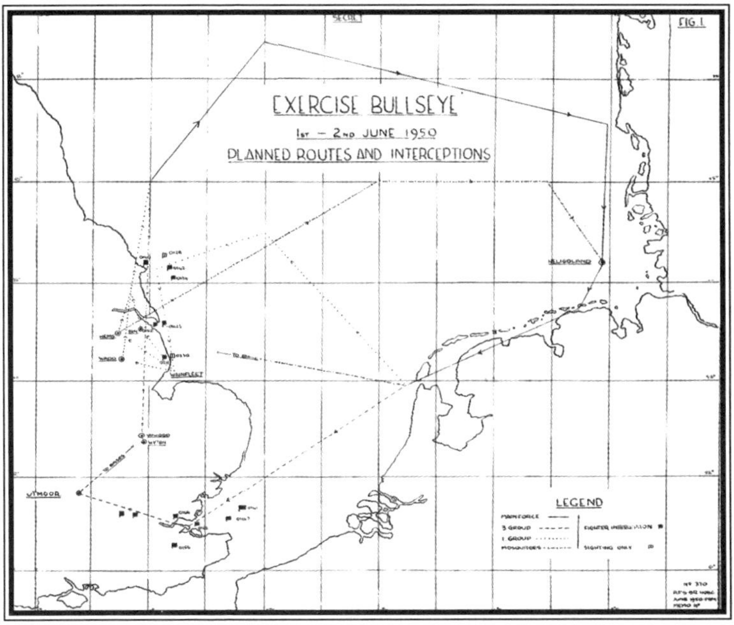

Map 8 Exercise 'Bullseye': five years after the Second World War, Heligoland was still being heavily pounded by the RAF. On 1–2 June 1950 it was test bombed by 88 Lancasters and Mosquitos in Exercise 'Bullseye'. Pleas of the 2,500 exiled islanders to be allowed to return to their homeland were rejected; and the British High Commissioner in Germany threatened demonstrators with imprisonment. (*Public Record Office*)

this country'. Whether or not those American B-29A bombers were sometimes carrying practice atomic bombs is not clear. The island's location and shape provided the USAF and the RAF with an invaluable training venue. As the Chiefs of Staff had stated to ministers on 2 February 1950:

> We would emphasise that the need for a live bombing range such as Heligoland is not confined to the mere dropping of bombs. The long sea crossing provides unique opportunities to simulate realistic operational conditions, not only for the two Bomber

> forces, but also for our Air Defence System, which obtains valuable training in the reporting and intercepting of large forces of aircraft approaching from the east. In addition these practice bombing raids enable the pre-flight activities, navigation, target marking and other techniques concerning the approach and method of attack to be fully tested and evaluated on each occasion.[20]

In addition to bombing runs by a few isolated aircraft dropping experimental weapons, mass raids were carried out by bombers. Codenamed 'Bullseye', these began on 5 April 1946 with an attack by pathfinding Mosquitos and 44 Lancasters carrying 1,000lb bombs. The event was believed to have been the first RAF mass training exercise since the war ended. A similar 'Bullseye' bombing of Heligoland occurred on 2 June 1950.[21] Although each of the 49 Lincolns involved was ordered to take vertical pictures of the bomb releases and impacts none of those photographs is now known to exist.

The Prime Minister, Clement Attlee, had been warned in a top secret note sent by the Defence Research Policy Committee that 'If the atomic bomb is to be effective and economically used, the accuracy with which it is dropped must be of the high order achieved in the last stages of the last war.' New navigation devices would have to be developed, and presumably tested, to achieve maximum precision. 'The effort on these allied problems of navigation and accurate bombing is wholly insufficient and we are falling behind our target dates.' The need for precision bombing skills to be kept at the highest pitch by means of practice – both for conventional and atomic bombs – was affirmed at a special meeting of the secret

HEROD Committee, held specifically to discuss crew training on 16 November 1951. According to the minutes of that meeting: 'It was agreed that practice bombs were essential for the training of the Air and Group crews who would be responsible for the delivery of atomic bombs.' Heligoland was uniquely placed in this regard, as was admitted in the Chief of Staff's 2 February 1950 briefing paper: 'Heligoland is the *only* suitable site within a reasonable distance of Great Britain; no British islands are suitable.'

By March 1950, the RAF was starting to take delivery of seventy B-29A bombers loaned from America. Although, because of the restrictive McMahon Act, those B-29A Washingtons were prevented from being fitted with A-bomb racks, in all other respects they were identical to the SAC's own Superfortresses. Each of the eight RAF squadrons which operated the B-29A Washingtons practised their precision bombing techniques at the Heligoland range, sometimes in joint exercises with the USAF. Seemingly for some time prior to the introduction of the Canberra bombers – and then the Valiants in 1955 – it was on such Washington flights that future V-bomber aircrews were trained.

Whatever hopes Britain might have had of using Heligoland as a site for an atomic bomb test would have been finally dashed in the autumn of 1951 by a seemingly chance remark in an obscure telegram sent by the British Embassy in Washington to the Cabinet Office in London. The telegram concerned the United States' huge inland nuclear weapons test site in Nevada, and stated that 'One of the earliest Nevada explosions of only 1 kiloton had caused considerable window damage at 75 miles.' This apparently freak accident doubtless had a profound effect on any thoughts Penney and his team might have had of carrying out an atomic test on Heligoland. The Nevada accident appears to have been caused by detonating the atomic bomb too close to the mountains, which had the effect of greatly exaggerating the blast and widening the area affected by an enormous distance. Penney, who was an expert in blast and seismological effects, must have been reminded of the huge explosion caused on Heligoland on 15 October 1944 when the Aphrodite bomber crashed in the Unterland, wrecking the Biological Institute there and demolishing 24,600 sq. yards of domestic property. In a report written on 29 November 1944, D.G. Christopherson of the Armament Department of the Ministry of Home Security noted that the scale of the blast damage appeared to have been influenced by the shock waves bouncing off the cliff. This was neatly illustrated with a bull's-eye target diagram.[22] It seemed likely that if an atomic bomb were tested in the shallow water off Sandy Island, shock waves would bounce off the cliffs of Heligoland and cause structural damage to buildings at Cuxhaven, just 30 miles across the Bight at the mouth of the Elbe, and perhaps even affect other towns and villages along the German North Sea coast. This put an end to the possibility of Heligoland being used for an atomic bomb test.

The obvious alternative was to use Eniwetok Range, the United States' testing ground – from where inhabitants had recently been exiled – in the Marshall Islands. Unfortunately, the timing for seeking permission to use that could hardly have been worse. As early as November 1945 Attlee and President Truman had signed the Washington Agreement to allow full and effective cooperation in atomic bomb development. Under the terms of this Dr Penney was involved with America's A-bomb tests at Bikini Atoll. But in August 1946 the United States Congress had passed the McMahon Act prohibiting the passing of classified atomic information to *any* foreign country – including Britain. Even so, at a working level some exchanges of data did continue to take place between America and Britain. Pressure on Dr Penney to get Britain's atomic bomb completed was further increased in August 1949 when the Soviet Union carried out its first atomic bomb test. Then in January 1950 disaster struck. Klaus Fuchs, the Imperial College traitor and the only other senior British scientist at the Bikini Atoll tests (where he helped to plan blast experiments against decommissioned warships), was arrested at Harwell, accused of passing secret information about Britain's atomic bomb programme to the Russians between 1942 and 1949.

The huge breach of trust caused by the discovery of Fuchs' treachery meant that all Anglo-American technical cooperation on the bomb was abruptly halted, hence the additional difficulty in finding a suitable test site to replace Heligoland. On 3 June 1950 Attlee received a grim top secret memo from his officials: 'As you know, from your recent talk with the US Secretary of State [Dean Acheson], the prospects of our getting an atomic energy agreement with the Americans are bleak. Meanwhile the Ministry of Supply will shortly be reaching the point when they must know whether or not they can count on using the American testing ground at Eniwetok.' In the face of this uncertainty, the HEROD team urgently began to search for a venue for testing Britain's bomb.

It is usually assumed that somehow or other the idea of testing the atomic bomb on the Australian island of Monte Bello just appeared. But other sites were considered. This is evident from a secret telegram Attlee sent to the Australian Prime Minister Sir Robert Menzies on 15 September 1950, in which he spoke about the problems of obtaining the use of Eniwetok: 'Meanwhile it is clearly advisable', wrote Attlee, 'if only as a precaution, to consider possible alternative sites in British Commonwealth territory.' The curious wording of this sentence is ambiguous: did he mean '*a* British Commonwealth territory' or several Commonwealth 'territories'? It seems that the plural was intended because Attlee continued: 'One possible site which has been suggested by our experts is the Monte Bello Islands.' The use of the phrase 'One possible site' is crucial because it indicates that there were other sites under consideration. Indeed, on 8 September 1949 Air Marshal William Elliot, recommending that an interdepartmental committee be established on the subject, prepared a list of possible areas for test sites, namely: Australia; Botswana (E. Kalahari); Canada (Eastern); Namibia (near Walvis Bay) and Gobabis (W. Kalahari); Rhodesia; and Somaliland (near Berber).[23] A report by the Chief of Staff under the heading 'Testing of UK Atomic Weapon', apparently naming these and other possible sites, was sent to the Chiefs of Staff and the inner circle of ministers on 31 August 1950. Was British-controlled Heligoland one such site? File AE (M)(50)9, which contains written proof of that discussion, was unwittingly made available to the Public Record Office in 1985. Apparently the Cabinet Office then attempted a cover-up. On 17 July 1990 an official from the Prime Minister's office at 10 Downing Street, which was then occupied by Margaret Thatcher, purposely went to that nuclear testing file and removed pages which presumably mentioned

Heligoland, leaving several incriminating handwritten notes declaring: 'This file has been removed and destroyed.' Coincidentally perhaps, the archive destruction began just a fortnight before the 100th anniversary of the Heligoland swap.

A surreptitious reconnaissance of Monte Bello, and the treacherous waters around it, was made by British military personnel in October 1950. 'Operation Hurricane' – the preparation of the site for a nuclear test – began in the spring of 1952 with the arrival from Britain of an aircraft carrier and a host of supply vessels bringing miles of cables and instruments to record the effects of contamination, blast, heat flash and other factors of interest.[24] Before leaving England the seismic and blast equipment had been tested in huge explosions at Shoeburyness in the Thames estuary.

The selection of Monte Bello saved Heligoland from utter destruction. In many respects there were astonishingly close geographical and logistical similarities between the two islands. Each had received a reconnaissance party, each had a shallow water area and each lay some 30 miles distant from the north-west point of a continent.

On 22 March 1951 the British High Commissioner in Canberra received a top secret telegram from London predicting the devastating effect the test would have on the inhabitability of the islands. It would

> contaminate with radio-activity the north group and that contamination may spread to the other of the islands. The area is not likely to be entirely free of contamination for about three years. During this time the area will be unsafe for human occupation or even for visits, by for example pearl fishermen who

> we understand at present go there from time to time, and suitable measures will need to be taken to keep them away.

Under the guidance of William Penney, the first British atomic bomb was exploded there on the morning of 3 October 1952 at a strength of 20 kilotons – equivalent to that of the Nagasaki bomb. It was placed in the hull of the disused frigate HMS *Plym*, anchored in shallow water, and when the first flash burst through the hull the temperature was nearly 1 million degrees. Britain had joined the nuclear club just fractionally later than the five years Portal had planned it would take. In November 1953 the Blue Danube bomb entered service with the RAF. Three weeks after the Monte Bello explosion the Prime Minister made a lengthy public statement in celebration of the successful test. On the effects it would have on the lives of the fishermen who had made their living around that Australian island, curiously Churchill said not one word. What he considered really mattered was that: 'No animals were used in the test, no mammals were seen in the affected area and such birds as there were had mostly been frightened away by earlier precautions.'

10

The Islanders Return

In Britain there was virtually no limit to the concerns expressed by the government and various influential naturalist institutions for the welfare of the seabirds and other wildlife on Heligoland. In October 1943 the Council of the Royal Society for the Protection of Birds had met at their headquarters in Victoria Street, Westminster, and resolved to recommend to the Foreign Office, after the close of hostilities, that Heligoland be acquired as an international ornithological observatory. Then on 11 May 1945 *The Times* printed a letter from an official of the Canoe/Camping Club of Grosvenor Gardens, London SW1, recommending the island be made a permanent bird sanctuary and controlled by an 'international committee of naturalists'. What really alerted the Foreign Office and concentrated its mind on the well-being of the birds was news received from New York that well-organised ornithologists were petitioning the United Nations to make Heligoland an international biological station. Much logistical planning, and indeed physical danger, was involved in conveying explosives across the Bight for the 'Big Bang' in early 1947. Many VIPs were invited to witness this vindictive attempt to make Heligoland uninhabitable. Curiously the celebrated explosion was twice postponed, from 15 and 31 March, and eventually took place amid much publicity on 18 April that year. The hitherto unexplained reasons for the delay were not the result of any technical hitch – but to allow time to scare off a colony of migratory guillemots!

It was all puffins before people. Since their evacuation from the island in April 1945 the Heligolanders had been cynically ignored and expediently forgotten. Their exile was quite unlike that experienced in the First World War when they were kept together in a Hamburg suburb. This time the traditionally close-knit seafaring community of two thousand islanders was fragmented into minute pieces and widely scattered across some 144 towns and villages in northern Germany. Often this meant there were usually only one or two islanders together, and scarcely ever more than a handful in any village. For a while it was feared that this really might be the end of Heligoland as a nation. But their instinct to hold together was too strong and somehow, person by person, they tracked one another down. Soon their efforts were reinforced by the establishment of a group which became known as the 'Heligoland Committee'. It consisted of eleven Heligolandish aldermen and was based at Cuxhaven, where the largest concentration of the exiles, about one hundred altogether, had been rehoused. The committee kept their people informed about matters of common interest while the 'refugees' evolved their own means of clinging to their independent culture. In addition to going to well-attended meetings at Cuxhaven, they formed local clubs where their songs, folk-dances and dialect were kept alive.

All the islanders shared a yearning to return home, an urge magnified when they had to spend their first Christmas away from the island. On 1 January 1946 the same sentiment prompted the Heligoland Committee to start a petition begging that England should again take back the island as one of her Crown Colonies. There were at that time around 250 Heligolanders who had been born under the British Crown – a factor which influenced the wording of their petition: 'It is impossible for us to believe that Great Britain, or its people, to whom a lot of other small nations are again thankful for their regained freedom and liberty, should have forgotten their former subjects, the natives of the Crown Colony of Heligoland.'

Belatedly the Committee sought the assistance of British Members of Parliament who might lobby on their behalf. Only one was much interested: Douglas Savory, the Unionist MP for Antrim South. During the First World War he had been an RNVR intelligence officer, in which capacity – while posted as an Assistant Secretary to the British Embassy in Stockholm – he had worked for Admiral Reginald Hall, the head of Naval Intelligence. Savory was by descent a Huguenot, and had been a Professor of European Languages at Queen's University, Belfast, where his concern for persecuted small nations in Europe led to him being a respected independent investigator into the Katyn massacre. It was partly his own family's history, combined with his concern that Germany had long been discouraging the Heligolanders' use of their distinctive dialect, that caused him to respond to their call. Effectively he became the Heligolanders' champion in British public life, a role that had been unfulfilled since the death of William Black and the disgrace of Erskine Childers.

The Foreign Office made no response to the petition, so in April the Heligolanders tried again, this time urging that if readmission to the British realm were impossible, they would like to be annexed to Denmark. From the Foreign Office there was a stony silence. In the House of Commons Savory asked Ernest Bevin, the Foreign Secretary, what was happening regarding the Heligolanders' petition – and quite incredibly he was told that the Foreign Office had 'lost' the document. Even if Bevin were not deceiving the House of Commons, although it seems that he was, the timing could scarcely have been more ironic. According to the *National Geographic* that summer the Foreign Office was readily responding to petitions from British ornithologists to select a time for blasting operations which would be least likely to disturb the birds nesting on the northern tip of the island.

Rather surprisingly, at this time there were official murmurings in London that seemed well disposed towards the notion of Heligoland once again becoming a British territory. Cabinet Office papers from March 1946 show that the Foreign Office was fairly amenable to suggestions of Heligoland becoming independent, annexed or even part of the British Isles. On 18 January 1947 the Foreign Office informed the Chiefs of Staff that, in view of the long-term requirement expressed by them, the question of the annexation of Heligoland had been reconsidered. Although there would be some political difficulty in that course, the Foreign Office felt that the territorial claims of the Netherlands, France and Luxembourg over Germany (as well as to the large areas of Germany in the process of detachment, namely Poland and parts of Russia), were likely to facilitate any claims put forward by Britain.

Yet under no circumstances ought the *islanders* be allowed to return to Heligoland. That was essentially the view of the Air Ministry, which was the only government department calling for Britain to regain possession of the island. According to declassified Cabinet Office papers, on 15 November 1946 – during the lull in the practice bombing when naval engineers were rigging the underground fortifications for the 'Big Bang' – the Chiefs of Staff informed the Foreign Office that they 'considered the retention of Heligoland as a bombing range to be of considerable importance'. Of the three political alternatives proposed by the Foreign Office, the Chiefs of Staff preferred annexation. Failing that, they were prepared to agree to 'other countries [presumably the United States] being permitted to use the island for bombing practice, provided control of the island was retained by us'. Unfortunately for the Heligolanders the Foreign Office had very little interest in their future. On 29 June 1949 Ernest Bevin indicated the mood of resistance to a full civilian reoccupancy of the island when he coldly told the House of Commons that the British-influenced Land government in Germany favoured the Heligolanders being permanently transferred for settlement to the Schleswig-Holstein island of Sylt, instead of back to their beloved homeland!

Undaunted by that and other discouraging replies, Savory courageously battled on at Westminster. Stoically persevering on behalf of the islanders, every few weeks he would seek parliamentary replies from senior ministers. Again and again he raised the matter in the House of Commons through questions directed to the Secretary of State for Air, Arthur Henderson. The replies he was given stated that the terrible destruction on the island had mostly taken place during the war, but he had evidence that that was not the case. Tactics used by officialdom to blunt the edge of such scrutiny included the besmirching of the inquisitors. This happened on 12 January 1952 when, as an effort to shake off a barrage of criticism, the parliamentary under-secretary of state at the Foreign Office wrote to Savory that there must be 'little substance' in the complaints made by a distinguished leading islander, Franz Siemens, because he represented protest groups 'created by himself'. There was also a glimmer of a possibility that Savory's correspondence in support of the islanders was being monitored by British Intelligence. This became

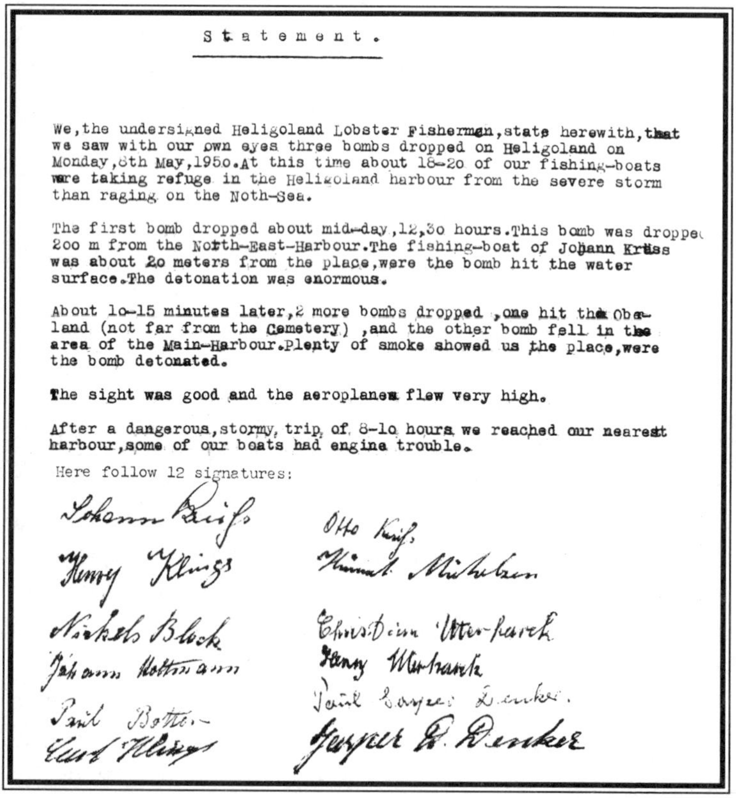

Statement.

We,the undersigned Heligoland Lobster Fishermen,state herewith,that we saw with our own eyes three bombs dropped on Heligoland on Monday,8th May,195o.At this time about 18-2o of our fishing-boats were taking refuge in the Heligoland harbour from the severe storm than raging on the Noth-Sea.

The first bomb dropped about mid-day,12,3o hours.This bomb was dropped 2oo m from the North-East-Harbour.The fishing-boat of Johann Krüss was about 2o meters from the place,were the bomb hit the water surface.The detonation was enormous.

About 1o-15 minutes later,2 more bombs dropped ,one hit the Oberland (not far from the Cemetery) ,and the other bomb fell in the area of the Main-Harbour.Plenty of smoke showed us the place,were the bomb detonated.

The sight was good and the aeroplanes flew very high.

After a dangerous,stormy, trip of 8-1o hours we reached our nearest harbour,some of our boats had engine trouble.

Here follow 12 signatures:

A vivid eyewitness account of the RAF dropping heavy bombs in the 1950s. *(PRONI)*

apparent to the professor on 13 July 1950, when he received a letter from Richard Kuchlenz, a Heligoland campaigner in Cuxhaven, who expressed puzzlement that an earlier letter from Savory had got 'lost in the post', and wondered: 'Do you think that my correspondence to you and yours is watched by certain people on your side?'

Despite Savory's endeavours, the bombing actually increased in ferocity, even though static explosions had destroyed all the remaining fortifications in the 1947 'Big Bang'. By far the heaviest bombing was Exercise 'Bullseye' on 2 June 1950. It was at that time that Savory at last hit upon a means of bringing the matter before the attention of the Commons. On the closing day, before the House adjourned for the autumn, it was customary for the Speaker to allocate time to various subjects which may be brought up 'On the Motion for the Adjournment'. Savory managed to get a petition signed by a very considerable number of MPs begging the Speaker to assign, on 28 July 1950, a certain period for the discussion of the fate of Heligoland. That he did, but he warned Savory that the entire proceedings must not exceed an hour.

As it was the first time since 1890 that the House of Commons had debated Heligoland, it was a historic occasion and ought to have been an influential one, too. But a consequence of the time restriction was that in the debate, which opened at 2pm, Savory could only present the case for the island very briefly. Speaking with one eye on the clock, and keeping a tight rein on the anger that surged within him, he presented the facts: describing the island, its place in Frisian history and its links with Britain. Passionately quoting the January 1946 petition he called for the island's return and a halt to the bombing.

The low attendance at the debate showed that then, even more than in the 1930s, there were very few MPs who understood what conditions were like on Heligoland. It was noticeable that each of the eight MPs who participated praised Professor Savory for his sincerity, kindliness and humanitarian views. He had, it was often said, 'the respect and affection of everyone in this House'. Nevertheless memories of the war were still strong and a few were unsympathetic that the bombing of their island was 'extremely inconvenient' for the Heligolanders. Others, considering the new Cold War reality that West Germany was now under Britain's protection, had differing views. The Sheffield MP John Hynd claimed that the use of 'a remote spot away from the mainland, where there is no inhabitation of any kind' was all Germany needed to do 'to contribute to the defence of Germany and of the rest of Western Europe'. Mr Reginald Paget MP, who had been a barrister at the Nuremberg war crimes trials, argued that to use as a bombing target 'an island of great history and tradition is an offence which will be resented by every German. If Western Europe is to be defended, these people must be our friends.'

For a while that afternoon it seemed that no island in the British Isles was safe from the possibility of being the target for future heavy practice bombing. The prospect was like an unwelcome prize in a pass-the-parcel parlour game. It was prompted by suggestions in the German press that Britain should use some Scottish island, instead of Heligoland, for bombing exercises. Studiously keen not to encourage the RAF to use any part of his Orkney and Shetland Islands constituency, Jo Grimond (later to become leader of the Liberal Party) suggested Rockall or 'islands around Ireland which are uninhabited'. Places such as the Channel Islands were suggested by other MPs. Such ideas would not have been out of place in Compton Mackenzie's comic novel set in the Outer Hebrides, *Rockets Galore* (1957). It went largely unnoticed at the time that the most far-reaching contribution in the debate was made by Lord Malcolm Douglas-Hamilton. The main supporter of Savory's argument, he was the member for Inverness and came from a distinguished land-owning family on whose property the fleeing Rudolf Hess had landed during the war. An RAF wing commander, he had gained great experience of flying over the Heligoland Bight during the war, and in 1945 he had been appointed commandant of the Air Training Corps in Scotland. Thus it was with some knowledge that he suggested some alternatives to Heligoland. He also strongly objected to the use of uninhabited Scottish islands and helpfully suggested that, if the only purpose of the Heligoland bombing range really was just navigational training, then a point *off* Heligoland would do just as well. His view was that a suitable site could be found among the uninhabited islands at the mouth of the Elbe, such as Scharhorn, Trischen and Neuwerk. To continue to use Heligoland for bombing simply because it had served as a base for offensive operations during the war – an excuse which the Secretary of State for Air was apt to use – would, as Douglas-Hamilton scathingly remarked, be as absurd a stance as continuing to bomb Cuxhaven and Wilhelmshaven.

The penultimate voice in the debate was that of Mr V. Yates, MP for Birmingham Ladywood, who summarised Savory's views well. He raged:

> I think it is an outrage to public opinion that an island to which the Germans, in their own country, could go to find beauty, culture and science, is now

> being completely laid in ruins. It does not seem to me to matter whether those people are Germans or Frisians, or of any other nationality. The fundamental consideration is: what is to be the future of those people who lived there and whose home it is? They at least ought to be consulted, if we believe in the right of self-determination.

With just minutes to go before Savory's historic hour-long Heligoland debate ran out of time, the Under-Secretary of State for Air, Aidan Crawley, rose to reply for the government. He opened by venturing that Savory 'will not expect me to answer for the mistakes of the government of Lord Salisbury or of any government between the wars'. Seldom can there have been such an ironic statement by a minister. Apparently unbeknown to Crawley it was virtually sixty years earlier (in July 1890) that Parliament had been told that Heligoland needed to be handed over because it was of sentimental and cultural value to the Germans, it had no foreseeable military use for Britain and it had not been a British possession for very long. Now, on 28 July 1950, Parliament was being told:

> Heligoland has not been in the possession of Germany for very long, it was only ceded to Germany in 1890, and insofar as it has any sentimental value for the Germans it can only be as a great military base from which two terrible wars were waged. I should hope that if any tradition was worth breaking, and if any sentiment was worth changing, then the German sentiment about Heligoland was such a one.

So keen was the junior minister to argue against the islanders returning to Heligoland that he divulged more details regarding Britain's technical needs for atomic bombs than perhaps he ought:

> We have not found anywhere else within range of these islands for normal bombing practice. It must also be in a part of the world where the climate is reasonable. We have had a look round parts of the world, and round a great many parts of the British Isles. The fact is, although there are a good many rocks sticking out of the sea, from this point of view none of them combines all the qualities that Heligoland has.
>
> Heligoland has the advantage of being geographically in a position which can give practice to all sorts of other units concerned with air defence. We have got to have an island which is of a certain size. It must stick out a certain distance from the sea in order to be a good radar target to be bombed from a height. . . . When all these considerations are taken into account, there is nowhere else which combines all the qualities which must be possessed by a target for live bombing practice from high altitudes, and if we are to have an effective bombing force, it is necessary to practise bombing with live bombs. Practice bombs have not the same ballistics; they are not so accurate, and they do not therefore give the bomb-aimers real training. Live bombs are quite different in their flight, and so on, and it is only when they are used that accuracy can be obtained.[1]

All this meant that there was 'no question of anybody's home being on that island, nor can there possibly be any question of more than a handful of people – of fishermen – gaining their living there again'. He claimed that only a week or two earlier he himself had flown round the island, within a few hundred feet of its cliffs, and had a very close look at it. Chillingly he described the battered island as 'the nearest thing to the Warsaw Ghetto I have seen in Western Europe'.

As a few of the debating MPs pointed out to the junior Air Minister, the question of the ongoing violation of the island by the postwar practice bombing could be expected to have some impact on the German people. In accord with the German press, which was publishing fiery articles protesting against the continued use of the island in peacetime as a target, the German Federal Parliament became interested. On 1 December 1949 it unanimously passed a resolution calling for the Federal Government to request Heligoland's return. On 3 May 1950 the government of Schleswig-Holstein passed a resolution calling on Britain to lift its ban on the islanders. Then in May 1950 the Helgolander-Komitte appealed to the Vatican for the support of Pope Pius XII. All this agitation was encouraged by a group called the 'Helgoland-Büros'. Otherwise known as the Heligoland Society, it was founded in Pinneberg that year by Henry Peter Rickmers, a distant descendant of the nineteenth-century Heligoland ship-owning merchant, Rickmer Rickmers. It lobbied various Europe-based institutions to broaden support for the displaced islanders. Its message went far. In Britain it got the newly founded Mebyon Kernow (Cornish National Party) to campaign for the islanders' return. Then on 1 July 1950 the Federal Council of Minorities convened in Holland and approved a unanimous resolution calling for an immediate stop to the bombing of the island, and begged Britain to allow the Heligolanders to return to their island and to grant them self-determination to decide for themselves to which state they wished to belong.

Meanwhile, the islanders were becoming impatient to return to their homeland, and some of their supporters favoured direct action. Initially this took the form of individual members of the Heligoland Society occasionally making a token landing on the island for a few hours. Soon a rival protest group called Helgoland-Aktion was founded by Prince Hubertus zu Löwenstein. A historian, from 1937 to 1946 he had lectured in American universities. Löwenstein was reputed to be a nephew of Lord Pirbright, who in 1888–92 had been under-secretary of state for the colonies. Helgoland-Aktion evolved from an earlier patriotic organisation of Löwenstein's called the 'Deutsche Bewegung' (German Movement), which campaigned for the restitution of Germany's lost lands. At the time, another of Löwenstein's campaigns was to prevent the Socialist-preferred new national anthem *Hymn to Germany* from replacing *Deutschland über Alles*, which had long been synonymous with German militarism.

Few Heligolanders were involved with Helgoland-Aktion, although it and the Heligoland Society used remarkably similar tactics, such as quick 'raids' on the island, in order to make their views known. Sometimes their rivalry became dangerous. In June 1950 there was an absurd rowing-boat race to the island, a boat representing each group setting off from different ports to see who would get to Heligoland first. But they had overlooked the hazardous waters of the Bight. One boat did not get far, the other nearly perished. For those willing to endure the perilous voyages, there was also the risk of unannounced practice bombings. There were never any British personnel on either Heligoland's main Rock Island or on Sandy Island; there were no signallers ashore to guide the bombers, nor was there often a duty guardship in the Bight. Even so, if there were protesters in the vicinity, the British forces in North Germany could invariably find some sort of boat to shoo them away.

All that changed at Christmas 1950. On 12 December that year two Heidelberg student protesters, Georg von Hatzfeldt and René Leudesdorff, reached the island undetected. They hoisted over the ruins a huge flag of the Communist World Peace Movement (designed by Pablo Picasso), sporting a huge letter 'E' signifying European unity, then moved on to the Oberland to establish their headquarters in the Red Tower. Never before had protesters attempted to occupy the island, and Hatzfeldt and Leudesdorff's use of the Red Tower came to be regarded as especially poignant. The former wartime anti-aircraft post still contained firing-control and plotting rooms, and as the only building remaining intact on Heligoland it came to be publicised as a historic symbol of Heligolandish defiance. Although these Heidelberg students were dubbed 'Communist squatters' by newspapers, Prince Löwenstein, aware of the publicity value of such stunts, hurriedly sailed to the island with a few supporters. They may have been few in number but their presence on the island at Christmas that year meant that for the first time since 1945 the island was inhabited once again. By the New Year there were sixteen people on Heligoland, five of whom were either press photographers or journalists. The presence of the latter meant the protest occupation received considerable, indeed worldwide, newspaper coverage. In Germany (where the publicity stunt was much approved of) Hatzfeldt and Leudesdorff appeared set to become minor national heroes.

For Britain, suddenly everything seemed to go wrong. On 29 December the High Commissioner in Germany, Sir Ivone Kirkpatrick, declared an Exclusion Zone on and around the island and threatened those who violated it with heavy fines and a year's imprisonment. The problem then was enforcement. Having no suitable ships of its own with which to send a platoon-strength force to evict the intruders, the Land Commission responsible for the area ordered the German-crewed minesweeping flotilla under its control to provide the necessary transportation. But opinions regarding the return of the island were no less strong in those warships than they were among civilians on the mainland, and the minesweepers' commodore refused to take the order. No officer could be found who was willing to obey the instruction. In due course it was only the flotilla commander who was disciplined. It has always been kept quiet since, but effectively what had happened was that a substantial portion of what remained of the German Navy had mutinied.

Resorting to desperate measures to do what was required of him, Major F. Messenger, the British officer in Cuxhaven responsible for Heligoland, embarked his force upon *Eileen*, the only vessel then available: a harbour tender. It was 1 January 1951 and the weather was foul. No sooner was the overcrowded boat out of the harbour than it hit heavy seas. It had been a very cold winter and an exceptional amount of thick sheet ice had formed on the estuaries and shallow waters off the Frisian coast. The tender steadily headed into the Bight through huge broken-off patches of this floating ice. Then disaster struck. In the dauntingly steep waves the spinning propellers of the tender happened to crash down on a jagged piece of ice, which smashed one propeller and knocked a blade off the other. The vibration from the unbalanced propeller became so severe that it threatened to cause an engine stoppage or the loss of more blades. Either would cause the vessel to stop, and without power it would very quickly capsize in such towering seas. Accounts of that voyage subsequently appeared in British newspapers and were remarkably redolent of the stories of such trips written many years earlier by the ornithologist Robert Lockley and Governor Barkly's young widow. Eventually Messenger's boat reached the island, and successfully removed the squatters and journalists. Not all survived. So deadly terrifying was the ordeal that one German journalist accompanying the platoon died, quite literally, of fright.

That loss of life was overshadowed by the Cabinet's apprehension of the possible repercussions in Germany were any squatters to be accidentally killed when practice bombing resumed. Regardless of all that, the Military Establishment was intent on fighting until the last minute to keep the island. Stalling for time, on 6 February 1950 the Secretary of State for Defence, Lord Alexander of Hillsborough, wrote a letter to the Prime Minister, Clement Attlee: 'I think we must bear in mind that we can expect continued pressure by the Germans for various concessions of this nature, which may be granted too easily in a piecemeal fashion unless we maintain a clear picture of our post-war policy towards that country.' On 14 February the fledgling West German Federal Parliament, led by Chancellor Konrad Adenauer, unanimously passed a motion demanding the island's return. There were other factors now for Britain to consider, too. A few months earlier all prospect had gone of using the island for a static shallow-water atomic bomb test, and it was widely accepted that to prevent further intrusions by protesters a radar station would need to be established on the island – and this option Britain was evidently unwilling to pursue.

Another possibly significant consideration at that time was that Britain's bombing of the island might also have been illegal. This unwelcome news had been brought to the government's attention a few months earlier by Douglas Savory in his adjournment debate on 28 July 1950. There he notified the junior Air Minister that the continuing postwar bombardment was entirely contrary to international law. The diligent Savory had consulted a distinguished professor of international law, L. Oppenheim, the author of *International Law*, an authoritative book that had been reprinted several times by Cambridge University Press. Oppenheim advised Savory that what Britain was doing was injudicious insofar as it was a clear breach of the Hague Convention. Article 3(a) states that: 'A measure of permissible devastation is found in the strict necessities of war. As an end in itself, devastation is not sanctioned by the law of war.' Yet the Labour government had been permitting 'devastation' to continue through almost five years of peace. It seems Britain had forgotten that as recently as the commencement of the last war it had been most careful to act within the letter of the Hague Convention when bombing German targets.

Savory also cited the 35th Conference of the International Law Association, which in 1928 resolved: 'Damage to or destruction of immovable property is only permitted for the purpose of attaining a specific military objective. Indiscriminate, wanton, and general devastation or destruction is prohibited.' There was a third potentially legal embarrassment looming for Britain. As recently as 1949 it had publicly agreed to the incorporation into the Geneva Convention of a fourth protocol concerning the protection of civilians.

Already the Heligolanders were turning their minds to appeals for money and gifts in kind. In February 1952 Savory forwarded to the Foreign Office a petition requesting just that. What, the Cabinet must have wondered, if they should go so far as to demand compensation, citing as grounds Britain's probable breaches of international law? Ministers would have had some justification in fearing for their careers. At the time a political scandal was coming to light regarding a Hampshire bombing range called Crichel Down, which had been seized from its former owners and improperly disposed of. The outcome of the Crichel Down affair was that the minister deemed responsible eventually had to resign.

For all these reasons, on 20 February 1951 the Cabinet's Defence Committee met with Prime Minister Clement Attlee, and it was decided that Britain should relent.[2] Accordingly, later that week the British High Commissioner in Germany, Sir Ivone Kirkpatrick, informed Chancellor Adenauer that by 2 March 1952 the bombing of Heligoland would cease and the islanders would be permitted to return.

In reaching that decision the Defence Committee rather assumed it would be able to secure the use of a nearby alternative bombing range. Evidently Savory's July 1950 debate had been of slight influence in another respect because it was there that the recommendation was made by Lord Douglas-Hamilton that the Grosser (Greater) Knechtsand, near Cuxhaven, could be used as a bombing range. A low-lying mudflat island of some 5 sq. miles, Grosser Knechtsand was situated at the mouth of the Elbe and was nearly submerged at high tide. The channel between the 'Grosser' and the Scharhorn had been immortalised in *The Riddle of the Sands* as the spot where the plucky yacht *Dulcibella* was nearly lured to her doom. So keen now was Adenauer to maintain Britain's ongoing military protection of West Germany that in December 1951 he reached a gentleman's agreement with London whereby the RAF would be allowed to bomb the Grosser. For a while it seemed as though Adenauer had over-reached himself. Germany's Parliament, the Bundestag, was decidedly unenthusiastic about the scheme, preferring to deny Britain use of the sandbank and suggesting the Shetland Islands instead.

In February 1952 *The Times* received a letter from a town councillor of Cuxhaven (which was just 10 miles distant from the Grosser), insisting that there was already serious unemployment in Cuxhaven, and that the town, which earned its living from fishing, coastal shipping and tourism, would be blighted by the new bombing range. Capitalising on the existing disgruntlement of north German fishermen, who had kept a bonfire burning for months near Cuxhaven in symbolic protest against the RAF's use of the Heligoland bombing range, Prince Löwenstein's nationalist group, Helgoland-Aktion, switched its attention to the Grosser. In March 1952 it organised a visit by fifty fishing boats to plant United Europe flags there. They organised a petition, signed by a thousand inhabitants of the mainland, which was sent to Dr Adenauer urging him to reject the bombing agreement, and pledged to impede the Grosser Knechtsand's military use by stationing a boat close by on sentry duty. In the absence of any official explanation at Westminster, the only opportunity British people had to make sense of what all this meant was in an editorial which appeared in *The Times* on 1 March, skilfully comparing the Grosser with Heligoland. The impending renunciation of British use of Heligoland was right, it said. 'Bombing and demolitions had rendered the island materially useless; they had not, however, destroyed the sentimental regard in which many Germans hold it. To have refused to relinquish it would have led to endless ill-feeling.' Nevertheless, there was a price to pay for measures for the defence of Germany. The Bundestag did eventually agree to allow bombing practice on the Grosser, but its reluctance to do so had shown it was not really concerned to honour Adenauer's agreement; it was 'more interested in preserving shrimping grounds'. The claim became ironic because two years later Britain waived its remaining rights to bomb the Grosser – a decision which had much less to do with the Cuxhaven townspeople's objections than with information supplied by ornithologists that such activities were damaging the feeding grounds of seabirds![3]

In Germany, Britain's relinquishment of Heligoland on 2 March 1952 became a day of national rejoicing. The *New York Herald Tribune* reported that the flag of Heligoland was even raised over Hamburg. Britain had made few concessions in terms of access during its final months of control of the bombing range: in June 1951 German fishing boats were allowed to seek shelter in the harbour when the weather was exceptionally stormy, and in September a few Heligolanders went ashore for a matter of hours to survey the damage. Then, just before the midnight deadline of the handover, some fishermen from Cuxhaven landed, lit bonfires on the island's southernmost tip and raised the island's distinctive flag. On the day itself four hundred guests of honour (few of them Heligolanders) were landed by boat. The ceremony re-establishing German administration was a comparatively simple state occasion led by the Prime Minister of Schleswig-Holstein, Dr Wilhelm Lupke, and civil servants from the district of Penningen, to which Heligoland was to be administratively attached. Among the guests was Prince Löwenstein, busily calling for the reintroduction of *Deutschland über Alles* as the German national anthem. Conspicuously, no leading Heligolander was involved in the acceptance. The islanders were merely allowed to be represented by their oldest inhabitant, who expressed thanks for the return of the island.

The proceedings were hauntingly redolent, in some respects, of the handover in August 1890. Grand speeches were made by important German statesmen about Heligoland – which to its people was simply their home. No longer was there a Kaiser Wilhelm to raspingly decree the island to be 'a strong place in the German Ocean against all enemies who care to show themselves upon it'. Now leading Germans took care to describe it in ambitiously idealistic terms as some sort of model for international conflict resolution. With a certain degree of selective amnesia, Premier Lubke denied that the island had ever been intended to be the 'Gibraltar of the North Sea'! It should now, he said, 'be a symbol of new hope, understanding and peace for Germany and Europe'. Chancellor Adenauer, using words which might have been spoken by the Kaiser himself, described the island as a magnanimous symbol of reconciliation: 'Set in the seas between Britain and Germany, Heligoland will be a token of peace and friendship between the two countries.' President Theodor Heuss, in a radio broadcast, pledged the island would be 'returned to peaceful purposes'.

The British government's failure to send anyone at all to this handover ceremony was all the more disgraceful given that it had been the cause of Heligoland's desolate condition. The extent of destruction was now more extensive than in 1945, more severe even than after the 'Big Bang' in 1947. Debris from the once-massive armaments was scattered everywhere. The island's rugged treeless plateau was pitted with craters. Even the rubble in the towns remained blackened from the RAF's phosphorus bomb experiments. The island was so littered with explosives that German government officials calculated it would be a further five years before they were cleared and the island made safe to be fully habitable.

Appropriately on an island whose function and origin was maritime, the first object constructed as a matter of priority was a temporary lighthouse. Ingeniously adapted for that purpose was the Red Tower, the only structure still standing. There being no other shelter on the island, for a while bomb disposal experts and construction workers had to live on board a ship berthed in the wrecked harbour. As soon as the handover ceremony had finished, bulldozers set to work clearing the piles of rubble. The entire Unterland was raised in height by one metre. Hitherto it had been so close to the high water mark that floodwaters had been known to reach 300 metres along the street to Heligoland's only post office. In the preceding months much effort had been expended by the government of Schleswig-Holstein in consulting with architects and representatives of the islanders as to what form the island's new houses should take. It was agreed that the narrow street plan, and most of the historic street names, should be as before; the houses would remain nestled at the foot of the cliff across the harbour, and also clustered on its southern ridge. However, such was the islanders' understandable disenchantment with the British that they decided to start anew in terms of the style of their houses. Psychologically wrong-footed, they took a decision they would later regret, to rebuild their homes in an uncompromisingly modern style rather than in the traditional form.

The envisaged cost of making the island inhabitable and reconstructing its civil buildings, hotels and harbours was estimated at between £11 million and £20 million – an immense amount at the time. Heavy shipping charges meant the cost of rebuilding houses on the island was so horrendously high it was equivalent to constructing homes for 20,000 people on the mainland. Nevertheless, such was the sentimental power of the place, in Bonn the coalition and opposition parties were agreed that the reconstruction of Heligoland was an all-German obligation. President Heuss and Chancellor Adenauer, having become patrons of a special Heligoland appeal fund, publicly called upon the already financially shattered German people for contributions in cost or kind. The Federal Government considered issuing a special series of Heligoland stamps, while Heuss and Adenauer endorsed an ingenious scheme whereby fragments of RAF bombs were mounted on wooden shields and sold as 'Helgoland Plaques' for the equivalent of 4 shillings each to raise funds.

The sale of these plaques throughout Germany, and presumably in East Germany as well, caused consternation. There was a possibility that some of the shrapnel could contain fragments of blue steel molybdenum, from the tail-fin and nose-cone sections of the experimental bombs the RAF had been dropping on Heligoland. Clumsily trying to deter the spread of these valuable fragments, in February 1954 the British authorities declared that they would be liable for customs duty on the mainland.

For all the German authorities' declared good intentions, the rebuilding was faltering. In early 1958 Sir Douglas Savory received via Franz Siemens a report by the Frisian Bureau of Michigan showing that, six years after the bombing had stopped, 65 per cent of the Heligolanders were still having to live on the mainland. Few houses had been constructed as practically all the rebuilding had been of maritime installations. Such lack of progress was being worsened by Britain's unwillingness to provide compensation. Savory was in a quandary: he was no longer at Westminster (having left Parliament in 1955); nor, since Lord Douglas-Hamilton had also stood down, was there any parliamentarian with a detailed knowledge of Heligoland; and besides Savory knew from experience that the Clerk of the House of Commons would deliberately refuse to accept any questions for which the Foreign Secretary could not be held responsible. Therefore, on 18 July 1958, Savory wrote to the Federal Chancellor, informing Adenauer of the concerns of Franz Siemens and all the other Heligolanders.

That helped accelerate the rebuilding programme. The recladding of damaged patches on the walls of the Red Tower in 1962, which was by then a permanent lighthouse, marked the end of the other planned phase of reconstruction. Domestic houses having been rebuilt, the new priority was to re-create public buildings which had formerly been part of the island's allure for tourists. In due course there appeared a seaside and health resort, an aquarium and a sanctuary for migratory birds. By 1961 a tourist office was established. The rebuilding which had taken place was of such quality that Heligoland had become one of the most modern holiday resorts in northern Europe, and a complete example in miniature of Germany's miraculous economic regrowth. In sporting terms the island returned to normality, participating in the Inter-island Games – a relatively unknown mini-Olympic competition between various European islands. In yacht racing it became the starting point for a biennial 550-mile race to Kiel. The island also won some renown for hosting the annual 'North Sea Week' regatta, which included feeder races from Cuxhaven and Bremerhaven. Being inescapably linked to Germany's submarine history, appropriately enough Heligoland was used in 1981 for filming several scenes for the celebrated television film *Das Boot*. Twenty years earlier crucial footage of the 'Big Bang' had been used in the credits of the film, *The Guns of Navarone*, albeit only fleetingly.

Thus it was that Heligoland remained totally forgotten by Britain. To the islanders' astonishment the British government eventually issued a celebrated expression of sorrow for its gratuitous wartime bombing of Dresden, at the far end of the Elbe – yet the gratuitous postwar bombing of the former British colony of Heligoland was not apologised for, either at the time of the March 1952 handover to Germany or subsequently. But by chance the German correspondent of *The Times* happened to make a visit to the island where he interviewed its Bürgermeister, the former leader of the Heligoland Society, Henry Rickmers. Now aged eighty-one, Rickmers recalls in broken English that in spite of his own bitterness after the war, he had long cherished a hope that it would be possible to re-establish the friendly relations with Britain which existed at the time when the island was under British rule. The 25th and 50th anniversaries of the historic 1890 cession had both fallen during a world war, and 1965 was going to be the first opportunity to celebrate such a jubilee in peacetime. That occasion was, Rickmers knew, being planned as an all-German celebration, so he was not hopeful that consideration would be given to any thoughts of Britain. Nevertheless the journalist was impressed and worked it into his article 'Heligoland Arises from the Ashes', which was printed on 14 May 1964. It ended with a recommendation, prompted by Rickmers: 'Perhaps the seventy-fifth anniversary of its transfer to Germany, when "God Save the Queen" last rang out over the island, could be a worthy occasion.'

The celebration on 10 August 1965 was certainly a great occasion, with a cavalcade of important visitors to the island, of whom the most prominent were the Federal Chancellor, Dr Ludwig Erhard; the Defence Minister; the Minister President of Schleswig-Holstein; and a host of officials and representatives of the German press. Chancellor Erhard had interrupted his election tour of north Germany to sail across from Wilhelmshaven in a corvette, making his first ever sea trip. Arriving just as the Kaiser had done in 1890 to take possession for Germany, he was warmly greeted in fine weather by the island's inhabitants and many holidaymakers. In spite of some competition, provided by Bremen's thousand-year celebrations on the same day, the total number of guests on the island on that day was over twelve thousand – or, to put it another way, six guests for every native of the tiny island.

From the very outset Erhard used the visit to emphasise the importance of reconciliation, and at the foot of the main landing stage he laid a wreath on the memorial to Hoffmann von Fallersleben, the German poet who wrote the words of the national anthem in August 1841. The Chancellor explained that the words of *Deutschland über Alles* were intended to encourage people to put Germany above the then existing collection of small quarrelling states, and that in the Wilhelmine period a wrong and dangerous interpretation had been put upon the words – that Germany must come above everything else in the world. The important phrase now, he said, in the new national anthem was 'unity, justice and freedom'.

The climax of the ceremonials was an open-air church service and a 'Festakt' at the highest point of the island beside the lighthouse. It seemed only appropriate that the day's jollifications should end on a solemn and impressive note as the crowd sat in darkness on the spot where Kaiser Wilhelm II had officially taken over the island. The religious service was simple, solemn and moving. The same hymns were played as in 1890 and the same music also accompanied the Festakt, which concluded with the mass singing of Fallersleben's 1841 national anthem. In an interview with the newspaper *Deutsche Welle*, which was afterwards printed in the official government bulletin, the Chancellor emphasised that Heligoland, once the symbol of unhealthy opposition to England, was now no longer a 'bulwark' – the Kaiser's description – against a traditional enemy. It was, on the contrary, a symbol of peace and of peaceful accomplishments.

Soon after *The Times* article appeared in May 1964 the British Consul-General in Hamburg, K.R. Oakeshott, hastened to the island to discuss details of the 1890 commemoration. The intended ceremony was a purely German affair, with many notables from the mainland. Bürgermeister Rickmers – for all his enthusiasm – was pessimistic about his ambition to have some British participation, although he hoped for some gesture from the British. Oakeshott reported this to the British ambassador in Bonn at the time, Sir Frank Roberts. This was the same Frank Roberts who, as a junior Foreign Office bureaucrat in the late 1930s, had drafted letters for Anthony Eden deflecting suggestions that Britain should recolonise Heligoland. Sir Frank ought to have got some inkling of just how much the island still meant to Germans in August 1964 when, as ambassador, he had attended an Anglo-German ceremony in Cologne marking the 50th anniversary of the Battle of Heligoland (the first sea battle between Britain and Germany during the First World War). The battle was still so relatively recent that present was a former naval stoker, Adolf Neumann, who was the only survivor of the flagship *Köln*, which had been sunk with all hands. Despite this, when the 75th anniversary of the cession was about to take place, British officials were hopelessly ill-prepared for it. A flustered Roberts later wrote to the Foreign Secretary, Michael Stewart: 'Although I had looked forward to this occasion as likely to prove useful for Anglo-German relations, I must confess that I had never expected that the result would be so strikingly favourable.'[4]

On 9 August 1965, the day before Chancellor Erhard's re-enactment of the Kaiser's arrival, a 'British evening' reception had been given by Bürgermeister Rickmers. It took place at the same hour as one held exactly seventy-five years earlier by Arthur Barkly. In the absence of a British consular presence on the island the Foreign Office had never bothered to keep track of the views of the islanders. Thus it had no means of knowing that, as memories of the bombings gradually faded, there was a resurgence of the traditional warmth towards the British, derived from memories handed down of benevolent British rule. A declassified report by Oakeshott about the commemorations reveals that a German admiral had confided that many Heligolanders believed the friendly atmosphere of the 'British evening' was the high point of the celebrations. Typical of the spirit of the Heligolanders was the fact that the island's own flag normally flew proudly at the top of a display of flags. Significantly, although the German Federal flag and the Union Jack tended to come next, the British flag – Oakeshott reported – 'sometimes had pride of place'. He went on:

> Everywhere I heard comments from the islanders about the tradition of the benevolence of the British Governors. An example of the regard in which we were subsequently held, in spite of war-time experience, was made to me by one of the two students who had squatted on the island thirteen years ago, that he would not have done so had he not been convinced of the fairness and generosity of the British.[5]

Yet although the Royal Navy had helped to improve relations by sending to the island the modern conventional submarine HMS *Opossum*, which some seven thousand people eagerly clambered over, the best the Foreign Office could manage, somewhat belatedly, was the presentation by Sir Frank to the islanders of two bound volumes of copies of official documents covering the eighty-three years of British administration. From Heligoland, goodwill towards the British spread to the seafaring northern parts of Germany with which British connections had always been closest. All this took place in the aftermath of the queen's successful state visit to Germany that summer. As Roberts himself saw on an official visit to the island via Cuxhaven, Bremerhaven and Bremen, the Heligoland celebrations were having a beneficial impact.

In the wider context of the 1890 settlement, Germany was willing to accommodate the ghosts of the past. During his fleeting visit to Heligoland on 10 August 1965 Chancellor Erhard went out of his way to explain in the context of Zanzibar that the 'colonial conception of the Wilhelmine period had completely disappeared in a Germany which now only wants to cooperate in development projects and through association with the EEC with overseas countries and more especially with the independent nations in Africa'. In contrast, British officialdom preferred to forget, tending to believe that Britain had no place in celebrations regarding a possession that was now another country's. In 1964, in a distant continent, Zanzibar was decolonised and became part of Tanzania. The next year official celebrations were held in Zanzibar to celebrate the end of the Second World War. Even so, the Foreign Office reprimanded Britain's Deputy High Commissioner there who dared to politely attend.[6]

Epilogue

Even in summertime now, when the seas in the Bight are too rough for ferries to disembark their passengers in the roadstead, the only means by which Heligoland can be reached is by light aircraft. Yet the difficulties involved in finding such a plane well illustrate why it is that the island has become almost entirely unknown to non-Germans. For today's British traveller the first stage is a scheduled Lufthansa flight from London to Hamburg's busy high-tech Fuhisbüttel airport. With just two propeller-driven planes, Helgoland Airlines is among the world's smallest national airlines, so much so that enquiries at Fuhisbüttel's information services and two or three speculative shuttle-bus trips to other terminals reveal nothing. Eventually it transpires that they might be flying from the executive aircraft hangars on the air freight side of the airport, but there is no such airline nameplate outside the flying club-style building. All is deserted. Only after several minutes' searching is a clue found – an old Helgoland Airlines poster showing times of departure. So this is the place. Eventually a pilot arrives and announces that the scheduled flight will be leaving for the island an hour early, so it can stop off and collect passengers from another airfield en route.

Appropriately enough, a sturdy and immaculately kept Channel Isles-built Britten-Norman Islander is the workhorse of Helgoland Airlines. Its jaunty Jolly Roger fluttering piratically at the cockpit window is removed and securely furled, and the twin engines thunder into life. Within minutes the rugged aluminium plane is airborne, en route to a military maritime reconnaissance airfield to collect a cargo of excitedly chattering German holidaymakers. Soon resuming its 150-km journey to the island, the plane heads north-west along the wide serpentine Elbe, passing first Brunsbüttel at the mouth of the Kiel Canal and then the resort of Cuxhaven. The ebbing tide exposes vast tracts of muddy saltflats, green with algae and criss-crossed with impromptu rivulets. This is all now a national wildlife park. The sight of those historic islets, the Scharhorn, Neuwerk and the Grosser Knechtsand, inevitably reminds the traveller that this was the sight Erskine Childers would have been seen from his seaplane on the Cuxhaven raid in 1914. Perhaps it was the last land the doomed Hampden bomber crews ever saw before they were all shot down in flames in 1939. At 120 knots the Britten-Norman continues at 2,000ft, blown around like a leaf in turbulence; while in the wild Bight below coastal merchant ships and sailing yachts, pitching heavily in the swell, claw through a white-horsed sea along the Lower Saxony coast.

Suddenly, through the aircraft's rain-streaked windscreen and whirling propellers, there it is: angular and red, its long outlying booms and moles stretching out to sea like tentacles. The plane flies over the airfield at nearby Sandy Island. Then in an unforgettable manoeuvre it banks sharply to port and plunges downwards in a controlled dive; levelling out, it skims over a beach and the edge of a sea wall, before gliding to a gentle landing on a wet concrete runway which seems scarcely longer than a football pitch. Spontaneously the German passengers cheer and applaud, relieved to have safely survived the stormy crossing; one wonders how many of them appreciate the history of this far-flung outpost of their country.

There is no standing on ceremony here. Everyone pitches in: passengers unload their own luggage, piling the rucksacks on to a handcart provided by the customs official, who also seems to operate the control tower. No passports are checked, and air fares (just £80 from the mainland) are trusted to be paid on arrival. When sterling travellers cheques are offered there is consternation. Amazingly these have never been seen before – an indication of how few British people have been here in recent years. Irrespective of the stormy weather the wind is surprisingly salt-free, clean and warm, indeed even gently soothing. Sandy Island is a one-horse hamlet, with barely made roads, and just one shop where bathers can get provisions. Low-lying and otherwise covered in untended gorse which grows to the fringes of its dunes and dazzling beaches, even now it has some sense of a faded wartime airfield. Readily visible are other indications of former military activities. Intact at the Dünenhafen, on the west side, is the 'L'-shaped mole created as the first (and only completed) step in Hitler's 'Hummerschere' seaport scheme.

To get from the airfield on Sandy Island to Heligoland's main island, a few hundred yards on the other side of the roadstead, involves a short trip in a waterbus. At Sandy Island's landing stage, if the wind has dropped, one might wonder why there should be a simple bus shelter-type structure, which is so over-engineered with curiously thick glass and hefty steel girders. As if by instinct a few tourists suddenly crowd inside, sensing something is about to happen. Sometimes even well-seasoned travellers get caught unawares. Almost without warning the waters of the roadstead, which had seemed to be calming down, become a seething cauldron of steeply pitched, white-crested waves. Rain and hail lash the transparent waterbus shelter, perceptibly rattling it to its foundations. Hoved to, for a while, the catamaran ferry that shuttles between Heligoland and Sandy Island struggles around the west mole. The trippers embarked, it battles back into the roadstead. As the ferry pitches and rolls along its short course to Heligoland's north harbour, it is quickly evident that it is no ordinary ferry. The three-strong crew are alert, yet calm and protective of their passengers; everywhere ropes are neatly coiled and safety equipment is gleaming, stowed ready for use. Too well they know the local phrase 'Nordsee ist mordsee' – literally the North Sea is murderous. Everything is prepared and used to coping with more severe seas than these.[1]

At first glance, the traveller who knows Heligoland only from Victorian paintings and postcards is struck with a profound impression that very little has changed. In the narrow Lung Wai, the high street where once stood warehouses crammed with merchandise for smuggling to the mainland in defiance of Napoleon's 'continental system', there are now duty-free shops selling luxury goods. The island depends a great deal on its VAT-free status and these wooden weatherboarded buildings are filled with liquor, cigarettes, perfume and confectionery. Near the landing stage, where Governor Arthur Barkly bade his historic farewell to the islanders in 1890, is the spot where Conversation House used to stand. On that very site there is now the Musikpavillon, a Sandy Island-style glass and steel structure around which visitors can linger in the open air to hear a German three-piece band singing perennial favourites like 'Tie a yellow ribbon round the old oak tree'.

In the summer it all seems noticeably carefree. On Heligoland there are no cars or bicycles. A handful of electric-powered delivery vans are used in the early mornings to haul packages up to the Oberland. Discreetly out of sight they use an obscure freight road through the uncovered remains of the old railway tunnel cut to haul Tirpitz's howitzers on to the high plateau. The road runs through the vast crater of the 1947 'Big Bang' and past an old people's home constructed with donations raised by Hamburg's 'Friends of the Heligoland Society'. At the crest is a tablet denoting the exact place where Werner Heisenberg, the father of Germany's atomic bomb project, figured out his method to unravel the secrets of the hydrogen atom. Within the crater is a clinic for sufferers of Parkinson's Disease; on its roof is painted a huge, distinctive Red Cross symbol. Perhaps it is there in case the RAF decides to return.

At the top of the lighthouse, where a powerful lantern runs on a well-oiled though surprisingly ancient-looking mechanism, the lighthouse-keeper remarks that when the weather is clear it is possible to make out the north German coast. A more fascinating sight from that vantage point over the plateau's grotesquely distorted and unrepaired surface are the many giant craters made by the British 'earthquake' bombs. There are other ill-disguised evidences of conflict on the edge of the precipices over the sea where disused gun mountings have been ingeniously resurfaced and made into bird-watching platforms.

Nearly all the houses on the Oberland, and indeed most of those in the Lower Town, have small gardens, and many are graced with window boxes or hanging baskets. There is still a street called Gouverneur Maxse-Strasse, and a Gätke Strasse, after the ornithologist who was part of the island's British administration in Victorian times. Nearby is the rebuilt St Nicolai Church, from the ceiling of which hangs a huge model ship, a replica of the one donated by Governor Maxse. On the wall outside, the German vicar shows visitors the metal plaque dedicated to Queen Victoria by a distant relative of Bürgomeister Henry Rickmers.

Shifting economic circumstances in Hamburg have had an effect on Heligoland. German reunification has opened up the Elbe to long-distance ferries and cruise vessels which previously only sailed downstream to the estuary. Heligoland's traditional status as a popular tourist resort has also been challenged by airlines offering European destinations. The fastest ferries now operating to the island sail from the historic nexus of landing stages on the Elbe in the St Pauli district of Hamburg. High-speed catamarans, in calm weather they can reach 36 knots and take passengers to Heligoland in just two hours. Their shallow draft allows them to dock at the outer harbour, just as Germany's torpedo-boats used to. By noon, five conventional elegant white-hulled ferry ships are anchored in the roadstead, having made the arduous crossing from various German coastal ports. Local wooden boats draw alongside and convey the trippers either to Sandy Island for a few hours' sunbathing or to Heligoland itself for some duty-free shopping. By 4 o'clock all the ferries have departed for the mainland. The tugs and pilot boats that sometimes call in to the outer harbour might boast the latest high-tech specification but the sea has not changed since Victorian times and neither has the frequency of their movements.

On the island still is a dedicated lifeboat service, with its corvette-sized rescue vessel ever ready and waiting. Appropriately enough, the helicopter hangar is sited on nearby dockyard land where the British Coastguard team was based in the nineteenth century. Picturesque sailing yachts are now neatly moored in the Südhajen harbour, which Kennedy's Aphrodite plane should have attacked in 1944. Parts of the subsequently destroyed U-boat shelter are still visible at low water. The statue of Karl Peters has gone, and so has the rest of the U-boat shelter. In its place now stands a yacht club and the world-renowned Biologische Anstalt Heligoland research station. Pointing to a wall map in his office the BAH's Professor of Studies notes with some bitterness a breach in the North Mole made many years ago by the RAF. Indeed, some of the bombs from the 18–19 April 1945 raids narrowly missed the lobster ground on the weather side of the island and are still there, trapped in the fissures of the rocks. However, in contrast to the scientists the fishermen are quite matter-of-fact about such annoyances. On rare occasions the lobstermen accidentally haul one to the surface, and simply call the German Navy in to disarm it.

If the weather is sometimes so awful that the ferries and light aircraft do not arrive, the Heligolanders are utterly unflustered. They dismiss it with a worldly shrug of the shoulders, for they know that the island can readily have four seasons in a day, and that better weather may come tomorrow. For them, grim weather is a reality for much of the year. From September until the spring the island is effectively 'closed', the ferries running, if at all, only twice a week. Heligoland winters remain a hidden world, which has not been well described since Frances Barkly's account of the time when her husband was governor. The islanders, left to their own devices to endure the winter, talk of seas of almost unimaginable ferocity. But these are a stoic people to whom survival is a matter of experience. When they go for walks on the windswept Oberland plateau in winter they put rocks in their rucksacks to prevent the wind blowing them over the edge.

If there is any lingering resentment of past British actions it is entirely directed at the RAF, whose leaders, the islanders believe, bombed Heligoland quite gratuitously. They are bewildered that the man they hold principally responsible, Sir Arthur 'Bomber' Harris, the head of Britain's Bomber Command, should have been nationally venerated by the unveiling of a statue to him in Whitehall. Despite the sins of history the older Heligolanders' affection for Britain has endured. Younger islanders tend to have a rather vague European outlook and refer to Heligoland's dependency coldly as just 'Dune', while the oldsters occasionally delight in using anachronistic English names like 'Sandy Island'. Traditionally, every summer in the harbour a rowing race is held, re-enacting the scramble to save the crew of HMS *Explosion*. On the evening of 9 August each year many of the 2,000 islanders gather at their civic centre, the Nordseehalle, to watch an annual pageant commemorating Governor Barkly's handover of the territory to Germany. A remarkable spectacle to witness, it shows the extent to which Heligoland remains in a mid-twentieth-century time-warp. Their culture is almost pre-

Rock'n'Roll. At the Nordseehalle, everyone is well washed and dressed in their Sunday best or blazers. During the performances a choir gathers on stage and heartily sings 'Men of Harlech' in German and 'The Leaving of Liverpool' in English.

Heligoland is less than 300 miles from the shores of Britain, but its people's affection for their former rulers continues to go unrequited. In 1990, when a special edition was made of the island's flag in respect of the 100th anniversary of the handover, Sir Frank Roberts privately sent a message of goodwill – but the British government coldly ignored the island. Since 1965 the nearest that the British public have come to being reminded of their cultural link with the Frisian Islands occurred in 1979 with the movie adaptation of *The Riddle of the Sands*, starring Jenny Agutter – but even that did not directly mention Heligoland. Instead, for the British, the island remains a curiously forgotten land.

Perhaps if the story of Britain's shameful treatment of Heligoland had been told in the English language, subsequent misdemeanours by the Foreign Office might have been forestalled. In 1890 it was widely assumed in government circles that the Heligoland–East Africa swap had established a constitutional precedent whereby all such relinquishments of territory should only be carried out with the approval of Parliament. And yet, as the years went by and Heligoland was forgotten, the Foreign Office found a means of reneging on that principle, by using Orders in Council. Elsewhere there came to be instances of a three-stage process – perhaps it should be called the 'Heligoland Syndrome' – by which British officials would unscrupulously round up islanders, deport them by boat into exile, and then use the forcibly vacated island for economic or military activities. This happened in 1847 to the Banabans in the West Pacific, in 1958 to the coconut gatherers on Christmas Island, and in 1971 to the inhabitants of Diego Garcia.[2]

Rarely were public-spirited individuals ready to champion the rights of such vulnerable peoples. There were exceptions, decent courageous parliamentarians such as Sir Bernard Braine, who – as William Black and Sir Douglas Savory had earlier done for the Heligolanders – in the 1960s and 1970s campaigned to scupper Foreign Office plans to hand over the Falkland Islands to the military dictatorship of Argentina. But Parliament has become too timid to speak out in favour of such islanders in opposition to sanctimonious Foreign Office bullying. Now, more than ever, there are many lobbyists who eloquently campaign for wildlife in colonial territories, but none is primarily concerned about the well-being of islanders. In 2001 the former islanders of Diego Garcia won the right to return to their homeland – not because British MPs spoke out on their behalf, but because they successfully took the Foreign Office to the High Court themselves, as the Heligolanders could. And now MPs seem to lack the intellectual verve to overcome the Foreign Office's plans to give Spain joint sovereignty of Gibraltar, in defiance of the Gibraltarians' wishes. Heligoland was once known as the 'Gibraltar of the North Sea'. So perhaps Gibraltar is set to become the 'Heligoland of the Mediterranean'?

In 1955 government meteorologists representing countries bordering the North Sea convened and agreed that sea areas they wanted altered on the maritime weather map should be given the names of sand-banks there already well known to mariners. Accordingly the Dogger sea area was halved, and its

NE section named Fisher; while Forties was also divided and its northern half named Viking. At that meeting every opportunity was taken by the German delegation to get the name of the area Heligoland Bight changed to 'German Bight'. The Germans argued that German Bight was the name by which the area had generally became known on their side of the North Sea. The validity of those assertions was doubtful but they were successful in getting the others to accept their demands. Unsurprisingly, the Heligolanders were never consulted[3] as to their views on the abolition of their distinctive Bight's name.

The loss of the term Heligoland Bight, which was to take effect in 1956, could have been resisted by the British government. However, the Meteorological Office was then still under the control of the Air Ministry which – becoming anxious that the postwar bombings should be forgotten – had reason to let the Bight further fade from public view. Furthermore, officials would have realised that the likelihood of parliamentary questioning by Sir Douglas Savory was diminishing. Savory's eyesight was deteriorating – which was possibly a contributory factor in a mysterious, and serious, accident he had falling down the Grand Staircase at Westminster – and in 1955 it was already known he was preparing to retire from the House of Commons.

No wonder yachts flying the Red Ensign are rarely to be seen in the Bight. The sea area's change of name has meant nothing to the occasional tempestuousness of the waters there. As recently as May 2002 *Yachting Monthly* reported that charts covering the treacherous area of shoals and twisting channels near the Frisian Islands are now quite woeful.[4] In a fresh breeze boats venturing into the area can anticipate exciting sailing conditions: fast, wet, and exhilarating; added to which there are tidal changes which can be radically altered by strong south-westerly winds and beguilingly capricious floods in the Elbe. Yet another requirement Erskine Childers would shiver to recognise there is that, to escape waves breaking on the shallows, in making a passage along the Saxony coast in stormy weather, yachts must hazard venturing outside the islands, proceeding many miles offshore – into the Bight and nearer to Heligoland.

With its traditions and British heritage, Heligoland is still a remote part of British life, ignored though it is. Every time the familiar tones of the Meteorological Office's Shipping Forecast sound out, the replacement of Heligoland by German Bight should remind us of a now largely forgotten place in British history.

Notes

Chapter 1: HMS *Explosion* Arrives

1. Gates, *The Napoleonic Wars 1803–1815*, pp. 42, 47.
2. Ibid, pp. 39, 82; Hill, *British Strategy in the Napoleonic Wars 1803–15*, pp. 47–9, 157–8.
3. Vale, *Correspondence, Despatches and other Papers of Lord Castlereagh*, vol. 6, pp. 168–8.
4. Hill, *British Strategy*, pp. 48–9; MPG 1/970.
5. Penning, *Geological Magazine*, 1876, pp. 282–4; CO 700/Heligoland 3.
6. L'Estrange, *Heligoland*, p. 6.
7. ADM 53/1067.
8. FO 933/22.
9. *The Naval Miscellany*, 'Seizure of Heligoland, 1807', 1902, pp. 380–3.
10. ADM 1/5121/22.
11. ADM 1/557, 2 September 1807.
12. *Dictionary of National Biography*; Marshall, *Royal Naval Biography*, vol. 1, 1823, p. 140.
13. ADM 1/557, p. 196.
14. Ibid, p. 197.
15. Ibid, pp. 200, 232, 234.
16. Ibid, p. 200; CO 118/1, p. 3.
17. ADM 1/557, p. 232.
18. CO 118/1, pp. 23, 25.
19. ADM 1/557, pp. 201, 205.
20. Ibid, pp. 197, 20121.
21. CO 118/1, p. 37.

22. ADM 1/557, p. 212.
23. Ibid, p. 216.
24. CO 118/1, p. 5.
25. ADM 1/557, p. 232.
26. CO 118/1, p. 26.
27. ADM 1/557, p. 228; CO 118/1, p. 116.
28. *The Times*, 15 June 1811.
29. *The Times*, 5 November, 20 December 1810.
30. ADM 1/557, p. 310.
31. CO 118/1, p. 96.
32. Holland, Rose *et al.*, *Cambridge History of the British Empire*, vol. 2, pp. 114–15, 279; W. Lindsay, *History of Merchant Shipping*, vol. 2; Galpin, *Grain Supply of England*, pp. 179–80.
33. Fieldhouse, *The Colonial Empires*, p. 76.

Chapter 2: Gibraltar of the North Sea

1. ADM 1/557, pp. 15, 234.
2. CO 118/1, p. 32; *An Account of the Interesting island of Heligoland*, 1811.
3. ADM 1/557, pp. 201, 234; Hindmarsh, *From Powder Monkey to Governor*, p. 146.
4. *The Times*, 15 June 1812, 3 February 1814.
5. Hindmarsh, *From Powder Monkey to Governor*, p. 152; CO 118/24, 7 October 1842.
6. *The Times*, 22 March 1825.
7. Black, *Blackwood's Edinburgh Magazine*, 'Heligoland – the Island of Green, Red and White', August 1890, p. 160.
8. CO 118/1, pp. 26, 110, 115; *The Times*, 22 March 1849.
9. Busch, *Bismarck*; *The Times*, 31 January 1849.
10. Hardinge, *The Life of Henry Howard Molyneaux Herbert*, vol. 3, pp. 34–40; CAB 18/8A; PRO 30/6/52.
11. CO 700, Heligoland, p. 6; *The Times* 19 October 1886, 23 June 1890.

12. Laurie, 'Pondicherry for Heligoland in 1871'; *The Times*, 7 June 1871.
13. Butler, *Bismarck*, p. 33.
14. Dugdale, *German Diplomatic Documents*, vol. 1, pp. 172–3.
15. Ibid, p.174.
16. PRO 30/29/22A/9.

Chapter 3: Rivalries in Africa

1. Foreign Office, *German Colonisation*, p. 69.
2. Ibid, pp. 21–2.
3. Dugdale, *German Diplomatic Documents*, vol. 1, pp. 170–5; Robinson and Gallagher, *Africa and the Victorians*, pp. 189, 205.
4. Aydelotte, *Bismarck and British Colonial Policy*, p. 71; Gillard, 'Salisbury's African Policy', p. 653.
5. Cecil, *The Life of Robert, Marquis of Salisbury*, vol. IV, pp. 291–2; Kennedy, *Salisbury 1830–1903*, p. 219.
6. Cecil, *The Life of Robert, Marquis of Salisbury*, vol. IV, pp. 291–4.
7. Foreign Office, *German Colonization*, p. 68.
8. Amery, *The German Colonial Claim*, 1939, p. 60.
9. Holland, Rose *et al.*, *Cambridge History of the British Empire*, vol. III, pp. 264–5.
10. Sanderson, 'The Anglo-German Agreement of 1890 and the Upper Nile', pp. 49–72.
11. Cecil, *The Life of Robert, Marquis of Salisbury*, vol. IV, p. 254.
12. *Atlas of the British Empire*, p. 123.
13. Foreign Office, *German Colonization*, p. 97.
14. McEwan, *Nineteenth Century Africa*, p. 252; Sanderson, 'The Anglo-German Agreement of 1890 and the Upper Nile', p. 62.
15. Stationery Office, *Germany*, vol. II, p. 202.
16. Palmer, *The Kaiser*, p. 130.
17. Foreign Office, *German Colonization*, p. 98.

18. Louis, 'Sir Percy Anderson's Grand African Strategy'; Cecil, *The Life of Robert, Marquis of Salisbury*, vol. IV, p. 282; Dugdale, *German Diplomatic Documents*, vol. 2, p. 30.
19. Sanderson, 'The Anglo-German Agreement of 1890 and the Upper Nile', pp. 49–72.
20. McEwan, *Nineteenth Century Africa*, p. 252; Cecil, *The Life of Robert, Marquis of Salisbury*, vol. IV, pp. 289–90; Dugdale, *German Diplomatic Documents*, vol. II, pp. 32–4.
21. Palmer, *The Kaiser*, p. 39.
22. Dugdale, *German Diplomatic Documents*, pp. 37, 41.
23. Foreign Office, *German Colonization*, pp. 99–100.
24. FO 881/6146.

Chapter 4: Queen Victoria Opposes

1. Buckle, *The Letters of Queen Victoria 1862–1901*, vol. 1, p. 606.
2. Ibid, p. 612.
3. Ibid, p. 614; CAB 41/21/42.
4. Robert Cecil, 'The Danish Duchies', *Quarterly Review*, January–April 1864, 236–87.
5. Spinner, *George Joachin Goschen*, p. 160.
6. CAB 41/21/42.
7. FO 93/36/31.
8. Spinner, *George Joachin Goschen*, p. 160.
9. Buckle, *The Letters of Queen Victoria*, vol. 1, p. 614; C. 6043.
10. *Hansard*, 29 June 1890, 1311.
11. House of Commons Debate, 19 June 1890, 1370.
12. House of Commons Debate, 24 June 1890, 1790.
13. CO 346/6.
14. House of Commons Debate, 25 July 1890, 922.
15. Robert Heron-Fermor, *A Speech in Condemnation of the Cession of Heligoland*, and *Prussia in Relation to the Foreign Policy of England*.

16. House of Lords Debate, 10 July 1890, 1258.
17. House of Lords Debate, 10 July 1890, 1259, 1262.
18. House of Lords Debate, 10 July 1890, 1260–1.
19. House of Lords Debate, 10 July 1890, 1275, 1287.
20. House of Lords Debate, 10 July 1890, 1274–5, 1290.
21. House of Commons Debate, 24 July 1890, 800.
22. House of Commons Debate, 24 July 1890, 957.
23. House of Commons Debate, 25 July 1890, 976; House of Commons Debate, 24 July 1890, 756.
24. House of Commons Debate, 24 July 1890, 787; Cecil, *The Life of Robert, Marquis of Salisbury*, p. 300.
25. Piggott, 'The Integrity of the Empire', p. 240.

Chapter 5: Swapped

1. Barkly, *Among Boers and Basutos*.
2. Boyson, *The Falkland Islands*, pp. 155–7.
3. Barkly, *From the Tropics to the North Sea*, pp. 120, 143.
4. CO 346/6: 1 February 1889, 18 July 1889, 28 April 1890.
5. Boyson, *The Falkland Islands*, p. 155.
6. CO 346/6: 5 August 1889, 17 February 1889.
7. Ibid, 10 March 1890.
8. Ibid, 1 July 1890.
9. Ibid, 21 July 1890.
10. Ibid, 2 July 1890.
11. Ibid, 18 August 1890.
12. Ibid, 5 August 1890.
13. Ibid, 23 July 1890, 31 July 1890.
14. ADM 53/12908: 6–8 August 1890.
15. CO 346/6.
16. *The Times*, 11 August 1890.
17. Barkly, *From the Tropics to the North Sea*.
18. ADM 53/12908: 9 August 1890.
19. *The Times*, 11 August 1890.
20. ADM 53/12908: 10 August 1890.
21. Barkly, *From the Tropics to the North Sea*.

22. CO 346/6: 4 October 1890, 20 April 1891, 24 July 1891, 3 August 1891.
23. Ibid, 4 October 1890, 24 October 1890.

Chapter 6: Riddle of the Rock

1. C. 4582–7.
2. Cecil, *The Life of Robert, Marquis of Salisbury*, pp.
3. Roberts, *Salisbury: Victorian Titan*, pp. 555–6. Hurd, 'The Kaiser's Dream of Sea Power', p. 218.
4. Dear, *The Champagne Mumm Book of Ocean Racing*, pp. 14–19.
5. Drummond, *The Riddle*, pp. 57–61.
6. Steinberg, 'The Copenhagen Complex', pp. 27–8; Kaiser Wilhelm II, *My Memoirs 1878–1919*, pp. 83–4.
7. Steinberg, 'The Copenhagen Complex', pp. 31–3, 38.
8. Marder, *From Dreadnought to Scapa Flow*, vol. 1, pp. 113–14.
9. Kennedy (ed.), *The War Plans of the Great Powers*, pp. 183–90.
10. Drummond, *The Riddle*, pp. 195–7; Kaiser Wilhelm II, *My Memoirs*, p. 232.
11. Black, 'From Heligoland to Helgoland'; Dugdale, *German Diplomatic Documents*, vol 3, p. 359.

Chapter 7: Churchill Prepares to Invade

1. Lockley, *I Know an Island*, p. 164.
2. Mackay, *Fisher of Kilverstone*, p. 455.
3. Ibid, p. 467.
4. *Everyman's Encyclopaedia*, 1932.
5. Ring, *Erskine Childers*, pp. 157–67.
6. Churchill, *The Aftermath*, 1926.
7. CAB 1/20/5.
8. *The Times*, 21 September 1917.
9. Hoehling, *The Great War at Sea*, p. 247; ADM 137/2712, ADM 137/2710; Foulkes, *The Story of the Special*

Brigade, p. 240.
10. Palmer, *The Kaiser*, p. 208.
11. Hoehling, *The Great War at Sea*, pp. 250–2.
12. Lockley, *I Know an Island.*
13. Fisher, *Records*, p. 244.
14. Ibid, p. 245.

Chapter 8: Project Hummerschere

1. Matheson, 'The Dismantling of Heligoland', p. 551.
2. ADM 195/52.
3. FO 371/23059/C23663.
4. FO 371/23059.
5. Longmate, *The Bombers*, p. 64.
6. AIR 34/681.
7. HO 196/29.
8. FO 371/2201.
9. Skentelbery, *Arrows to Atom Bombs*, HMSO, pp. 169–70.
10. Cooper, *Beyond the Dams to the Tirpitz*, p. 196.
11. *The Times*, 20 April 1945; Brickhill, *The Dam Busters*, p. 257.
12. *The Times*, 5 May 1945.
13. ADM 179/537.

Chapter 9: 'Big Bang'

1. *The Times*, 15 May 1945.
2. ADM 1/18270.
3. PRO 30/26/197.
4. BJ 1/267.
5. Cathcart, *Test of Greatness*, pp. 43–4
6. Richards, *Portal of Hungerford*, pp. 361–3
7. *Daily Telegraph* 14 April 1947, 18 April 1947; *Daily Express* 19 April 1947.
8. PRO 30/26/197; ADM 1/20734.
9. Nanson, 'Heligoland', p.7; ES/221.

10. FO 371/55.
11. ES 1/3.
12. AIR 20/7272; AIR 27/2397.
13. AVIA 65/1153.
14. Macbean and Hogben, *Bombs Gone*, p. 269; Rhodes, *The Making of the Atomic Bomb*, p. 589.
15. D 2/16.
16. AVIA 6/12298.
17. AIR 29/1295, p. 16.
18. AIR 2/10012.
19. Macbean and Hogben, p. 272.
20. PREM 8/1375.
21. AIR 20/4752; AIR 14/4216.
22. HO 196/28.
23. AIR 8/2349.
24. Bird, *Operation Hurricane*, p. 94.

Chapter 10: The Islanders Return

1. House of Commons Debate, 28 July 1950, 910.
2. PREM 8, Cabinet Defence Committee, 20/2/51.
3. FO 1032/2492.
4. FO 371/187181; *The Times*, 31 August 1964.
5. FO 371/183181.
6. FO 371/187181.

Epilogue

1. Collyer, *Rain Later, Good*, pp. 48–51
2. Drower, *Britain's Dependent Territories*, pp. 12, 146–5, 176–8.
3. Met Office, *Sea Areas Used in BBC & GPO Bulletins for Shipping*, 2001.
4. Durham, 'Poole to Sweden', *Yachting Monthly*, May 2002, pp. 39–40.

Bibliography

Primary sources

Private papers

Savory, Sir Douglas

D/3015/4/4 *Sermon at Savory's Memorial Service*

D/3015/1/4/17 *Letter from Kuclenz, 13 July 1950*

D/3015/1/4/42 *Letter from Foreign Office, 12 January 1952*

D/3015/1/4/82 *Frisian Information Bureau Bulletin, December 1957*

D/3015/1/4/94 *Unpublished Manuscript of book by Prof. Paul Hubbell on 1890 Heligoland Treaty*

Savory, Douglas *From the Haven into the Storm: Memoirs of Professor Sir Douglas Savory* [Unpublished Manuscript]

Wallis, Sir Barnes

D 2/16 *War Weapons*

D 2/18 *War Weapons*

D 5/5 *Development of War Weapons*

D 5/6 *Report by Air Commodore P. Huskinson on his visit to USA*

British Government papers

ADM 1/52 H *Heligoland, 1890–1921*

ADM 1/557 *Admiral Russell, 1807*

ADM 1/5121/22 *Attack upon the Danish Island of Heligoland*, 1807

ADM 1/8461/153 *Beatty letter to Balfour*, 21 June 1916

ADM 1/8568/260 *Heligoland: Petition of Islanders for the retention of the small boat Harbour*, 1 September 1919
ADM 1/18233 *Heligoland: Use as RAF Live Bombing Range*
ADM 1/18270 *Occupation of Heligoland and Dune: Report of Proceedings 11–14 May 1945 by Lt. Commander C. Aylwin, RN*
ADM 1/20734 *Demolition of Fortifications on Heligoland Island, 18 April 1947 (Operation 'Big Bang')*
ADM 37/425 *Heligoland, 1807 (Island)*
ADM 37/8607 *Heligoland, 1813–15 (Yard)*
ADM 53/825 *Ship's Log: HMS Majestic, July 1806–April 1809*
ADM 53/1067 *Ship's Log: HMS* Quebec, *1805–1809*
ADM 53/12908 *Ship's Log: HMS* Calypso, *20 January 1890–12 January 1891*
ADM 53/67544 *HMS* Vindex: *Copy of log, October 1916*
ADM 179/537 *Risk to shipping of reopening Heligoland Bight*, May 1945
ADM 186/567 *Report on the Seaplane Operation against Cuxhaven, 25/12/1914*
ADM 195/52 *Heligoland: Engineering Staff of NIACC 1890–21*, February 1921
AIR 1/656/17/122/544 *Air Reconnaissance in W. Portion of Heligoland Bight (December 1917)*
Admiralty *North Sea Pilot*, Vol. 4, 1887
AIR 2/5060 *Operation JB: Air Co-operation with the Navy*
AIR 2/10012 *Heligoland: Policy and use by RAF*, 29 January 1948
AIR 2/13777 *Herod Committee – Part 1*
AIR 8/2349 *Atomic bombs: testing*
AIR 14/3826 *Exercise 'Bullseye'*
AIR 20/4752 *'Bullseye' Exercises*
AIR 20/6727 *USAF/RAF Collaboration, 1948*
AIR 20/7272 *Anglo-American Bomb Trials (1945–1946) against special concrete targets at Watten, Farge and Heligoland*, Vol. 1, Reports, 1947
AIR 20/7273 *Anglo-American Bomb Trials (1945–1946)*

against special concrete targets at Watten, Farge and Heligoland, Vol. 2, Illustrations, 1947
AIR 20/8149 *Bombs: Tallboy and Grand Slam*
AIR 27/2397 *Bombing of Heligoland*
AIR 29/1295 *Armament and Instrument Experimental Unit (Martlesham Heath), 1946–50*
AIR 34/672 *Heligoland (Weapons Analysis), April 1941–May 1945*, British Big Bomb Studies, Air Ministry RE8
AIR 34/681 *Heligoland: Submarine basin* (September 1940–October 1944)
AVIA 6/12298 *Trials of 1,000 lb (Emulsion Project)*, May 1948
AVIA 6/16181 *Final Trials of Experimental Design for the 1,000 lb MC Bomb (The Emulsion Project)*
AVIA 6/17799 *The Ballistics of Blue Danube*, May 1949
AVIA 6/18589 *Analysis of Gas Samples from the Heligoland Trials on Ammonium Nitrate*, Royal Aircraft Establishment, February 1949
AVIA 6/19446 *The Effect of High Release Speed on the Design of Blue Danube*
AVIA 65/1153 *10,000 lb HC, MC Bomb – Air Staff Requirement OR 1001 – 'Blue Danube', 1946–57*
BJ 1/267 *Seismology, Heligoland Explosion on 18.4.47 (including explosions in Germany, Bikini, etc.)*
C. 6043 *Despatch to Sir Edward Malet respecting the Affairs of East Africa*, 17
C. 6046 *Correspondence Respecting the Anglo-German Agreement Relative to Africa and Heligoland*, July 1890
C. 7582–7 *Report on the German Colonies in Africa and the South Pacific*, Foreign Office, miscellaneous series, no. 346 (1894)
CAB 1/10/43 *Action at Heligoland: Information obtained from a German Officer*, 30 November 1914
CAB 1/20/5 *Questions on Heligoland*, September 1916
CAB 18/8A *Proceedings of the Colonial Conference*, 1887
CAB 41/21/39 *House of Commons business, negotiations with Germany and African Territories*, 17 May 1890

CAB 41/21/41 *Africa Frontiers (negotiations with Germany)*, 4 June 1890

CAB 41/21/42 *African Negotiations*, 8 June 1890

CAB 41/21/44 *Negotiations with Germany over Heligoland, Zanzibar and Pemba*, 10 June 1890

CAB 41/21/45 *Divergence of opinion between Salisbury and Cabinet, re. legislative programme*, 5 July 1890

CAB 41/41/4 *Letter to Queen Victoria*, 22 June 1890

CN1 /12 *Demolition of fortifications, 1947*

CO 71/78 *Heligoland: Index of Correspondence, 1842–1866* December 1952

CO 118/1 *Heligoland 1807–1808: Despatches, Offices and Individuals*

CO 346/2 *Heligoland: Register of Correspondence, 1858–1866*

CO 346/6 *Heligoland: Register of Correspondence, 1889–1910*

CO 371/65296 *German General Economic*, 1947

CO 537/17 *Heligoland* (1890–1910)

DEFE 15/1889 *A Survey of Theoretical Work on Atomic Bomb Effects Carried out in the HER Project up to July 1951*, December 1951

ES 1/1 *Craters: Cratering from Atomic Weapons, 1946–1959*

ES 1/3 *'Charybdis' underwater explosions: base surge (1947–1955)*

ES 1/221 *AWRE, Aldermaston, Blast Effect Papers, 1947–54*

ES1/267 *Buildings for HER project: Shoeburyness, 1947–1950*

ES1/268 *Buildings for HER project: Shoeburyness, 1951–53*

ES 1/330 *Development of Foulness, 1945–51*

FO 64/1341 *Natives of Heligoland electing to remain British subjects, 1891–3*

FO 84/2032 *Minute to Queen Victoria by Lord Salisbury on the constitutional issue re Heligoland*

FO 93/36/24 *Germany. Agreement: Africa and Heligoland*, 1 July 1890

FO 93/36/31 *Germany. Preliminary Agreement: Africa and Heligoland*, 17 June 1890

FO 371/2201 *Proposal for annexation of Sylt and Heligoland*, 17 February 1944

FO 371/183181 *Speech by British Ambassador at Heligoland reception*, 9/8/1965

FO 371/23059 *Heligoland: Refortification*, 1939

FO 881/6146 *Correspondence respecting the Negotiations between Great Britain and Germany relating to Africa, April to December 1890*, December 1891

FO 933/22 *Thornton Papers, Correspondence from FO, January–September 1807*

FO 933/24 *Thornton Papers, Letterbook April–October 1807*

FO 936/1202 *Claims in Respect of Buildings*

FO 1006/238 *Evacuation of Germans from Heligoland*; F.A. Messenger, 6/1/1951

FO 1032/2492 *'Shelduck'*, 1954

Foreign Office *German Colonisation*, Historical Section Handbook No. 35, February 1919

Foreign Office *The Kiel Canal and Heligoland*, Historical Section Handbook No. 41, 1920

Foreign Office *Tanganyika*, Historical Section Handbook, No. 113, 1920

GFM 33/2217 *Linking the North Sea and the Baltic, 1888–October 1905, Dept. 1A*

HO 196/29 *Incident on Heligoland Airfield, September 1944* June 1890

MPG 1/970 Heligoland

Naval Intelligence *Germany: Coast Defences and Coast Defence Ordnance:* Division Report No. 579, September 1902

PREM 8/474 *Heligoland*

PREM 8/1375 *Chief of Staff Committee, 2/2/50*

PREM 8/1546 *Tube Alloys*

PRO 30/6/52 *Papers concerning Royal Commission on the Defence of British Possessions and Commerce Abroad*

PRO 30/26/197 *Demolition of fortifications on Heligoland (Operations 'Big Bang' and 'Little Bang')*

PRO 30/29/22A/9 *Confidential Correspondence Describing a Conversation on Heligoland with Count Munster*, 28 December 1884
Stationery Office *Germany*, Vol. 2, HMSO, 1944
WO 32/5382 *Heligoland: Disposal of, 1919*
WO 205/653 *Reduction of Frisian Islands and Heligoland, 1945*

Secondary sources

Books – German

Busch, F.O., *Das Buch von Helgoland*, Schneider 1935
von Hagen, M.C., *Geschichte und Bedeutung de Heligoland-vertrages*, Berlin, 1916
Hallier, Ernst Hans, *Die Vegetation auf Helgoland*, Hamburg, 1863
Krüss, James, *Historie von der Schönen Insel Helgoland*, Sinemis, 1988
Rickmers, Henry and Woosnam, Frank, *Helgoland eine Insel auf dem Wege nach Europa*, Niederelbe-Verlag, 1992
Sell, Manfried, *Der Deutsch-Englische Abkommen von 1890 über Helgoland*, Berlin, 1926
Schreiber-Loetzenburg, Arno, *Helgoland und seine Verwalung sect*, 1890, Carl Heymanns, 1927

Books – English

Adenauer, Konrad, *Memoirs*, Weidenfeld & Nicolson, 1966
Amery, L.S., *The German Colonial Claim*, Chambers, 1939
Amery, Julian, *Life of Joseph Chamberlain*, London, 1951
Ashton, Rosemary, *Little Germany: Exile & Asylum in Victorian England*, OUP, 2000
Oglander, C., *Roger Keyes*, Hogarth, 1951
Aydelotte, William, *Bismarck and British Colonial Policy*, University of Pennsylvania, 1937
Bacon, R., *Lord Fisher*, Hodder & Stoughton, 1929

Barkly, F.A., *Among Boers and Basutos*, Roxburghe Press, 1896

——, *From the Tropics to the North Sea*, Roxburghe Press, 1898

Bartlett, C.J., *The Long Retreat*, Macmillan, 1972

Baylis, J., *Ambiguity and Deterrence: British Nuclear Strategy, 1945–1964*, OUP, 1995

Bayly, C.A., *Atlas of the British Empire*, Facts on File, 1989

Bayly, Lewis, *Pull Together: The Memoirs of Admiral Sir Lewis Bayly*, Harrap, 1939

Benson, Arthur and Esher, Viscount, *The Letters of Queen Victoria, 1862–1901*, John Murray, 1908

Bird, Peter B., *Operation Hurricane: A Personal Account of the British Nuclear Test at Monte Bello*, Square Mile, 1989

Black, William G., *Heligoland and the Islands of the North Sea*, Blackwood, 1888

Blakeley, Brian, *The Colonial Office 1868–92*, Duke University, 1972

Boyson, V.F., *The Falkland Islands*, Clarendon Press, 1924

Brackenburg, Mark, *Frisian Pilot*, Stanford, 1979

Braybrooke, Richard, *Memoirs of Samuel Pepys*, Frederick Warne, ND

Brickhill, Paul, *The Dam Busters*, Evans, 1951

Bruce, Anthony, *An Illustrated Companion to the First World War*, Michael Joseph, 1984

Bryant, G. Isaac, *The Postage Stamps of Heligoland and their History*, Popular Philatelic Library, 1895

Buckle, G.E., *The Letters of Queen Victoria, 1862–1901*, 2 vols, John Murray, 1930

Busch, Moritz, *Bismarck: Some Secret Pages of his History*, Macmillan, 1899

Butler, A.J., *Bismarck: The Man and the Statesman*, vol. 2, Smith Elder, 1898

Campbell, D. *The Unmistakable Aircraft Carrier*, Paladin, 1986

Cathcart, Brian, *Test of Greatness: Britain's Struggle for the Atom Bomb*, John Murray, 1994

Cecil, Gwendolen, *The Life of Robert, Marquis of Salisbury*, Hodder & Stoughton, 1932
Childers, Erskine, *The Riddle of the Sands*, Nelson & Sons, 1904
Churchill, W.S., *The World Crisis 1911–1918*, Landsborough, 1960
Clowes, William, *Her Majesty's Colonies*, Clowes, 1886
Collyer, Peter, *Rain Later, Good*, Thomas Reed, 1998
Colomb, John, *The Defence of Great Britain*, Stanford, 1880
Cooper, Alan, *Beyond the Dams to the Tirpitz*, William Kimber, 1993
——, *The Dambusters Squadron: Fifty years of 617 Squadron RAF*, Arms & Armour, 1993
Cox, Tom, *Damned Englishman: A Study of Erskine Childers*, Exposition Press, 1975
Cromer, Lord, *Modern Egypt*, Macmillan, 1908
Cunningham, Viscount, *A Sailor's Odyssey – The Autobiography of Admiral of the Fleet Andrew Cunningham*, Hutchinson, 1951
Darstaedter, Friedrich, *Bismarck: and the Creation of the Second Reich*, Methuen, nd
Deacon, Richard, *The Silent War: A History of Western Naval Intelligence*, David & Charles, 1978
Dear, Ian, *The Champagne Mumm Book of Ocean Racing*, Severn House, 1985
Division of Naval Intelligence, *Warships of the British Commonwealth*, US Government Printing Office, 1944
Dreyer, R.F., *The Mind of Official Imperialism*, Hobbing, 1987
Drower, George, *Britain's Dependent Territories: a Fistful of Islands*, Dartmouth, 1992
——, *Overseas Territories Handbook*, Stationery Office, 1998
Drummond, Maldwin, *The Riddle*, Nautical Press, 1985
Dugdale, E.T.S., *German Diplomatic Documents*, vol. 1, Methuen, 1928
Eckhardtstein, Baron von, *Ten Years at the Court of St James, 1895–1905*, Thornton

Edward, F. Knight, *The Harwich Naval Forces*, Hodder & Stoughton, 1919
Evans, Richard, *Death in Hamburg*, OUP, 1887
Eyck, Erich, *Bismarck and the German Empire*, George Allen, 1948
Fieldhouse, D.K., *The Colonial Empires*, Macmillan, 1965
Fisher, Lord, *Records*, Hodder & Stoughton, 1919
Fopp, Michael, *The Washington File*, Air-Britain, 1983
Foulkes, C., *The Story of the Special Brigade*, Blackwood, 1934
Franke, H.D., *The Challenge to Marine Biology*, BAH, 1995
Galpin, W.F., *Grain Supply of England in the Napoleonic Wars*, University of Michigan, 1925
Garvin, J.L., *Life of Joseph Chamberlain*, Macmillan, 1931
Gates, *The Napoleonic Wars 1803–1815*, Arnold, 1997
Gätke, Heinrich, *Heligoland as an Ornithological Observatory: the Result of Fifty Years' Experience*, Douglas, 1895
Geiss, I., *German Foreign Policy 1871–1914*, Routledge, 1976
Grenville, J.A.S., *Lord Salisbury and Foreign Policy*, Athlone, 1964
Hamilton, George, *Parliamentary Reminiscences and Reflections*, vol. 1, 1917; vol. 2, Murray, 1922
Hardie, Frank, *The Political Influence of Queen Victoria, 1861–1901*, London, 1938
Hardinge, Arthur, *The Life of Henry Howard Molyneux Herbert, Fourth Earl of Carnarvon 1831–1890*, vol. 3, OUP, 1925
Hastings, Max, *Bomber Command*, Michael Joseph, 1979
Hawkins, J., *Keeping the Peace: The Aldermaston Story*, Leo Cooper, 2000
Headlam, James, *Bismarck and the Foundations of the German Empire*, 1899
Henshall, Philip, *The Nuclear Axis: Germany, Japan and the Atom Bomb Race 1939–45*, Sutton, 2000
Herken, Gregg, *The Winning Weapon: The Atomic Bomb in the Cold War*, Alfred Knopf, 1980

Heron-Fermor, R., *A Speech in Condemnation of the Cession of Heligoland*, Brighton, 1890
Hertslet, E., *The Map of Africa by Treaty*, HMSO, 1909
Hill, Christopher, *British Strategy in the Napoleonic War 1803–15*, Manchester
Hindmarsh, Stewart, *From Powder Monkey to Governor: Life of Rear Admiral Sir John Hindmarsh, 1785–1860*, Access, 1995
Hinsley, F.H., *British Intelligence in the Second World War*, HMSO, 1981
Hislam, Percival A., *The Admiralty of the Atlantic*, Longmans, 1908
Hoehling, A., *The Great War at Sea*, Corgi, 1967
Holland Rose, J., Newton, A. and Benian, E., *The Cambridge History of the British Empire*, vol. 2, CUP, 1940
Hollingsworth, L., *Zanzibar under the Foreign Office, 1890–1913*, Macmillan, 1953
Hough, Richard, *First Sea Lord: An Authorised Biography of Admiral Lord Fisher*, Allen & Unwin, 1969
——, *The Great War at Sea 1914–1918*, OUP, 1983
Howard, Christopher, *Splendid Isolation: the Latter Years of the 3rd Marquess of Salisbury*, Howard, 1967
Hull, I.V., *The Kaiser and his Entourage*, CUP, 1982
James, William, *A Great Seaman*, Witherby, 1956
——, *The Eyes of the Navy, A Biography of Admiral Sir Reginald Hall*, Methuen, 1955
Jane, Fred T., *Jane's Fighting Ships, 1919*, Sampson Low Marston, 1919
Jane, Lionel Cecil, *The Action off Heligoland, August 1914*, Oxford Pamphlets, no. 48, 1915
Jellicoe of Scapa, Lord, *The Grand Fleet 1914–16*, Cassell, 1919
——, *The Submarine Peril*, Cassell, 1934
Jellicoe, John, *The Crisis of the Naval War*, Cassell, 1920
Joelson, F.S., *Germany's Claims to Colonies*, Hurst & Blackett, 1939
Jones, H.A., *The War in the Air*, Vol. 2, OUP, 1928

Jones, R.V., *Most Secret War*, Hamish Hamilton, 1978
Kemp, P.K., *The Papers of Admiral Sir John Fisher*, Naval Record Society, 1960
Kennedy, Aubrey, *Salisbury 1830–1903: Portrait of a Statesman*, John Murray, 1953
Kennedy, Paul, *The Rise and Fall of the Anglo-German Antagonism, 1860–1914*, Allen & Unwin, 1980
Kennedy, Paul (ed.), *The War Plans of the Great Powers 1880–1914*, Allen & Unwin, 1985
Keyes, Roger, *The Naval Memoirs of Admiral of the Fleet Sir Roger Keyes*, Butterworth, 1934
Kinsey, Gordon, *Orfordness – Secret Site: A History of the Establishment 1915–1980*, Terence Dalton, 1982
——, *Bawdsey: Birth of the Beam*, Terence Dalton, 1983
——, *Martlesham Heath*, Terence Dalton, 1983
Kirkpatrick, Ivone, *The Inner Circle*, Macmillan, 1959
van der Kiste, John, *Kaiser Wilhelm II: Germany's Last Emperor*, Sutton, 2000
Knight, Edward F., *The Falcon on the Baltic: A Coasting Voyage from Hammersmith to Copenhagen in a Three Ton Yacht*, W.H. Allen, 1899
Knutsford, Viscount, *In Black and White*, Arnold, 1926
Kohl, Horst, *Bismarck's Reflections and Reminiscences*, Dent, 1899
Kubicek, Robert, *The Administration of Imperialism: Joseph Chamberlain at the Colonial Office*, Duke University, 1969
L'Estrange, M., *Heligoland, or Reminiscences of Childhood*, John Parker, 1851
Lambi, I., *The Navy and German Power Politics 1862–1914*, Allen & Unwin, 1984
Lindsay, W., *History of Merchant Shipping*, Long Marston, 1877
Lockley, Robert, *I Know an Island*, George Harrap, 1938
Longford, Elizabeth, *Victoria R*, Weidenfeld & Nicolson, 1964
Longmate, Norman, *The Bombers: The RAF Offensive against Germany, 1939–1945*, Hutchinson, 1983

Lovell, R.I., *The Struggle for South Africa, 1875–1899: a Study in Economic Imperialism*, Macmillan, 1934

Lyne, R.N., *Zanzibar in Contemporary Times*, Hurst & Blackett, 1905

MacBean, J.A. and Hogben, A.S., *Bombs Gone: The Development and Use of British Air-dropped Weapons from 1912 to the Present Day*, Patrick Stephens, 1990

Macclelland, C., *The German Historians and England*, CUP, 1971

MacDonogh, Giles, *The Last Kaiser: William the Impetuous*, Weidenfeld & Nicolson, 2000

McEwan, P.J.M., *Nineteenth Century Africa*, OUP, 1968

Mackay, Ruddock, *Fisher of Kilverstone*, OUP, 1973

Macmillan, Mona, *Sir Henry Barkly, Mediator and Moderator*, Balkema, 1970

Mallmann Showell, J., *The German Navy in World War Two*, Arms and Armour, 1979

Marder, Arthur, *Portrait of an Admiral: The Life and Papers of Sir Herbert Richmond*, OUP, 1952

——, *British Naval Policy 1880–1905*, Putnam, 1941

——, *From Dreadnought to Scapa Flow*, OUP, 1965

Menaul, Stewart, *Countdown: Britain's Strategic Nuclear Forces*, Robert Hale, 1980

Messenger, Charles, *'Bomber' Harris and the Strategic Bombing Offensive, 1939–45*, Arms and Armour, 1984

Morley, J., *The Life of William Ewart Gladstone*, 3 vols, Morley, 1903

Moyes, Philip, *Bomber Squadrons of the RAF and their Aircraft*, Macdonald, 1965

Musgrove, Gordon, *Pathfinder Force: A History of 8 Group*, Crécy Books, 1992

Naval Intelligence, *A Handbook of German East Africa*, HMSO, nd

Nesbit, Roy Conyers, *RAF Coastal Command in Action 1939–1945*, Sutton, 1997

Packenham, Simona, *Sixty Miles from England: The English at Dieppe 1814–1914*, Macmillan, 1967

Palmer, Alan, *The Kaiser: Warlord of the Second Reich*, Weidenfeld & Nicolson, 1978
Patterson, A. Temple, *Tyrwhitt of the Harwich Force*, Military Book Society, 1973
Penson, Lillian, *Foreign Affairs under Lord Salisbury*, London, 1962
Peters, Karl, *New Light on Dark Africa*, Ward Lock, 1891
——, *England and the English*, 1903
Popham, Hugh and Robin, *Thirst for the Sea, the Sailing Adventures of Erskine Childers*, Stanford Maritime, 1979
Porter, Ian and Armour, Ian D., *Imperial Germany 1890–1918*, Longman, 1991
Raeder, Karl, *Struggle for the Sea*, William Kimber, 1959
Raleigh, Walter, *The War in the Air*, Vol. 1, OUP, 1922
Rhodes, Richard, *The Making of the Atomic Bomb*, Simon & Schuster, 1986
Richards, Denis, *Portal of Hungerford*, Heinemann, 1977
Ring, Jim, *Erskine Childers*, John Murray, 1996
Roberts, Andrew, *Salisbury: Victorian Titan*, Weidenfeld & Nicolson, 1999
Robinson, Derek, *Just Testing*, Collins Harvill, 1985
Robinson, R. and Gallagher, J., *Africa and the Victorians*, Macmillan, 1981
Robinson, Robert, *USAF Europe*, vol. 2, Signal Publications, 1990
Rohl, John, *The Kaiser and his Court*, Rohl, CUP, 1994
Roskill, Stephen, *Churchill and the Admirals*, Collins, 1977
Ryder, A.J., *The German Revolution of 1918*, Routledge, CUP, 1967
Saunders, Hilary St George, *Royal Air Force 1939–43*, vol. 3, 'The Fight is Won', HMSO, 1974
Schaffer, Ronald, *American Bombing in WWII*, OUP, 1985
Shannon, Richard, *Gladstone: 1865–1898*, 2 vols, Penguin, 1999
Shephard, Gordon, *Memoirs of Brigadier-General Gordon Shephard*, Hazell, Watson & Viney, 1924

Skentelbery, Norman, *Arrows to Atom Bombs: A History of the Ordnance Board*, HMSO, 1975
Somervell, D.C., *The British Empire*, Christophers, 1942
Spinner, Thomas J., *George Joachin Goschen*, CUP, 1973
Stanley, Dorothy, *The Autobiography of Sir Henry Morton Stanley*, Sampson Low, 1909
Steinburg, Jonathan, *Yesterday's Deterrent: Tirpitz and the Birth of the German Battle Fleet*, Macdonald, 1965
Bywater, H. and Ferraby, H., *Strange Intelligence: Memoirs of Naval Secret Service*, Constable, 1931
Stresemann, Erwin, *Ornithology: From Aristotle to the Present*, Harvard University Press, 1975
Taylor, A.J.P., *Germany's First Bid for Colonies*, Macmillan, 1938
——, *Bismarck: The Man and the Statesman*, Hamish Hamilton, 1955
——, *The Struggle for Mastery in Europe*, 1963
Temperley, H. and Penson, L., *A Century of Diplomatic Blue Books, 1814–1914*, 1938
Tirpitz, Alfred von, *My Memoirs*, Hurst & Blackett, 1919
Titus, A. Costanding, *Bomb in the Backyard: Atomic Testing and American Politics*, University of Navada, 2001.
Topham, Anne, *Memories of the Kaiser's Court*, Methuen, 1914
Townsend, Mary, *Origins of Modern German Colonialism, 1871–1885*, Columbia, 1921
——, *The Rise and Fall of Germany's Colonial Empire, 1884–1918*, Macmillan, 1930
Vale, Charles W., *Correspondence, Despatches and Other Papers of Lord Castlereagh*, vol. 6, William Shoberl, 1851
van de Vat, Dan, *The Grand Scuttle*, Hodder & Stoughton, 1982
Walker, Mack, *German Home Towns, 1648–1871*, Cornell, 1971
Waller, Horace, *Heligoland for Zanzibar*, Stanford, 1893
Wesseling, H.L., *Divide and Rule: The Partition of Africa 1880–1914*, Praeger, 1996

West, Nigel, *MI6: British Intelligence Service Operations, 1909–1945*, Weidenfeld & Nicolson, 1983
Wichterich, Richard, *Dr Karl Peters*, Keil Verlag, 1934
Wilhelm II, Kaiser, *My Early Life*, Methuen, 1926
——, *My Memoirs: 1878–1918*, Cassell, 1922
Wilhelm, Crown Prince, *Memoirs*, Thornton Butterworth, 1922
Wilkinson, Burke, *The Zeal of the Convert: the Life of Erskine Childers*, Colin Smythe, 1976
Williams, R.H., *Defending the Empire*, Yale University Press, 1991
Williamson, D.G., *Bismarck and Germany, 1862–1890*, Longman, 1986
Williamson, Samuel, *The Politics of Grand Strategy*, Harvard, 1969
Wynn, Humphrey, *RAF Nuclear Deterrent Forces*, HMSO, 1994

Articles

Air International, 'B-29: First of the Superbombers', September 1989, 141–4
Alward, G.L., 'The Future of Heligoland, and its Special Interest to the Fisheries', *Grimsby News*, November 1918
Black, William G., 'Heligoland – the Island of Green, Red and White', *Blackwood's Edinburgh Magazine*, August 1890, 160–71
——, 'From Heligoland to Helgoland', *National Review*, vol. 58, 1911, 317–22
Cecil, Robert, 'The Danish Duchies', *Quarterly Review*, January–April 1864, 236–87
Charlton, Edward, 'Dismantling Heligoland', *Smith's Dock Monthly*, June 1923
Doughty, Katharine, 'The Gates of Empire', *United Service Magazine*, May 1919, 146–50
Drower, George, 'A Rethink on Britain's Dependent Territories', *Round Table*, January 1989, 12–15

Durham, Dick, 'Poole to Sweden', *Yachting Monthly*, May 2002, pp. 9–40

Frisbee, John, 'Project Aphrodite' *Air Force Magazine*, August 1997, 57

Gillard, D.R., 'Salisbury's African Policy and the Heligoland Offer of 1890', *English Historical Review*, October 1960, 631–53

Hurd, Archibald, 'The Kaiser's Dream of Sea Power', *Nineteenth Century and After*, August 1906, 215–23

Obituary of Heinrich Gätke, *The Ibis: A Quarterly Journal of Ornithology*, vol. 3, 1897, 291–4

Illustrated London News, 'Heligoland', 26 April 1947, pp. 433–6

——, 'Heligoland', 19 April 1947, pp. 408–9

Jones, Stuart E., 'Demolishing German's North Sea Ramparts', *National Geographic*, November 1946, 635–44

Laurie, W.F.B., 'Pondicherry for Heligoland in 1871; and Heligoland ceded to Germany in 1890', *The Asiatic Quarterly Review*, July 1890, 36–52

Lewin, Evans, 'The Heligoland Mistake', *The Contemporary Review*, July 1916, 68–77

Louis, W. Roger, 'Sir Percy Anderson's Grand African Strategy, 1883–1896', *English Historical Review*, April 1966, 292–314

Matheson, J.C., 'The Value of Heligoland', *The Royal Engineers Journal*, June 1921, 257–61

——, 'The Dismantling of Heligoland', *The Royal Engineers Journal*, December 1923, 547–51

Nanson, M.R-C., 'Heligoland', *The Coast Artillery Journal*, November–December, pp. 2–7

Naval Miscellany, 'Seizure of Heligoland', *Navy Records Society*, vol. 20, vi, 1902, 375–86

Nomad, 'Forgotten Pages: Heligoland', *United Empire*, vol. 16, May 1925, 288–9

Penning, W.H., 'Waste of Insular Land by the Sea', *Geological Magazine*, 1876, 282–4

Piggott, Francis, 'The Integrity of the Empire: The Offer of

Cyprus to Greece', *The Nineteenth Century*, January 1916, 240–52

Sanderson, George, 'The Anglo-German Agreement of 1890 and the Upper Nile', *English Historical Review*, January 1963, 49–72

Savory, Douglas L., 'Heligoland Past and Present', *Contemporary Review*, no. 1097, 1957, 273–8

Steinburg, Jonathan, 'The Copenhagen Complex', *Journal of Contemporary History*, July 1966, 23–46

Surt, W., 'Anglo-American Amity: Transferring B-29s to the RAF', *Air Power History*, Winter 1944, 30–9

Webster, C.K., 'Foreign Policy of Castlereagh (1812–1815)', *Cambridge Historical Journal*, vol. V, 1935

Useful websites

www.allstates.flag.com	Heligoland flag & history
www.atomictourist.com	Nuclear test sites
www.chicheleyhall.co.uk	Admiral Beatty's mansion
www.deutsche-schutzgebiete.de	Heligoland–Zanzibar Treaty
www.helgoland.de	Heligoland official site
www.kulturenet.dk	Royal Danish Naval Museum
www.mayabooks.co.uk	Ecological data
www.nationaltrust.org.uk	Orfordness
www.zanzibar.net	Zanzibar

Index